Sawan

COMPUTERS
OUR LIFELINE

5

Based on NEP

AF482530

MANOJ PUBLICATIONS

COMPUTERS
Our Lifeline - 5

Publishers:

MANOJ PUBLICATIONS

761, Main Road, Burari, Delhi-110084 (INDIA)

Mobile : 09999476076, 09868112194,
08178823569, 08178854810

Email : info@manojpublications.com

For online shopping visit our website :

Website : www.sawanonlinebookstore.com

ISBN : 978-81-310-1643-5

Concept:

Puneet Gupta
M.B.A. (William & Mary, U.S.A.)

Edited by:

Davinder Singh Minhas
Rohan Kumar

PREFACE

This is the Age of Computers. In every nook and corner of the globe, computers have made their presence felt, be it school, office, post office, bank, shop, mall, hotel, restaurant, airport, railway station, Metro station and so on. Needless to say, they have become our lifeline as we can't do anything without them. In order to keep pace with the modern world, it is important to familiarise our children with computer applications right from the start. They ought to be taught the uses of computer in a lucid, interesting and enjoyable style: from basic to intermediate to advanced level.

Keeping in view the requirements of students, all the books in the series—Computers : Our Lifeline—have been designed to meet the purpose of acquiring a sound in-depth knowledge on computers with their uses. The contents of the books are based entirely on recently approved NEP (National Educational Policy).

The chapters in all the books contain a fairly good amount of illustrations which make the text very easy to understand. There are many computer books flooding the market. Our books are the books with a difference in order that they are well equipped with exhaustive exercises which test a student's mental horizon by making him take Formative Assessment as well as Summative Assessment. The knowledge of the latest software with their applications and types of computer language have been made available. Nay, students have been introduced to coding, the process of designing computer apps. The main goal of books in the series is to make a student computerate, *i.e.* computer literate.

We sincerely hope that all the books in this series will prove fruitful both to students and teachers. We shall be highly pleased to receive constructive suggestions in order to make the series more qualitative in the forthcoming editions.

– Author

CONTENTS

Computer - Its Generations

Hi friends, welcome to the new class. You guys are looking more smarter than ever! Well friends, do you know that as we humans have different generations, computers also have generations.

 ## GENERATIONS OF COMPUTER

Just like we have the generation of people in our family like grandfather, father and children, similarly, the computer also has different generations.

Today's modern computer has come into existence after a long journey of inventions and discoveries. The history of computer development is often referred to in reference with the different generations of computers. A generation refers to the state of improvement in the product development process. With each new generation, the computer and its devices are becoming smaller, more advanced and powerful than the previous generation. The term 'generation' is also used in the different advancements of new computer technology.

The following are the developments of the computer:

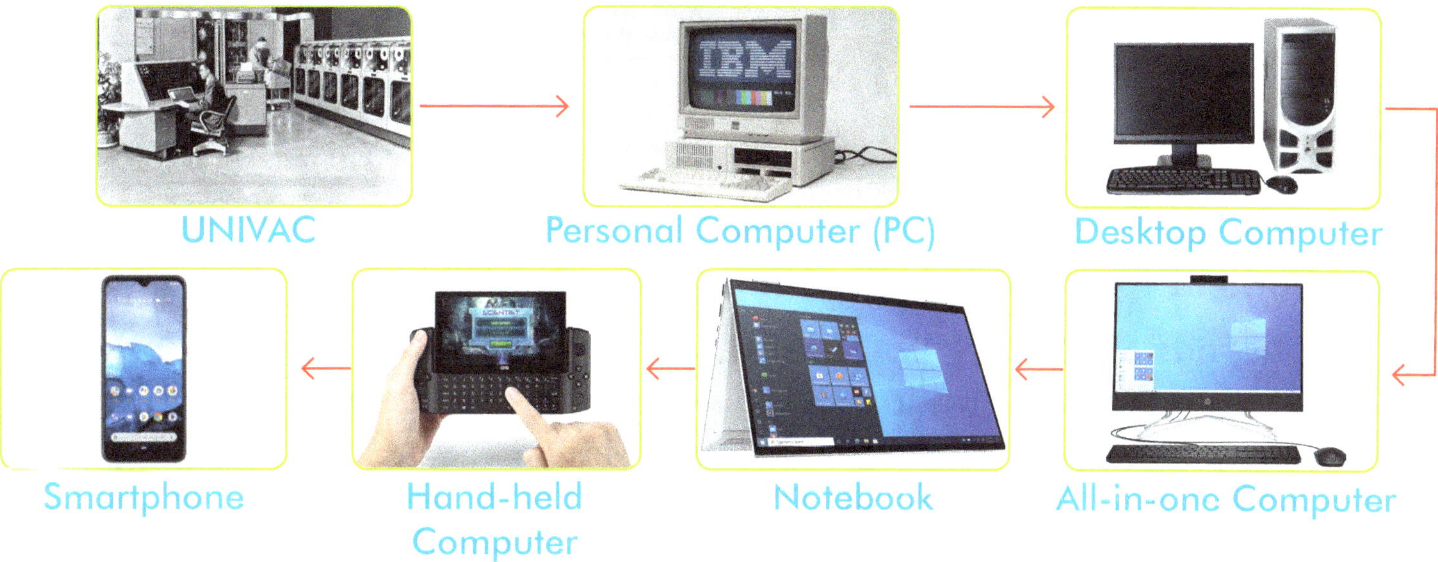

As you see in the above picture—with each new generation, the computer has got smaller and more advanced than its previous generation.

Computers in the past had very less features. Day by day as the technology developed and new features were added, they became more powerful, efficient and reliable. Each development phase of computer is referred as the generation of computer.

First-Generation Computers (1946-1959)

In the first-generation computers, thermionic valves or vacuum tubes were used.

⇒ These computers used Machine language to instruct the system.

⇒ These computers were very large in size.

⇒ These computers were very expensive but slow and often undependable.

⇒ In the First Generation computers, paper tapes and punched cards were used as secondary storage device.

⇒ ENIAC (Electronic Numerical Integrator and Calculator), EDVAC (Electronic Discrete Variable Automatic Computer), UNIVAC (Universal Automatic Computer) are the examples of the First-Generation computers.

UNIVAC

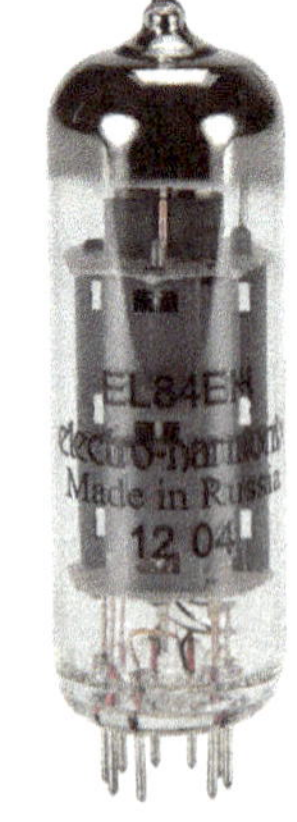

vacuum tube

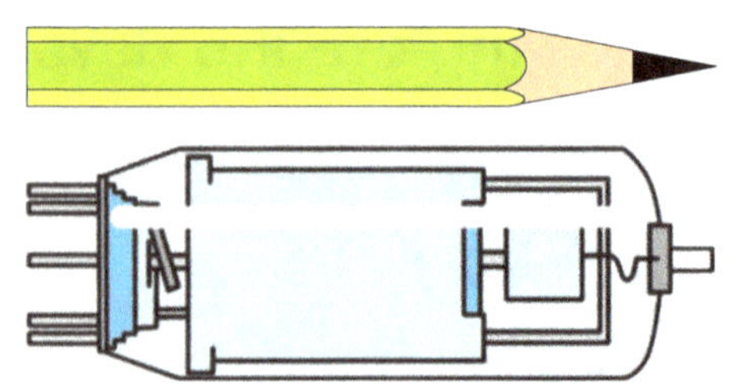

vacuum tube

Limitations of First-Generation Computers

⇒ Thousands of vacuum tubes were used in these computers that generated a lot of heat. They had to be cooled down by air conditioners only.

⇒ These computers were very large, quite slow with less memory, very expensive and not very reliable.

Due to the limitations and drawbacks of the first-generation computers the more advanced computers developed, which were the second-generation computers.

Second-Generation Computers (1957-1963)

⇒ The invention of transistors marked the commencement of the second generation.

⇒ Transistors were highly superior to the Vacuum tube that made the computer more reliable and consume low electricity. They occupied less space.

⇒ During this period, Magnetic cores were also invented for storage.

⇒ Second-generation computers were the first computers that stored their instructions in their memory. The capacity of memory was around 128 KB (kilobyte).

⇒ These computers used symbolic language, *i.e.* Assembly language instead of Machine language.

⇒ IBM 1401, IBM 7094, CDC 3600, Mark III and UNIVAC 1108 are the examples of Second-Generation Computers.

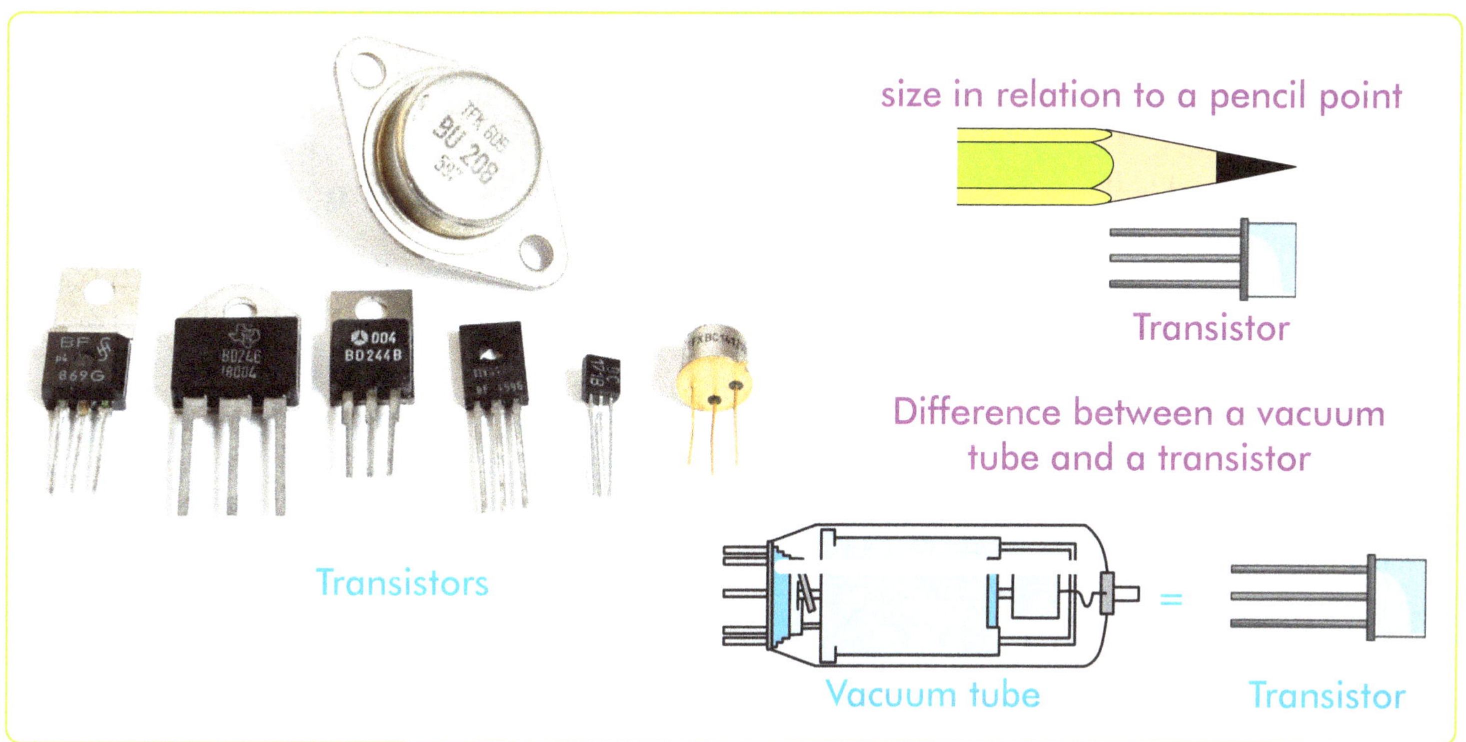

Limitations of Second-Generation Computers

⇒ Second-generation computers also produced a lot of heat, and they too had to be cooled down by air conditioners.

⇒ Speed and memory was still low.

Due to the limitations and drawbacks of the second-generation computers, the more advanced computers developed, which were third-generation computers.

Third-Generation Computers (1965-1971)

⇒ The Integrated Circuits (IC) replaced the Transistors which marked the start of the third-generation. The Integrated circuit (IC) is also called the chip.

⇒ The inventors of Integrated Circuits were Jack St. Clair Kibly and Robert Noyce.

⇒ The Third-Generation Computers proved to be highly reliable, a bit less expensive and faster. The size of the computer became smaller than that of compared to the computer of the previous generation.

⇒ During this generation, mainframe computers were developed; for example, IBM 360 series, ICL 1900 series, etc.

⇒ The capacity of memory was around 1 MB (megabyte).

⇒ The language used in the Third Generation Computers was High level language (FORTRAN and COBOL).

⇒ In the Third-Generation Computers, users interacted with keyboards and monitors which interfaced with an operating system.

⇒ This period witnessed the areas of application which concentrated mainly on education, business, science and engineering.

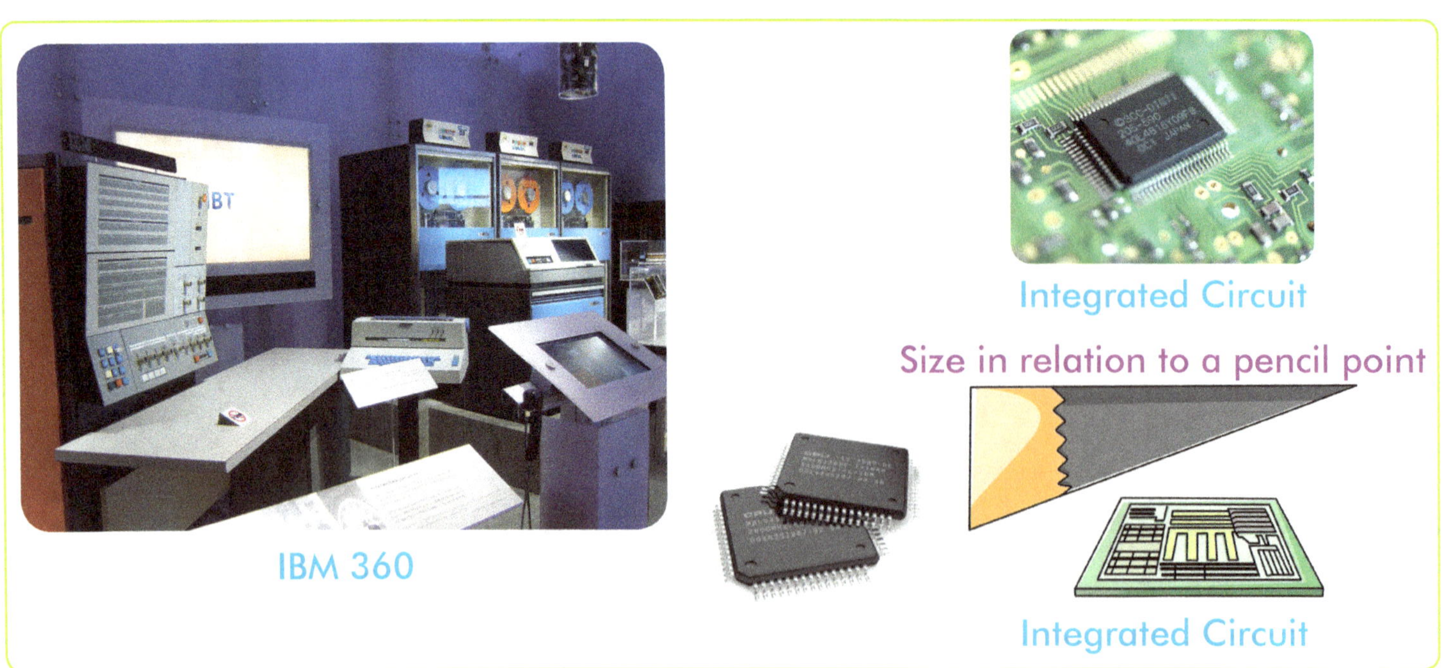

One tiny integrated circuit is equivalent to thousands of transistors.

Fourth-Generation Computers (1972-2010)

⇒ The beginning of this generation of computers was marked by the advent of the microprocessor chip.

⇒ The Intel 4004, the first microprocessor of the world, was invented by Dr. Ted Hoff, an engineer with the Intel Corporation. This technology is considered as Very Large Scale Integration (VLSI). The examples of the Fourth-Generation Computers are Intel 4004, Apple, IBM 370, etc.

⇒ The powerful operating system was developed with the processing speed, faster access and increased memory capacity.

⇒ The Fourth-Generation Computers became more powerful and they could be linked together to form a network, which ultimately led to the development and rapid evolution of the Internet.

⇒ The size of the computer in this era has become very small as compared to the size of the previous generation. For example, the computer of the first generation which occupied an entire room could now fit in the palm of the hand.

⇒ The programming languages used were C, C++, Java etc.

⇒ In 1981, IBM introduced its first personal computer (PC) for the home user. In 1984, Apple introduced the Macintosh.

Intel 4004

Intel Core i7

Personal Computer from IBM

Macintosh from Apple

Fifth-Generation Computers (2010 to present)

⇒ Fifth-Generation Computers use artificial intelligence which means decisions will be taken by the computer.

⇒ In these computers, large numbers of processors are used for more efficient performance. Voice recognition is a special feature in these computers.

⇒ ROBOT is the example of the fifth-generation of computers.

LET'S HAVE A LOOK

- Valves and Vacuum tubes were used in the first generation of computers.
- The first-generation of computers used Machine language to instruct the system.
- Transistors were invented during the second generation of computers.
- Integrated Circuits (IC) were used in the third generation of computers.
- The fourth generation of computers witnessed the advent of microprocessor chip.
- Fifth-Generation Computers used artificial intelligence that made the computer take all decisions.

BRAIN TEASER

1. Answer each of the following in one word or line:

a. In which generation of computers were vacuum tubes used?

b. In which generation of computers were transistors used?

c. Give one example of High Level Language.

d. What does IC stand for?

e. Name the first microprocessor of the world.

f. Write the example of the Fifth-Generation Computers?

2. Answer the following in brief:

a. Define the different generations of computers.

b. How were the Integrated Circuits (ICs) superior to transistors?

c.   What were the disadvantages of the First-Generation Computers?

d.   What is IC? How was it better than the components of the First-Generation Computers?

e.   How did the microprocessor help in the development of the modern computer?

f.   What will be the use of the Fifth-Generation Computers?

3.   Write the full forms of the following abbreviations:

a.   ENIAC

b.   EDVAC

c.   IC

d.   UNIVAC

e.   VLSI

4.   Fill in the blanks:

a.   In the First-Generation Computers, ___________ language was used for giving instructions to the system.

b.   The transistor was invented in the ___________ generation of computers.

c.   The Fifth Generation Computers use ___________.

d.   The first microprocessor was invented by ___________.

e.   Integrated Circuit was invented by ___________ and ___________.

f.   The Integrated Circuit is also called ___________.

g.   In 1981, ___________ introduced its personal computer (PC) for the home user.

5. Multiple Choice Questions

Tick (✓) the correct answer:

a. Which one was used in the first generation?

   i. Vacuum Tube ☐   ii. Microprocessor ☐   iii. Transistor ☐

b. Which generation used integrated circuit?

   i. First ☐   ii. Second ☐   iii. Third ☐

c. Language used in the first generation is:

   i. Assembly ☐   ii. High level ☐   iii. Machine ☐

d. IBM 360 is an example of:

   i. First ☐   ii. Second ☐   iii. Third ☐

e. Which one is the example of the second generation?

   i. EDVAC ☐   ii. IBM 1401 ☐   iii. CDC 1700 ☐

f. Number of generations of computer:

   i. 8 ☐   ii. 4 ☐   iii. 5 ☐

6. Match the following generations given in Column A with their components in Column B:

Column A	Column B
a. Ist generation	(i) Transistors
b. IInd generation	(ii) Integrated Circuits
c. IVth generation	(iii) Vacuum Tubes
d. IIIrd generation	(iv) VLSI

ACTIVITY TIME

Make a project in your class about the different generations of the computer with the help of your teacher.

2 Computer Language

Dear children, as you all know, a language is required to communicate with each other. Different countries have different languages to communicate. Similarly, in order to communicate with the computer, a special language is required that is understood by the computer. In this chapter, we shall study about the different types of computer languages.

COMPUTER LANGUAGE

A system of communication is called a language. A language that is understood by the computer is called computer language. A computer language is a special type of language, consisting of various types of commands and rules, that is used to do different types of tasks in the computer and understood by the computer.

A computer language is a set of words, symbols and codes that is used to write a computer program. The process of writing these instructions (program) is called programming. The people who can write these programs are called programmers.

Computers only understand the Machine Language to carry out their jobs.

Computer languages are classified into two major categories: Low-Level Language (LLL) and High-Level Language (HLL).

Here is the chart showing the categorisation of computer language.

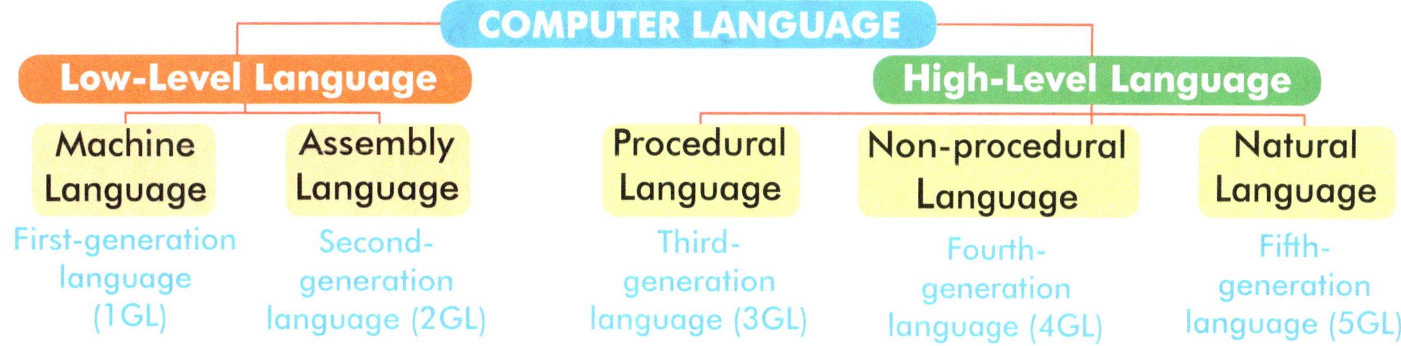

LOW-LEVEL LANGUAGE (LLL)

A low-level language is often closer to the computer. It is described as the machine-oriented language. A low-level language is directly understood by the computer.

The two categories of low-level languages are Machine languages and Assembly languages respectively.

Machine Language

Machine language is also known as the first-generation language (1GL). It is the only language which the computer can understand directly.

Machine language is a Binary Language which is in the form of 0s and 1s. The '0' stands for the absence of electric pulse (OFF) and '1' stands for the presence of electric pulse (ON).

Machine language has dual advantages — high speed and very low utilisation. But understanding and learning a machine language is not an easy task.

Machine language is machine-dependent i.e. Machine language programs run only on the computer for which they were developed. It is not compatible with other computers.

As you all know, the computer is a machine and it only understands the machine language directly. So, no translators are required to translate the programming code.

Assembly Language

Assembly language is also known as the second-generation language (2GL). It is a Symbolic Language, where computer programs consist of symbols or mnemonic codes in place of 0's and 1's. It is easy to understand as compared to the machine language.

The computer is not able to understand this language because the computer understands the machine language only. Therefore, it is required to convert this language to the machine language so that the computer may understand this program. For this, an Assembler is required which is used for the conversion of assembly language to machine language.

A program written in Assembly language is the source program and the program which gets converted into the Machine language by the Assembler is called Object program. For example, ADA is an Assembly language.

HIGH-LEVEL LANGUAGE (HLL)

A High-Level Language is a language which is commonly used by the user/programmer for writing programs. It is an English-like language which is easily understandable by the user. But again, this language is not understood by the computer and, therefore, needs a convertor which can convert this language to a computer understandable language (Machine language). For this purpose, we use Interpreter/compiler which translates the High Level Language into the Machine Language.

High-level languages often are machine-independent. A machine-independent language can run on many different types of computers and operating systems.

For example, C, C++, COBOL, BASIC, LOGO, etc. are High-Level Languages.

Three main categories of high-level languages are: Procedural language, Non-procedural language and Natural language.

Procedural Languages

A procedural language is also called third-generation language (3GL). In this language, the programmer writes instructions that tell the computer what to accomplish and how to do it.

A procedural language instruction is written as a series of English-like words, like ADD for addition, etc. It also uses arithmetic operators, such as * for multiplication and + for addition. These English-like words and arithmetic notations make easy for the programmer to write the program. E.g., BASIC, COBOL, PASCAL, FORTRAN.

Like an assembly language program, the procedural language is called the source program, which must be translated into machine language before the computer can understand it. Compiler or an interpreter is the program used to perform the translation for the third-generation languages.

Non-procedural Language

A non-procedural language is also called fourth-generation language (4GL). In this language, the programmer only specifies what the program should accomplish without explaining the manner. It enables users and programmers to write English-like instructions or interact with a graphical environment to retrieve data from files or a database.

Non-procedural languages typically are easier to use than procedural languages. Users with very little programming background can develop programs using non-procedural languages. Visual Basic, Oracle, JAVA, etc. are the examples of non-procedural languages.

Natural Language

A natural language is sometimes called fifth-generation language (5GL). It is often associated with expert systems and artificial intelligence. It allows the programmer to enter requests that resemble human speech.

For example, in the fourth-generation language (4GL), if you will write a program to obtain the names of the students whose marks exceed 80 it might be written as:

SELECT FIRST-NAME, LAST-NAME FROM STUDENT WHERE marks > 80.

A natural language version of the same program might be written or spoken as TELL ME THE NAMES OF STUDENTS WITH MARKS OVER 80.

INTERPRETER/COMPILER

The computer understands only one language, *i.e.* machine language. So, the instructions given in high level language are first translated into the machine language with the help of Interpreter or compiler.

Compiler

A compiler is a software that translates the whole high level language program into machine language at once. It displays the errors, if any, in the form of message. It takes less time to execute.

Interpreter

An interpreter is also a software that translates one line at a time of high level language program. It displays the errors one line at a time and it goes to the next line only after the correction of the error. It takes much time to execute.

COMMONLY USED PROGRAMMING LANGUAGES

Some commonly used Programming languages are:

C A programming language, developed in the early 1970s by Dennis Ritchie at Bell Laboratories.

BASIC Beginners All Purpose Symbolic Instruction Code.
It was developed by John Kemeny and Thomas Kurtz.

FORTRAN FORmula TRANslation is one of the first high-level programming languages used for scientific applications.

ALGOL ALGOrithmic Language is the first structured procedural language.

COBOL COmmon Business Oriented Language. It is a programming language designed for business applications.

RPG Report Program Generator. It is used to assist businesses with generating reports and to access/update data in databases.

LOGO Language of Graphics Oriented. It is an educational tool used to teach programming and problem-solving techniques to children.

C++ It is an object-oriented programming (OOP) language. It is an extension to C.

Java It is an object-oriented programming (OOP) language developed by Sun Microsystems.

Visual Basic It is a programming language that is based on the BASIC programming language, developed by Microsoft.

Visual C++ It is a programming language based on C++.

Delphi Borland's Delphi is a powerful program development tool that is ideal for building large-scale enterprises and Web applications.

Prolog PROgramming LOGic, used for the development of artificial intelligence applications.

HTML Hypertext Markup Language. It is a special formatting language used to format documents for display on the Web.

JavaScript It is an interpreted language that allows a programmer to add dynamic content to a Web page.

Python   Python is widely regarded as a programming language that's easy to learn, due to its simple syntax, a large library of standards and toolkits, and integration with other popular programming languages such as C and C++.

Python is used in a wide variety of applications, including artificial intelligence, financial services, and data science. Social media sites such as Instagram and Pinterest are also built on Python.

LET'S HAVE A LOOK

- A system of communication is called a language.
- A language that is understood by the computer is called computer language.
- A computer language is a set of words, symbols and codes that is used to write a computer program.
- The people who can write these programs are called programmers.
- Machine Language is a Binary Language which is in the form of 0s and 1s.
- An Assembler is required which is used for the conversion of assembly language into machine language.
- We use Interpreter/compiler which translates the High-Level Language Machine Language.
- A procedural language is also called third-generation language (3GL).
- A non-procedural language is also called fourth-generation language (4GL).
- A natural language is sometimes called fifth-generation language (5GL).

BRAIN TEASER

1. Answer each of the following in one word or line:

   a.   Which language is understood by the computer?

   b.   Which language is also called Binary Language?

   c.   Which language is also called Symbolic Language?

   d.   Name the two types of Low-Level Language.

e.   Name the translators used to translate High-Level Language into Machine Language.

f.   Name any four programming languages.

2.   Answer the following in brief:

a.   What is Machine Language?

b.   What is the use of Assembler?

c.   What is the use of compiler and interpreter?

d.   How is a machine language different from an assembly language?

e.   Distinguish between source program and object program.

f.   What is the difference between HLL and LLL?

3.   Write the full forms of the following:

a.   HLL

b.   FORTRAN

c.   BASIC

d.   COBOL

e.   LLL

4. **Multiple Choice Questions:**
   Tick (✓) the correct answer:

   a.   The language also known by binary language:
        i.   Machine language ☐   ii.   High Level Language ☐
        iii. Assembly Language ☐

   b.   The program used to translate HLL into machine language:
        i. Assembler ☐   ii. Compiler ☐   iii.   Mnemonic codes ☐

   c.   Example of Assembly language:
        i. ADA ☐   ii. C++ ☐   iii.   HTML ☐

   d.   A non-procedural language is also called:
        i. 3GL ☐   ii. 4GL ☐   iii. 5GL ☐

   e.   A programming language developed by Dennis Ritchie at Bell
        Laboratories:
        i. JAVA ☐   ii. C ☐   iii.   LOGO ☐

   f.   A language used for the development of artificial intelligence
        applications:
        i. Prolog ☐   ii. C++ ☐   iii.   Delphi ☐

5. **Fill in the blanks:**

   a.   ____________________ and ____________________ are the two categories of computer language.

   b.   The machine code is represented by ____________________.

   c.   Low level languages are ____________________ dependent languages.

   d.   ____________________ and ____________________ are the programs that translate HLL into the machine language.

   e.   ____________________ is the first structured procedural language.

6. **Write 'T' for true or 'F' for false in the boxes:**

   a.   The people who write the programs are called users. ☐

   b.   The computer understands only the Machine language. ☐

   c.   Machine language uses binary digits, 0 and 1. ☐

   d.   Assembly language is also called the Procedural language. ☐

   e.   High-level languages are machine-independent. ☐

Formative Assessment-1
(Chapters 1-2)

1. Complete the table to compare the generations of the computer.

Generation	Period	Device used	Example
1st			
2nd			
3rd			
4th			
5th			

2. Complete the following:

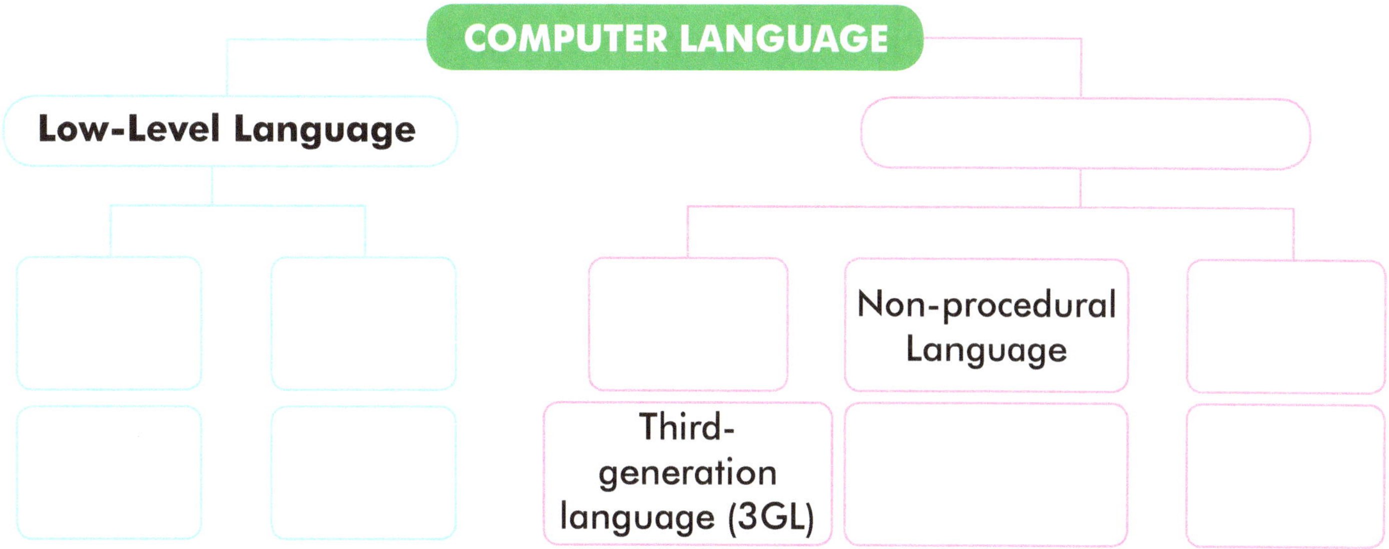

COMPUTER LANGUAGE

Low-Level Language

Non-procedural Language

Third-generation language (3GL)

3. Make a list of some commonly used High Level languages.

a. _______________

b. _______________

c. _______________

d. _______________

e. _______________

f. _______________

g. _______________

h. _______________

3 Files and Folders in Windows 10

Hi students! In the previous class, you learnt about decorating Windows 10. One of the main functions of Windows 10 is to manage your work in different files and folders. In this chapter, we will learn about these files and folders and how to manage them properly.

Managing and organizing tasks in Windows is done with the help of files and folders.

Here, we will learn to manage files and folders in proper manner.

FILES

A file is the basic unit of storage. A file differentiates one set of information from another in the computer. Each file has a name. A file name is a unique combination of letters of alphabet, numbers and other characters that identify a file.

Document File

A file is a collection of information, like a program, a set of data used by a program, or a user-created document. It is a collection of data that a user can restore, change, delete, save or send to an output device, such as a printer or an e-mail program. A file in a computer is represented by an icon.

FOLDERS

A folder is an object that contains multiple files. A folder is a specifically named location on a storage medium that contains related documents.

In order to provide a storage system for the files on your computer, Windows uses folders. Folders are like a filing cabinet that are used to organise information. A folder contains programs and files. A folder can have both files and additional folders called sub-folders. A folder in a computer is also represented by an icon. By looking at these icons you can differentiate between the folders.

An empty folder   A folder containing files   A folder containing sub-folders

DISC/DRIVE

A disc is a circular object on which you store your files and a drive is the device that reads from and writes to storage media, including discs. Often these words are used as though they were the same thing.

Your files and folders are stored on the hard disk on your computer or on some kind of removable media like a floppy disk, a CD or DVD, a USB drive or other removable disk.

This PC allows the user to access and see the local drives and external drives available in the computer.

Local drives : These drives display the hard disk (storage device) of your computer. When you double-click on this icon, a window appears to display the contents of the hard disk drive.

External drives (Removable Storage)-(DVD RW Drive) : These drives show the data in your CD-ROM or pen drive you insert in your computer.

You can double-click on this icon to view the contents of the disk drive.

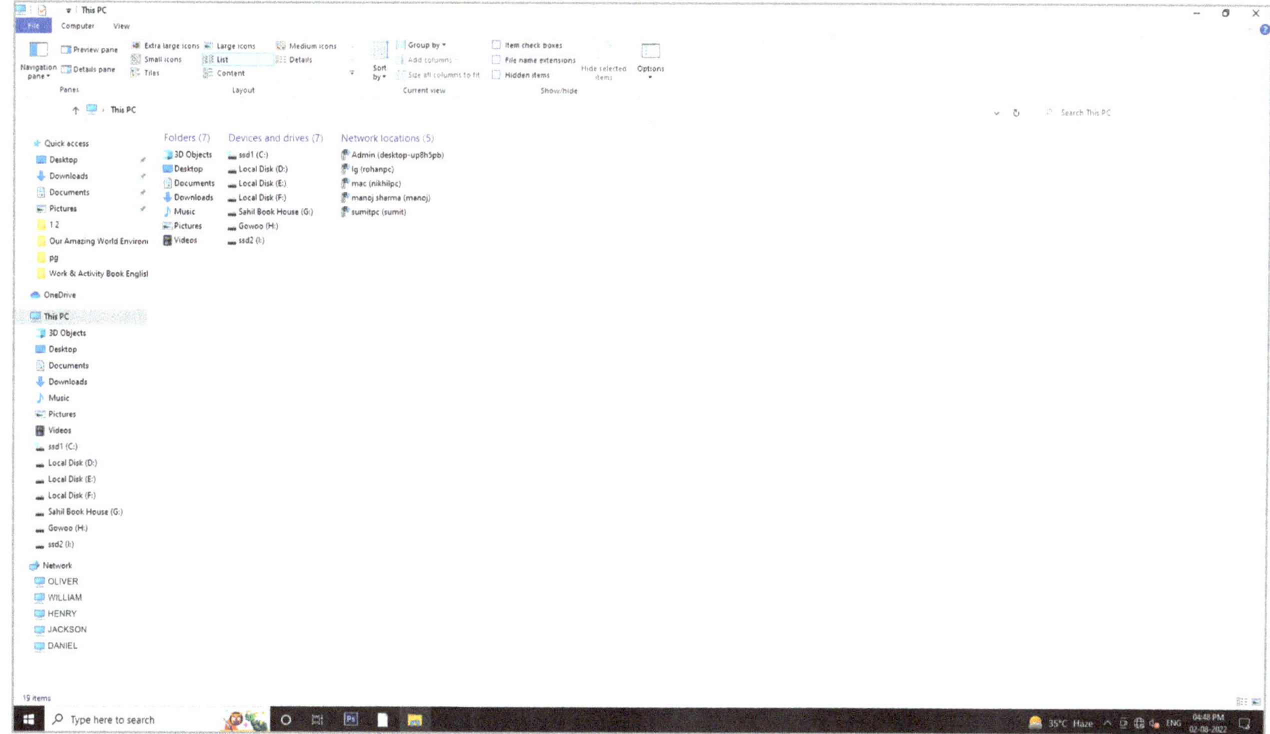

PATH OF FILES AND FOLDERS

A path is the route the user must follow to reach a folder or file from the drives. A path always starts with a drive letter.

Example: The path C:\Windows\calculator.exe is to the file that starts Calculator.

Difference between a folder path and a file path

A folder or a directory folder is a container wherein you store the files. Files are anything from picture files to word documents. The path to a folder is the address where the folder is kept on your computer. This applies full files as well. The path to a file is the address where it is kept on the computer.

ORGANIZING FILES AND FOLDERS

Files and folders can be organized in the common folders provided within Windows by default.

Documents : All text document files, like word processing files, spreadsheet and presentation, are stored in Document folder by default.

Pictures : All image files, you get from a camera, scanner or downloaded from the Internet, get stored in the Picture folder by default.

Music : All music or sound files, copied from an audio CD or downloaded from the Internet, are stored in Music folder by default.

Video : All video or movie files taken from a digital video camera or downloaded from the Internet are stored in Video folder by default.

Downloads : All programs and files downloaded from the Internet are stored in Download folder by default.

VIEWING FILES AND FOLDERS

Each program you have on your computer created a set of files and folders on your hard drive when it was installed, including Windows itself. If you want to open or work with those files, you first need to view them.

1. Double-click on (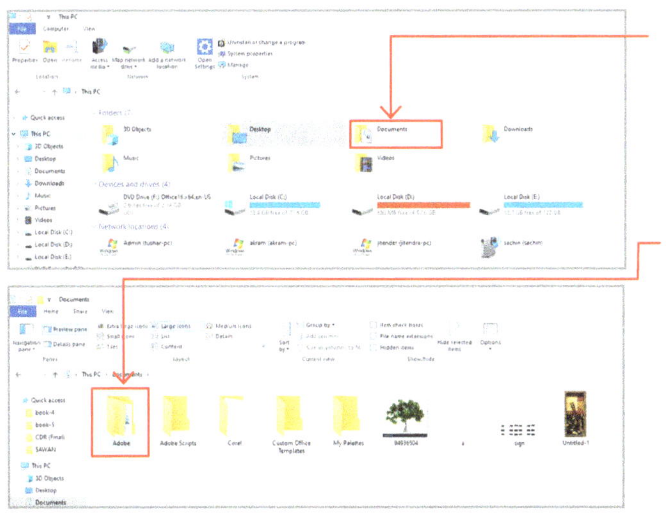) This PC icon on the desktop. This PC window will appear.

2. **Double-click** the location where your file/folder is located. Windows 10 displays the contents of folder including sub-folders.

3. **Double-click** the folder you want to view.

4. If the files you want to view are stored in a sub-folder, **double-click** the sub-folder.

Windows 10 displays the contents of the sub-folder.

CHANGING THE VIEW OF FILES AND FOLDERS

Windows provides a number of ways to arrange and identify your files while viewing them. The information can be viewed in different forms as follows:

Large Icons or Extra Large Icons: The images on a folder icon are displayed in Thumbnail View. It enables users to identify quickly the contents of the folder.

Small Icons: It displays your files and folders as small icons. The file name is displayed under the icon.

List view: It displays the contents as a list of files or folder names preceded by small icons. This view is useful if your folder contains many files and you want to scan the list for a file name. In this view, you can sort your files and folders.

Details view or content view: It gives us detailed information about files, including name, type, size and date modified.

Tiles view: It displays more information about the file.

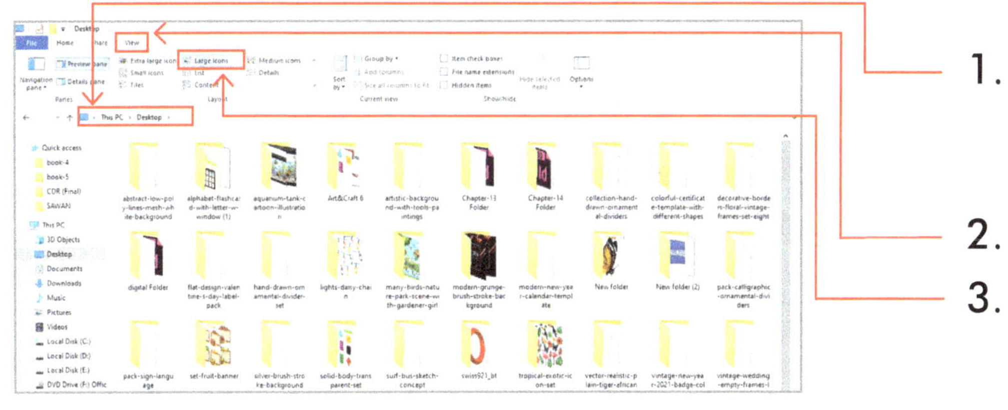

1. Open the **folder** containing files you want to view.

2. Click on **View** tab.

3. Click the type of **view** you want.

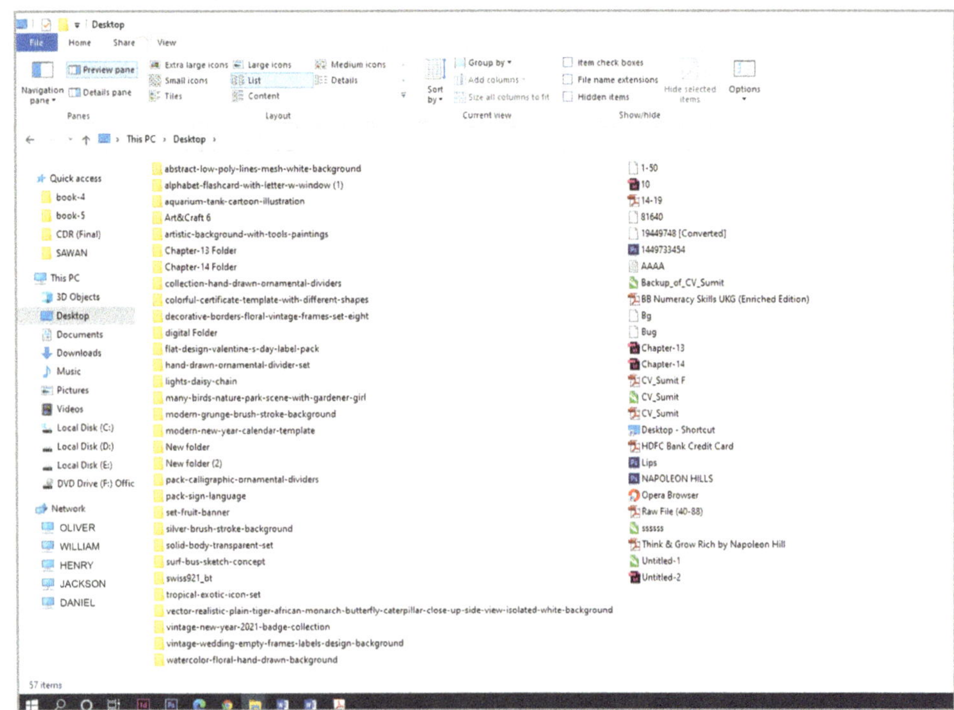

Windows changes the file view.

In this example, we change Large Icon view into List view.

🖱 SELECTING FILES AND FOLDERS

To perform any action with any file or folder, the first step is to select it so that Windows 10 may know exactly the file/folder wherein you want to work. Selected files appear highlighted on your screen.

The technique of selecting the folder or file is the same. The following are the various steps to select a file or a group of files.

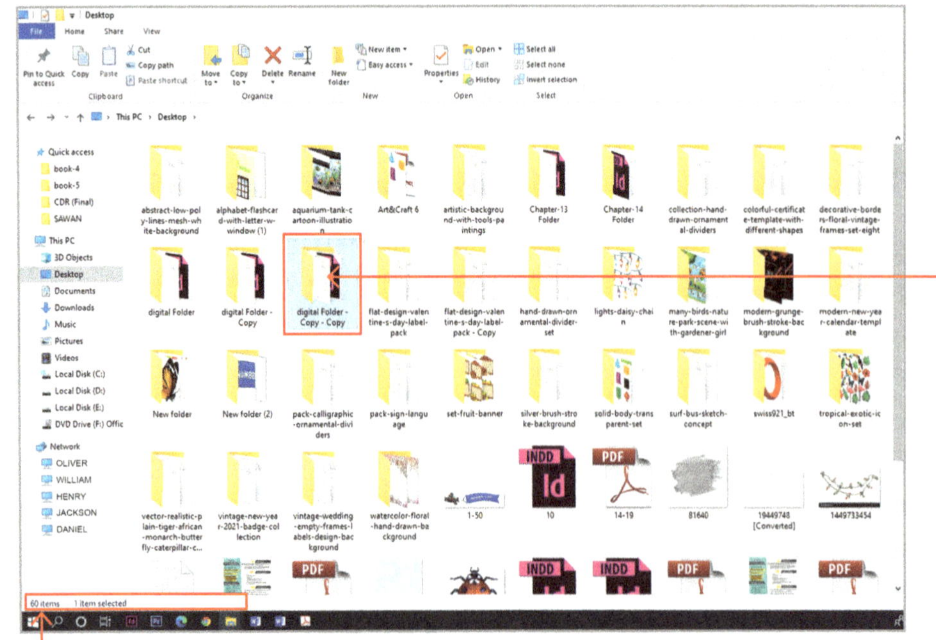

Selecting One File

1. Open the folder containing file.

2. Click the file you want to select.

The file is highlighted.

Information about the file appears in this area.

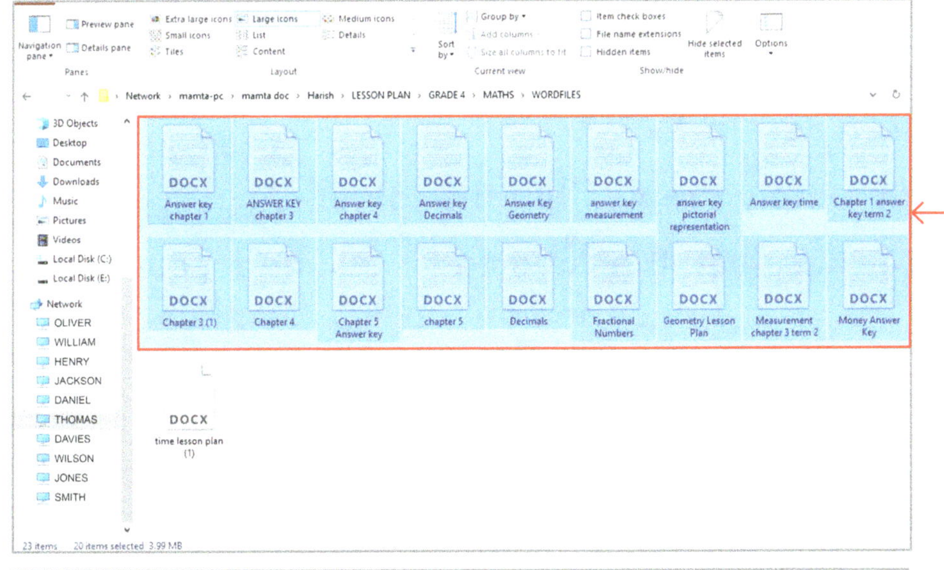

Selecting Multiple Files

1. Open the folder containing files.

2. Click the file you want to select.

3. Press and hold down the Ctrl key as you click each file you want to select.

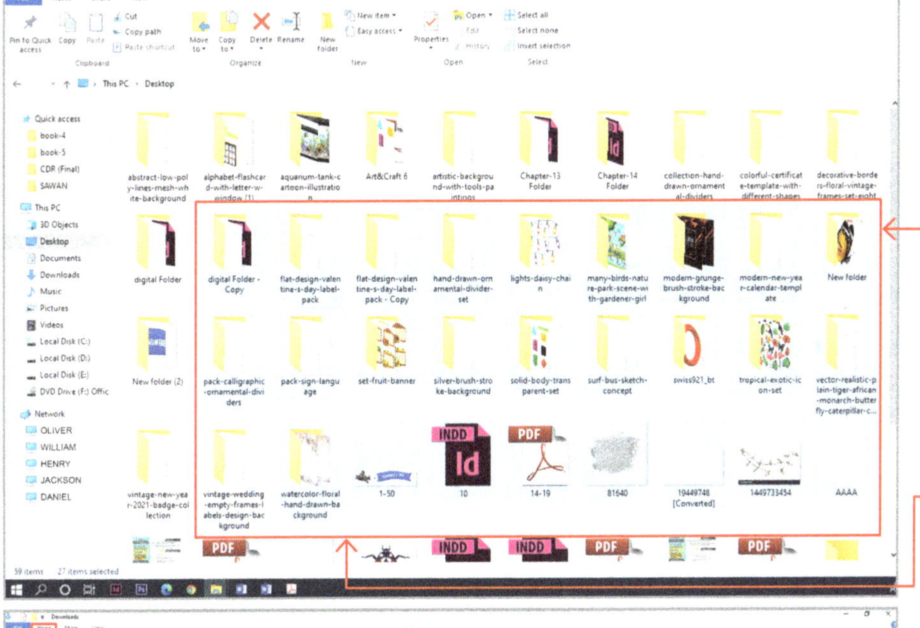

Selecting A Group of Files

1. Open the folder containing files.

2. Position the mouse pointer slightly above and slightly to the left of the first file in the group.

3. Click and drag the mouse pointer down and to the right until all the files in the group are selected.

Selecting All Files

1. Open the folder containing files.

2. Click on Home tab.

3. Click on Select All in Select tab. Windows selects all files in the folder.

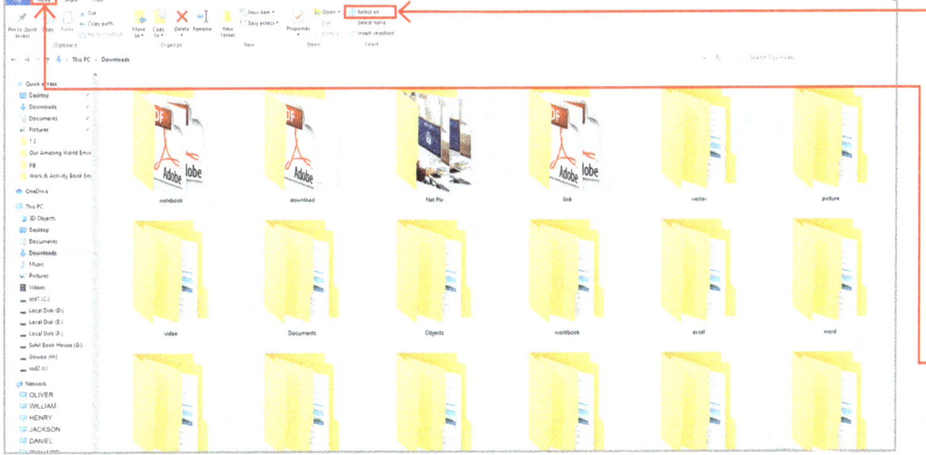

Deselecting File

⇒ To deselect **a single file** from a multiple-file selection, hold down **Ctrl** Key and click the file you want to deselect.

⇒ To deselect **all files**, click an empty area within the folder.

⇒ To reverse the selection—deselect the selected files and select the deselected files—click on **Home Tab** and then on **'Invert Selections'** under **Select tab**.

Note

Although you learn specifically about selecting files in this section yet the technique for selecting folders is exactly the same.

*Shortcut key for selecting all files command is **Ctrl + A**.*

COPYING FILES OR FOLDERS

A file or a folder can be copied from one location to another location or one folder to another folder.

When you **copy** a file/folder, the file/folder will remain in its original location and will also appear in the new location.

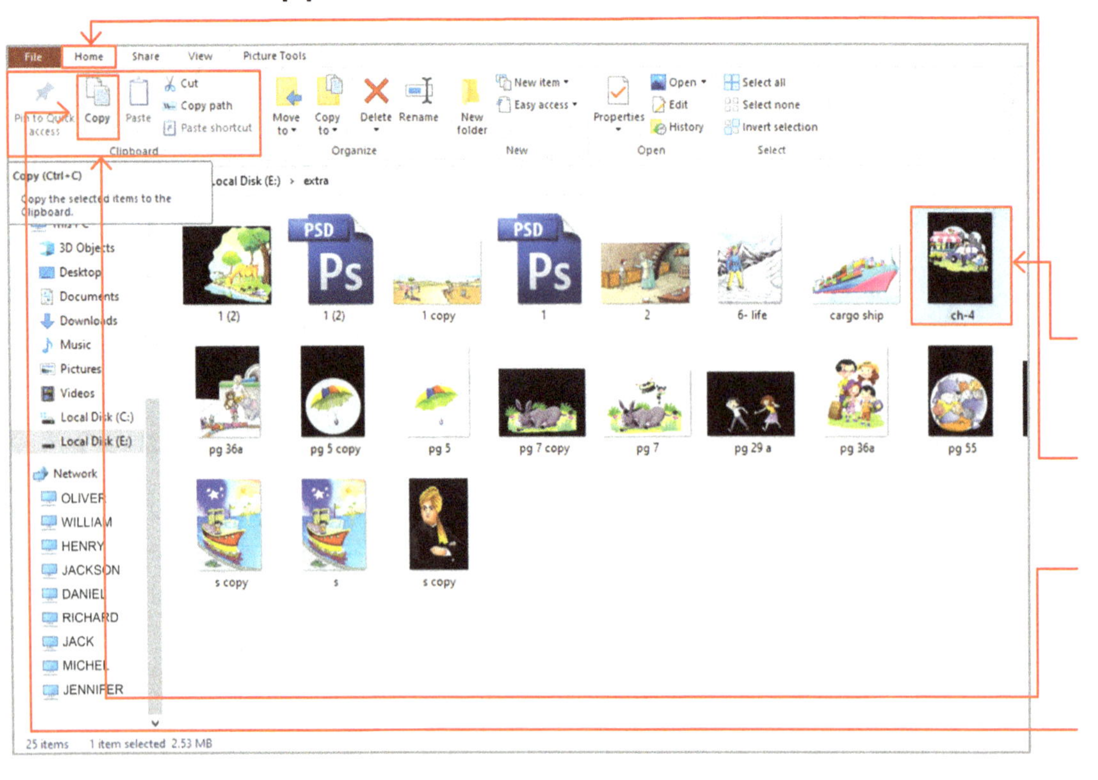

1. Open the folder containing the file you want to copy.

2. Select the **file/folder**.

3. Click on **Home** tab.

4. Go to **Clipboard** tab.

5. Click on **Copy**.

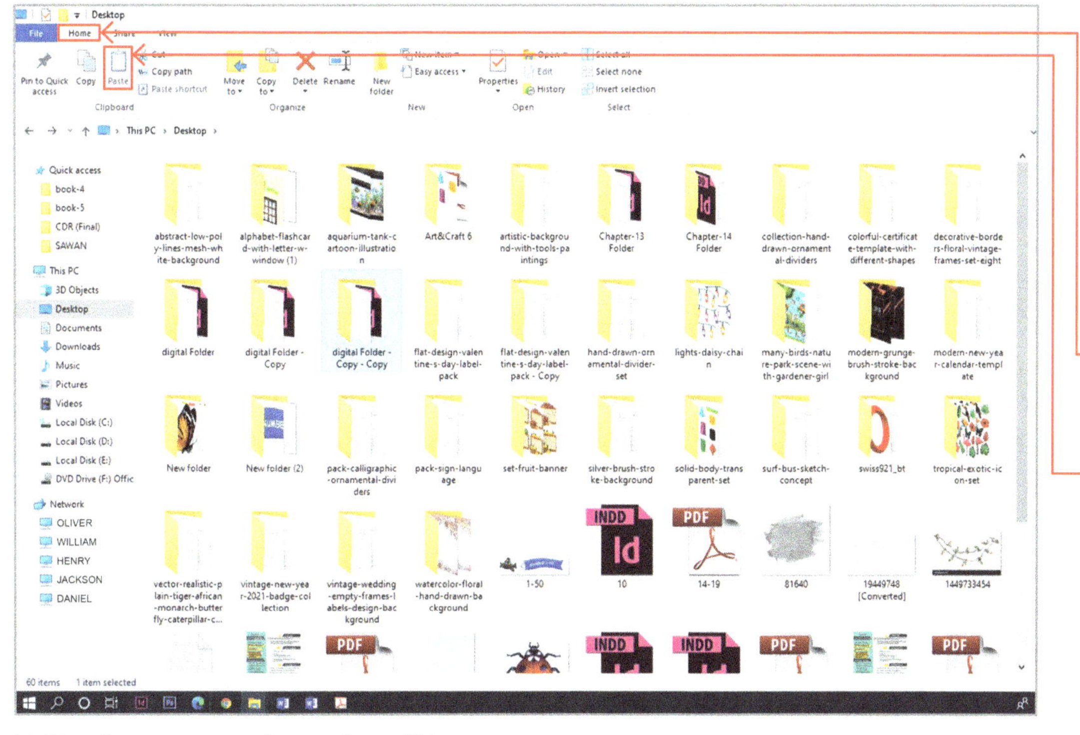

6. Navigate the folder where you want your file to paste.

7. Click on **Home** tab

8. Click on **Paste** in **Clipboard** tab.

Windows copies the file.

MOVING FILES AND FOLDERS

A file/folder can also be moved from one location to another location or one folder to another folder.

When you move a file/folder, the file/folder will disappear from its original location and will appear in the new location.

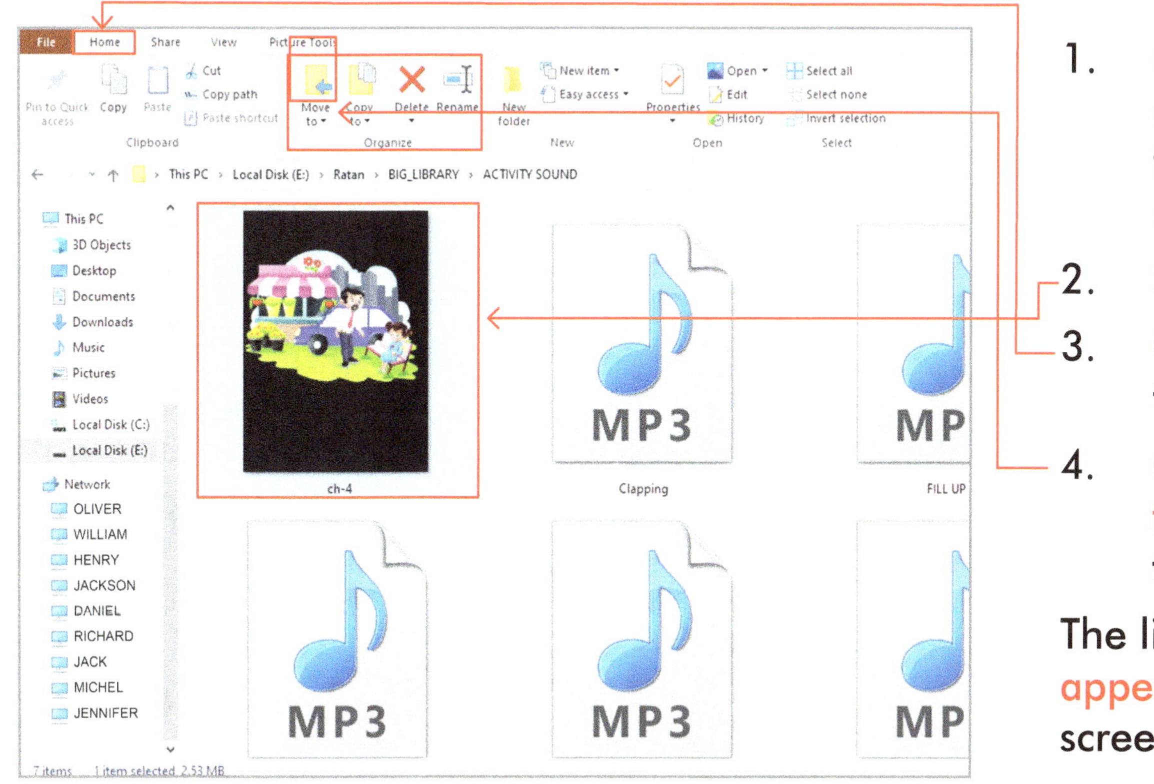

1. Open the folder containing the file you want to move.

2. Select the **file**.

3. Click on **Home** tab.

4. Click on **Move to** in **Organize** tab.

The list of **folders appears** on the screen.

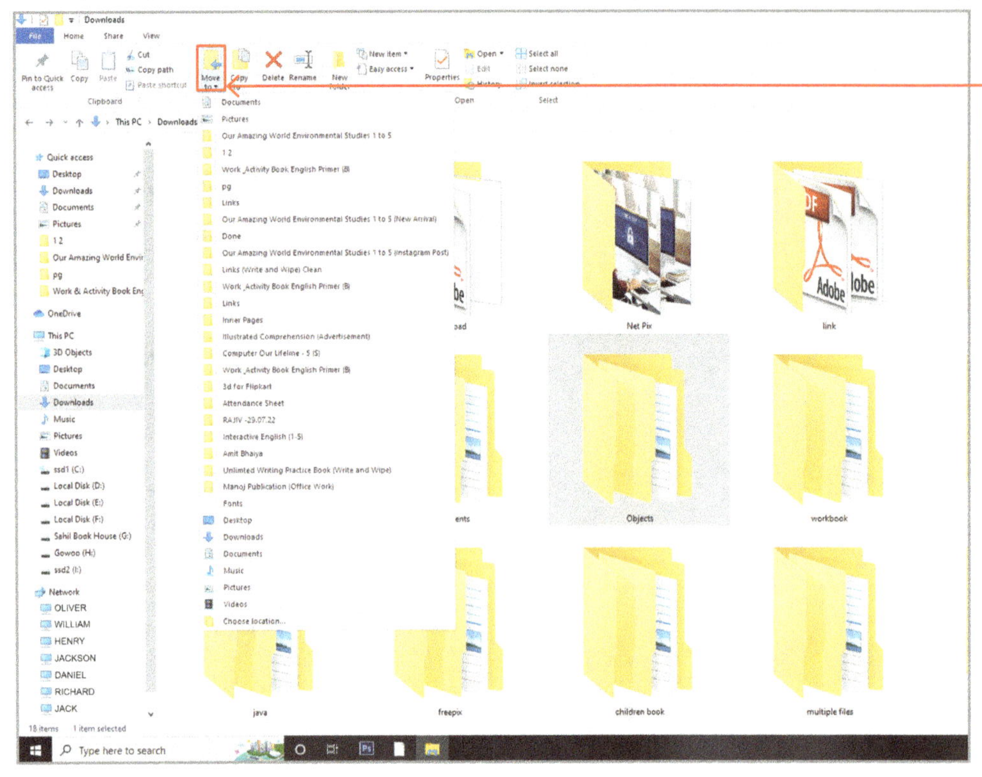

5. **Click on the folder where you want to paste your file.**

Windows moves the file into the Selected folder.

 CREATING A NEW FILE

The most common way to create new files is by using a program. But you can quickly create a new file directly at any location without starting any program or application. To create a new file, follow the steps as:

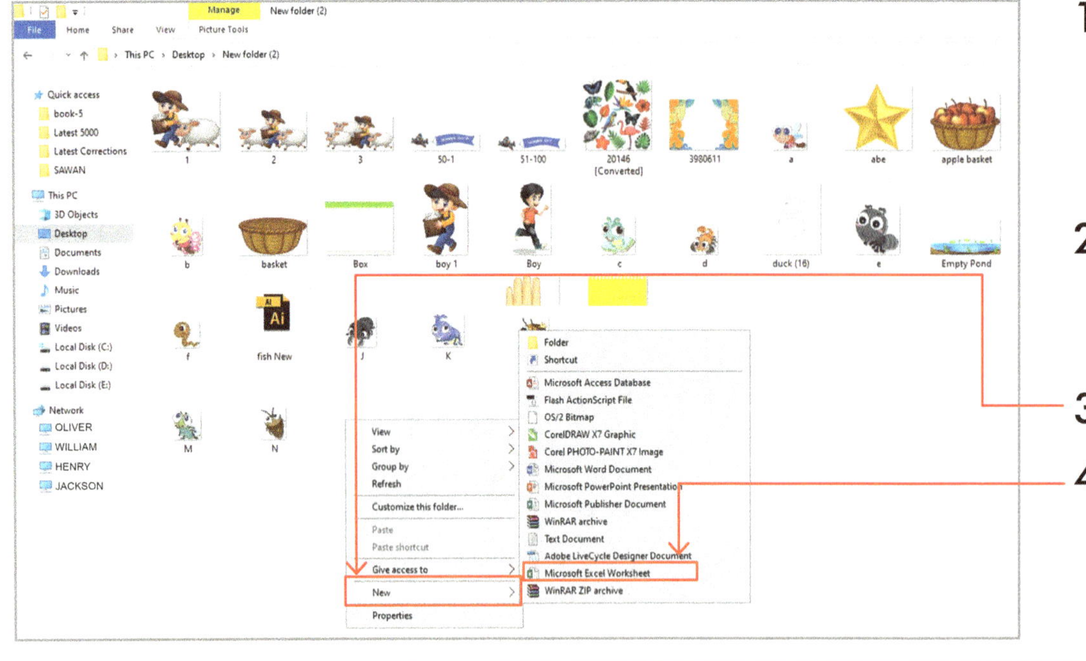

1. Open the folder in which you want to create a file.

2. Right-click an empty section of the folder.

3. Click on New.

4. Click the type of file you want to create.

Note

If you click Folder, Windows 10 creates a new sub-folder.

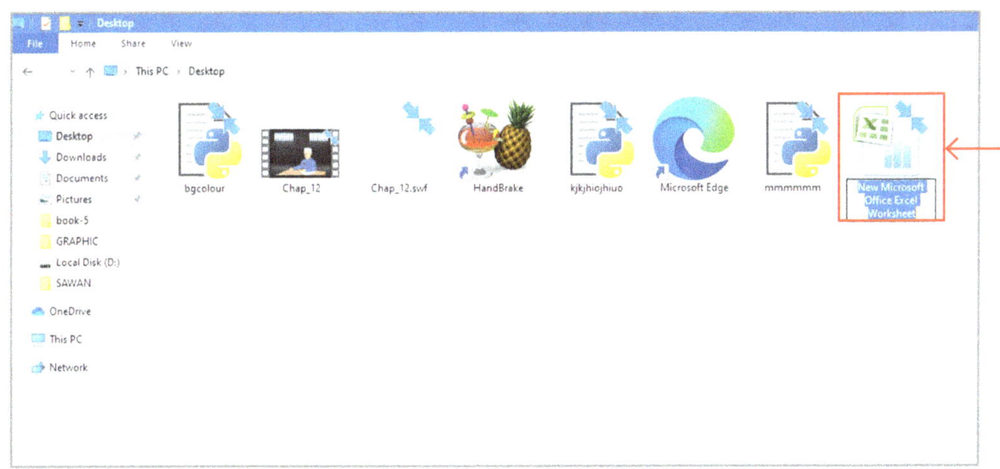

An icon for the new file appears in the folder.

5. Type the name you want to use for the new file and press the Enter key from the keyboard.

CREATING A FOLDER ON THE DESKTOP

You can create a personal folder to organize the files stored in your computer. You can also create a folder on the desktop. To create a folder on the desktop, the steps are:

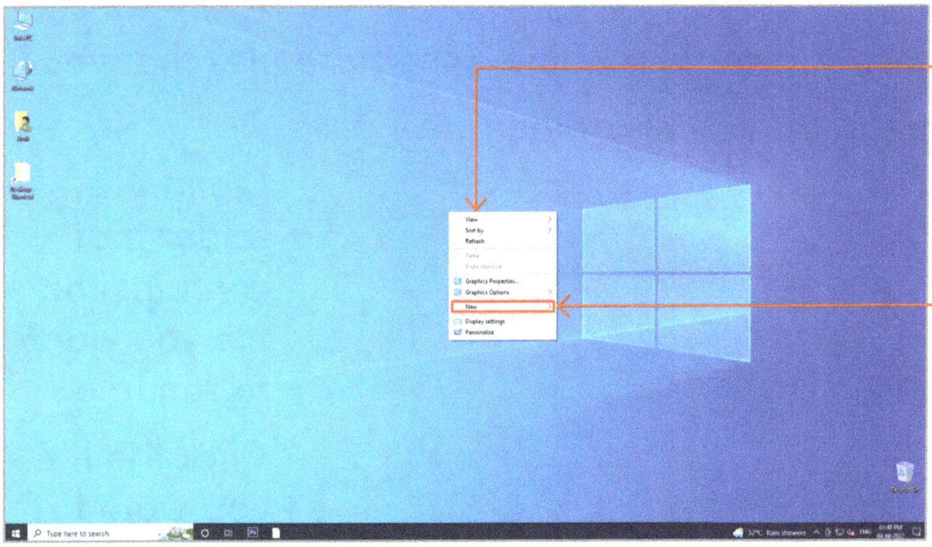

1. **Right-click** the mouse on a blank area on your desktop.

A menu appears.

2. Click on New.

A sub-menu will appear.

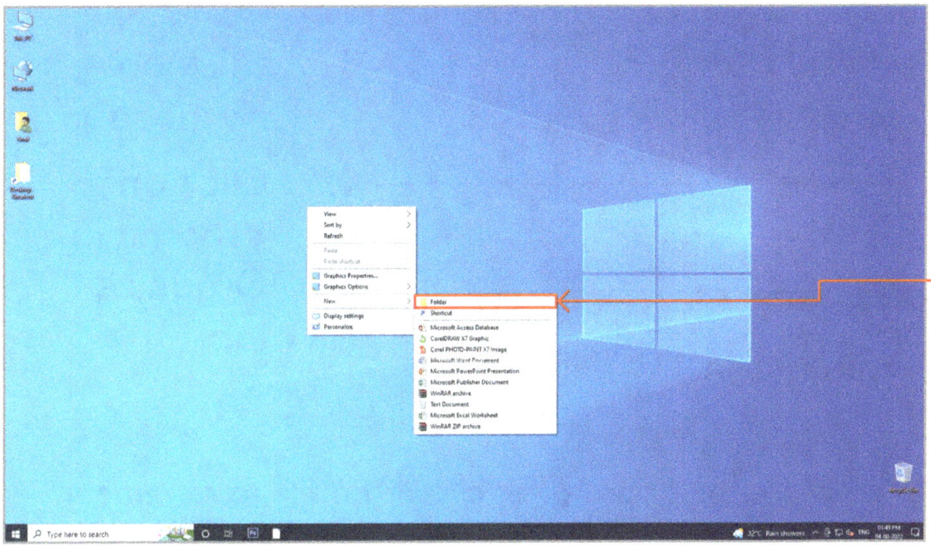

3. Click on Folder.

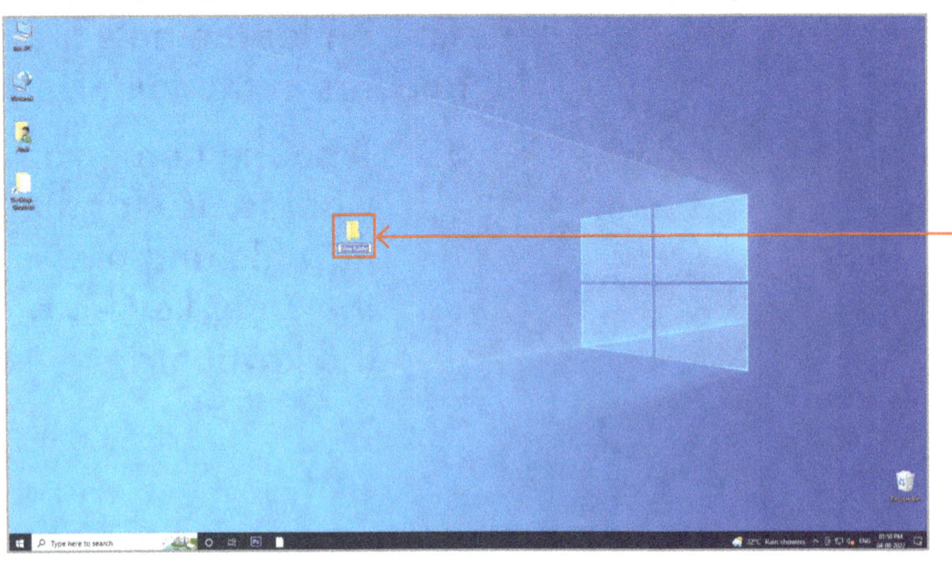

An icon for the new folder appears on the desktop.

4. Type the name you want to use for the new folder.

5. Press the **Enter** key.

RENAMING A FILE/FOLDER

You can rename a file/folder in order to describe its contents in a better way. A file/folder can be renamed exactly in the same way.

One thing to keep in mind that you should rename only those files that you have created. The steps for renaming the file/folder are:

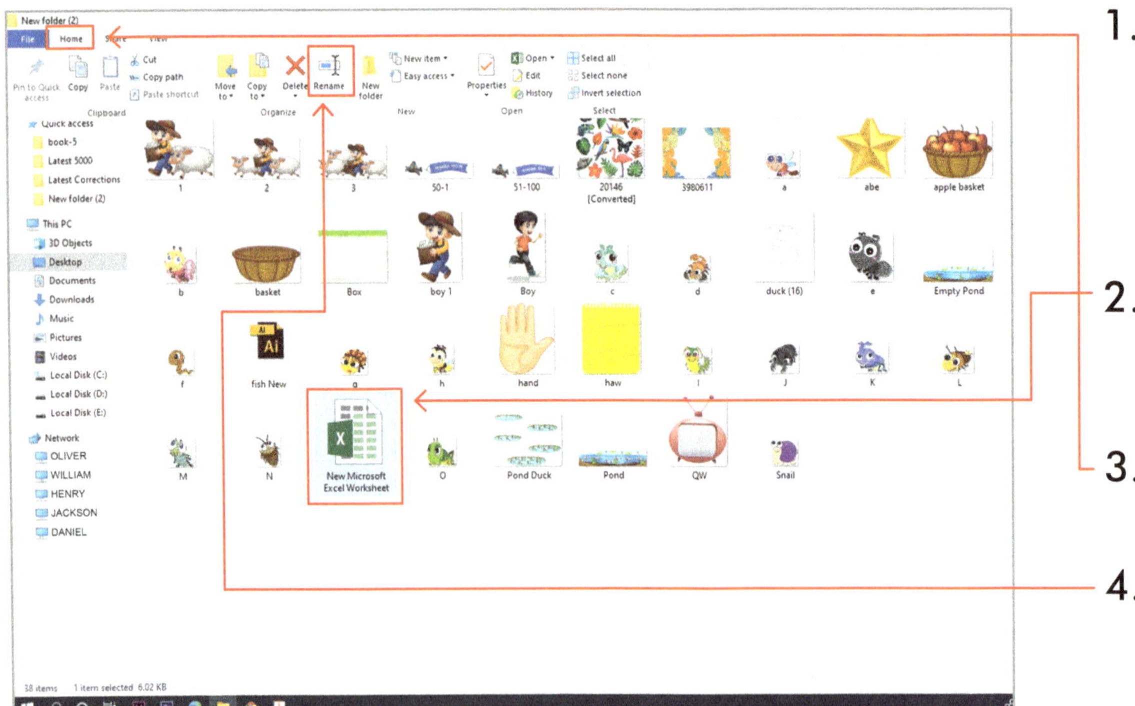

1. Open the folder that contains the file you want to rename.

2. Click the file you want to rename.

3. Click on **Home** tab.

4. Click on **Rename** in Organize tab.

A text box appears around the file name.

Note

You can also press F2 key from the keyboard after clicking a file to rename it.

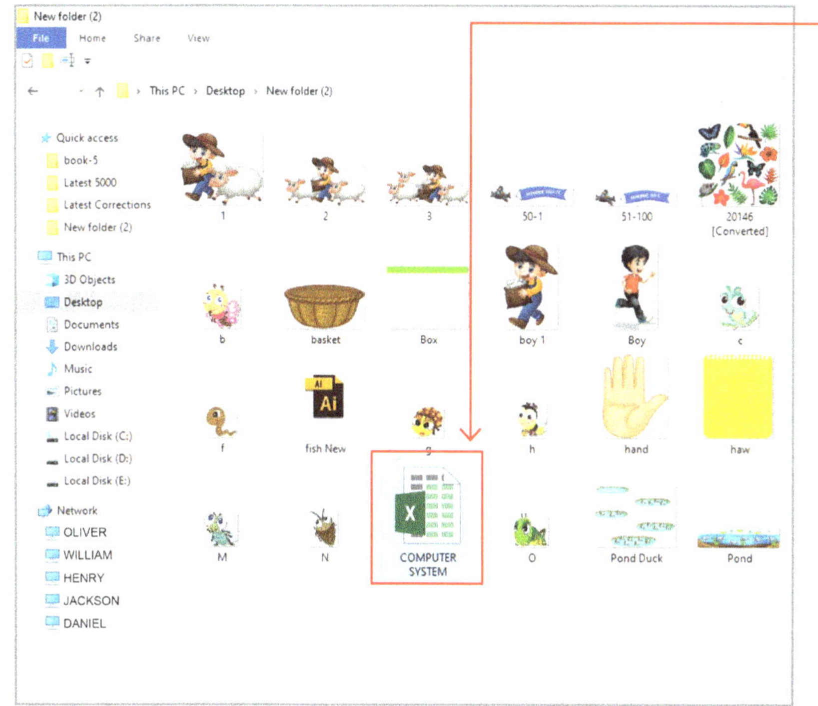

5. Type a new name for the file and then press the **Enter** key.

A file name cannot contain the / \? " < > or ! characters.

If you change your mind while typing a new file name, you can press the **ESC** key to return to the original file name.

The new name appears under the file's icon.

DELETE A FILE/FOLDER

A file/folder that is no longer required can be deleted from the memory of the computer. The deleted file/folder goes into the **Recycle bin**. Recycle Bin is the place where you can keep unwanted files before being permanently deleted. If you want to delete the file permanently, you have to delete it from the Recycle Bin. Follow the steps to delete a file/folder:

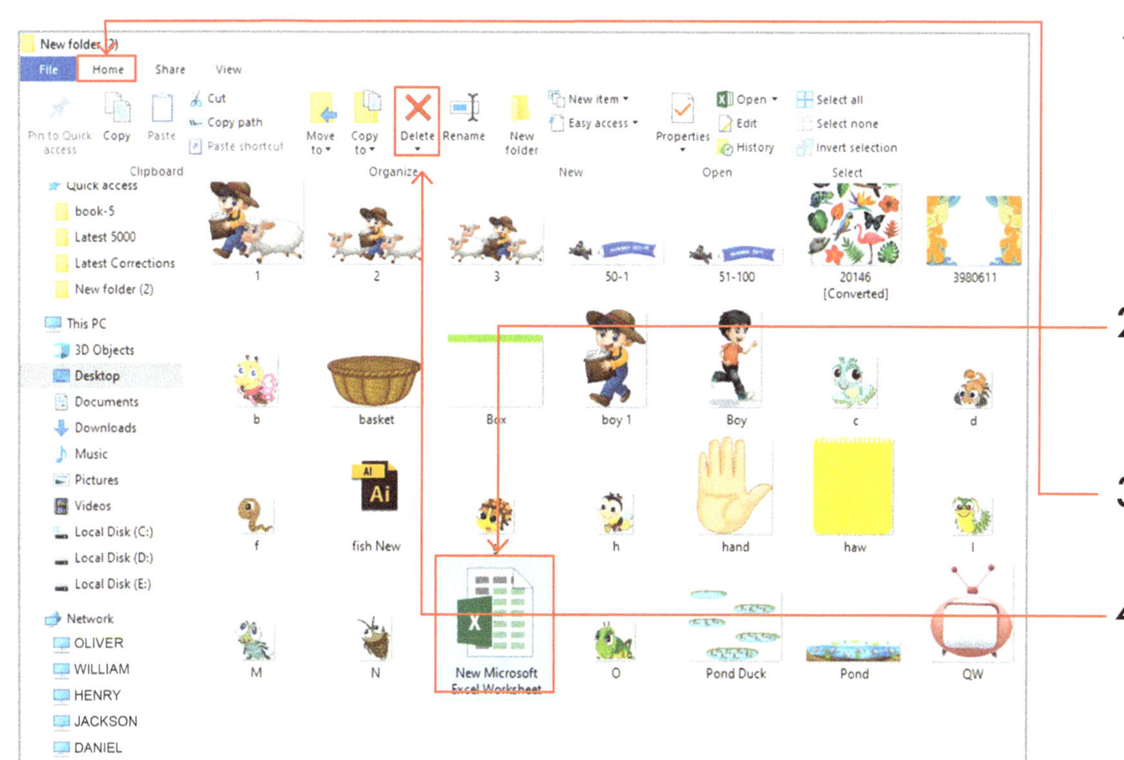

1. Open the folder that contains the file you want to delete.

2. Click the file you want to delete.

3. Click on **Home** tab.

4. Click on **Delete** in **Organize** tab.

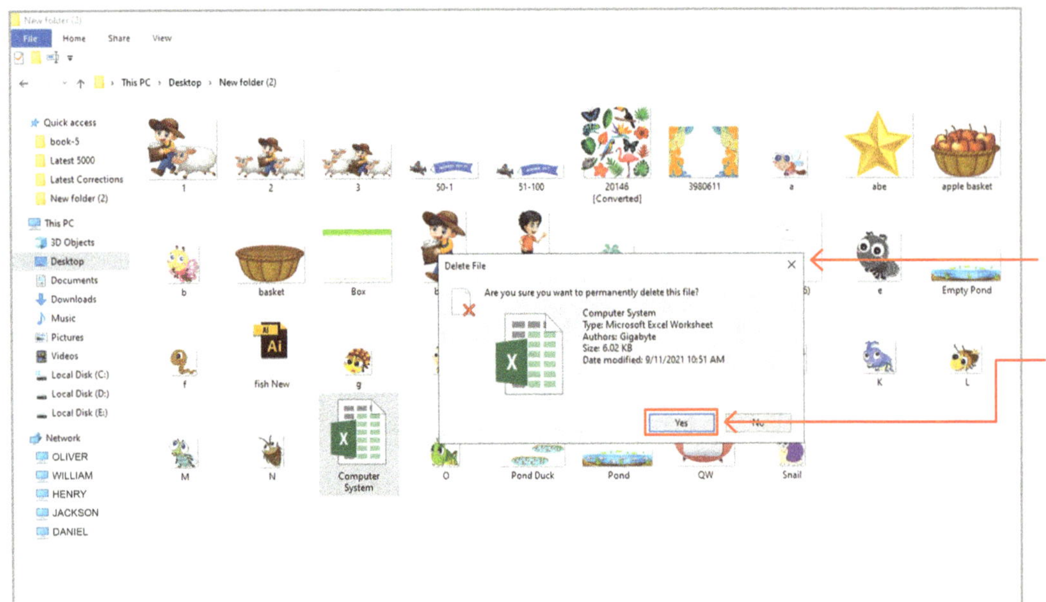

The **Delete File** dialog box appears.

5. Click on **Yes**.

The file disappears from the folder.

> ### Note
>
> *Another way to delete a file is to click and drag it to the desktop Recycle Bin icon.*
>
> *Make sure you delete only those documents that you have created yourself or that someone else has given to you. Do not delete any of the* Windows 10 system *files or any files associated with your programs, otherwise your computer may get a problem.*

RESTORING A DELETED FILE/FOLDER

The file/folder that is deleted goes to the **Recycle bin** and remains there until it is not removed from there.

Any file/folder is in the Recycle Bin can be again restored to its original location, if required. The steps are:

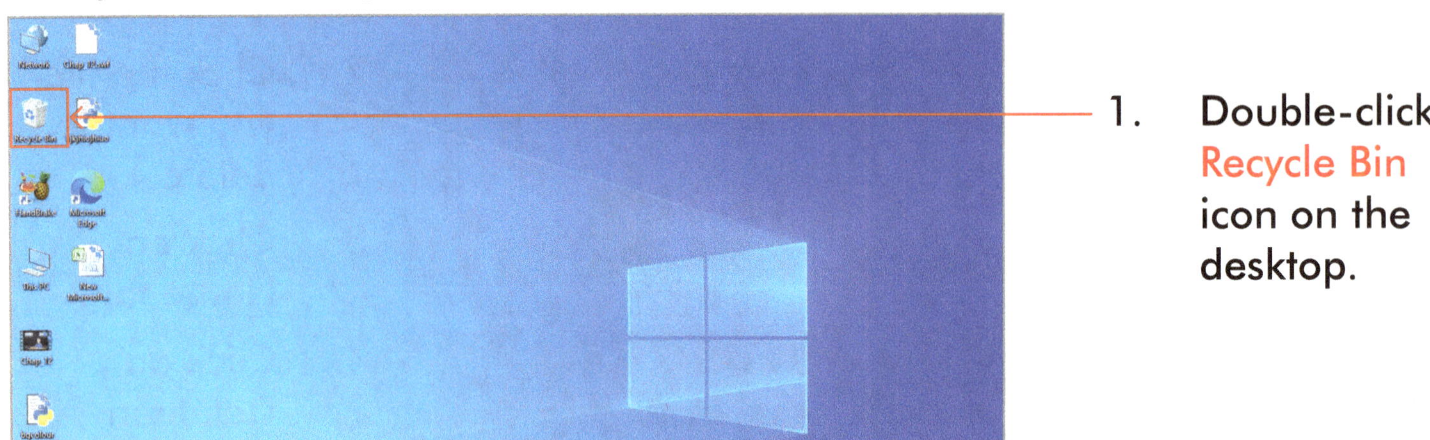

1. Double-click **Recycle Bin** icon on the desktop.

The Recycle Bin window appears, displaying all the files you have deleted.

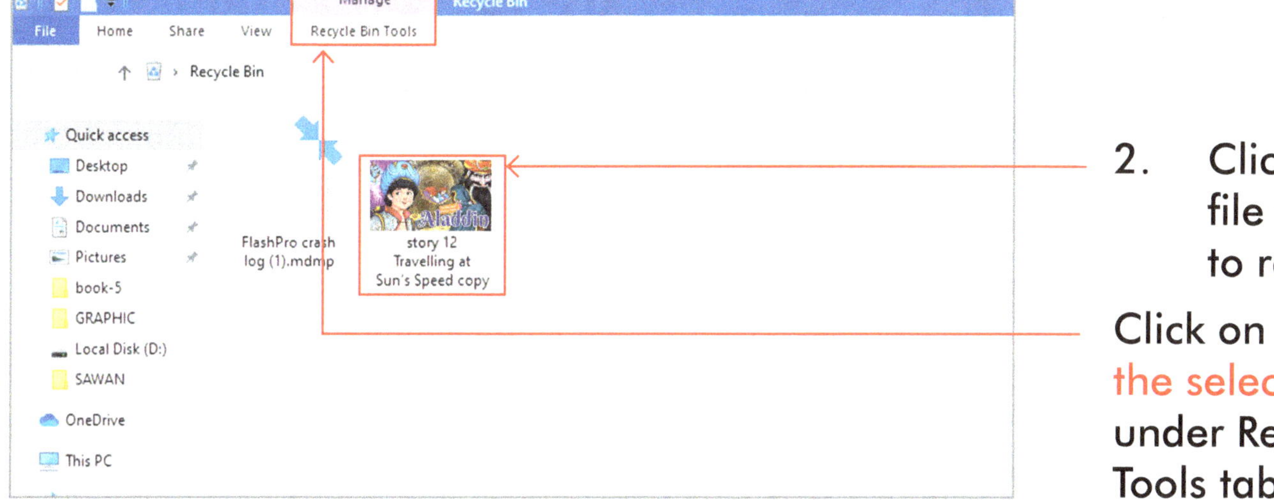

2. Click on the file you want to restore.

Click on Restore the selected items under Recycle Bin Tools tab.

The file disappears from the Recycle Bin and reappears in its original folder.

EMPTYING THE RECYCLE BIN

The file/folder that is in the Recycle bin can permanently be deleted from there if it is no longer required. Once the file/folder is deleted from the Recycle bin, it cannot be restored again.

The appearance of the Recycle Bin shows whether it contains deleted files folder or not. ( ) contains deleted files. ( ) does not contain deleted files.

The Recycle Bin can be made empty by:

1. Open the Recycle Bin by double clicking its desktop icon.

2. Click on Empty the Recycle Bin button on the Recycle Bin Tools tab.

    The Delete Multiple Items dialog box appears.

3. Click on Yes to delete permanently all the files in the Recycle Bin.

SEARCHING FOR A FILE/FOLDER

In your computer, there are thousands of files stored in various folders throughout the hard drive. You might have trouble locating a specific file. Windows 10 offers various ways to find files and folders with ease. Search option offers the most direct way to locate a file/folder. Use 'Search option' if:

⇒   You are looking for common file types.

⇒   You remember all or part of the name of the file or folder you want to find.

You can search from the Start menu or use the Search box in a folder window.

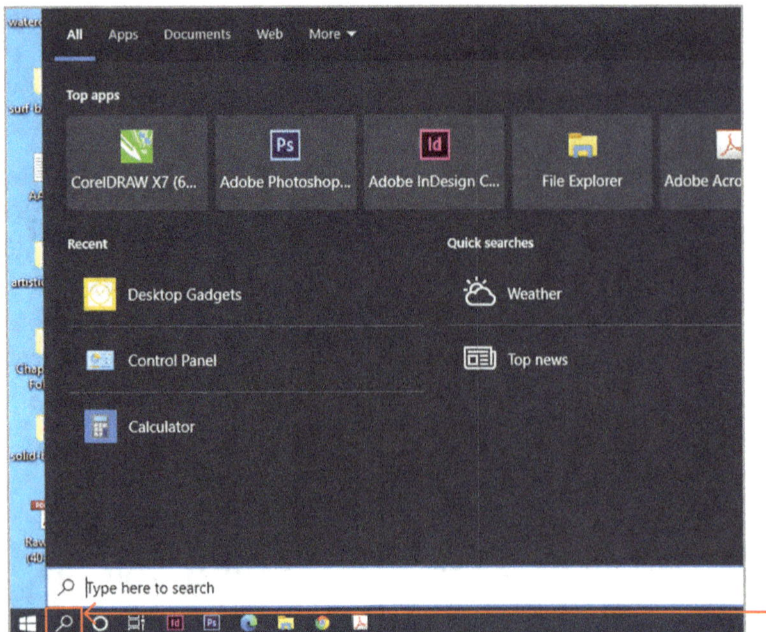

SEARCH FROM THE START MENU

1. Click on Search button.

The Search box appears on the screen.

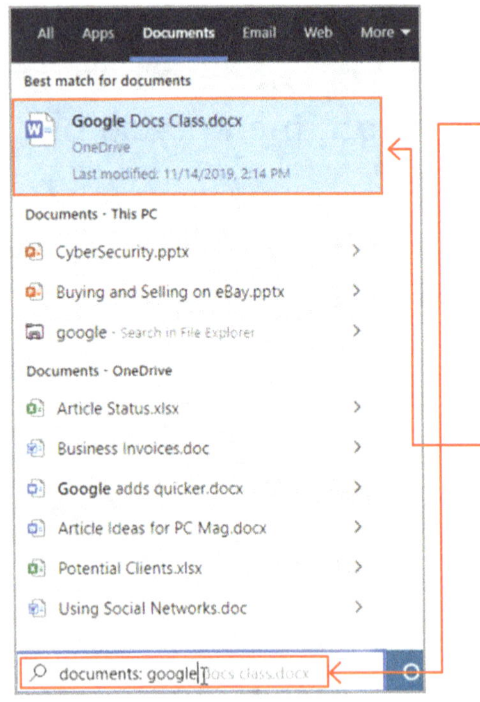

2. Start typing your search text.

As you type, Windows 10 displays the programs, documents and other data on your system with a name that matches your search text.

3. If you see the program or document you want, click on it to open.

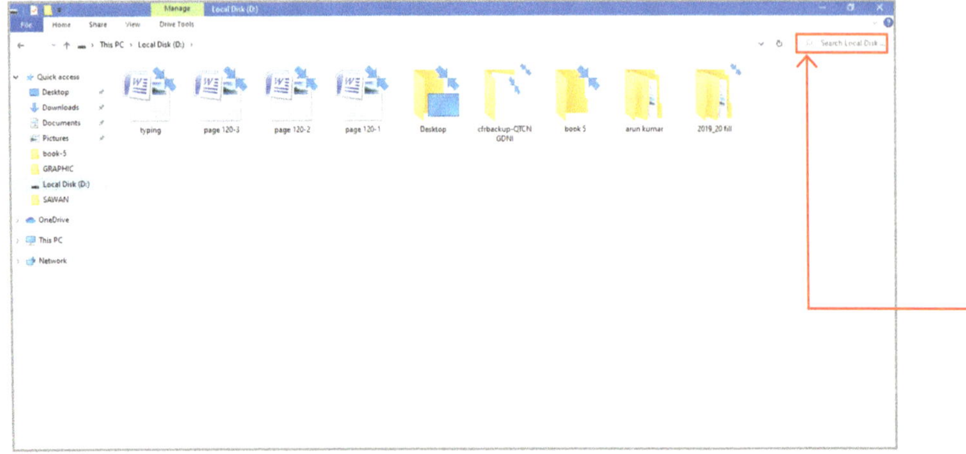

SEARCH FROM A FOLDER WINDOW

1. Open the folder in which you want to search.

2. Click on the Search box.

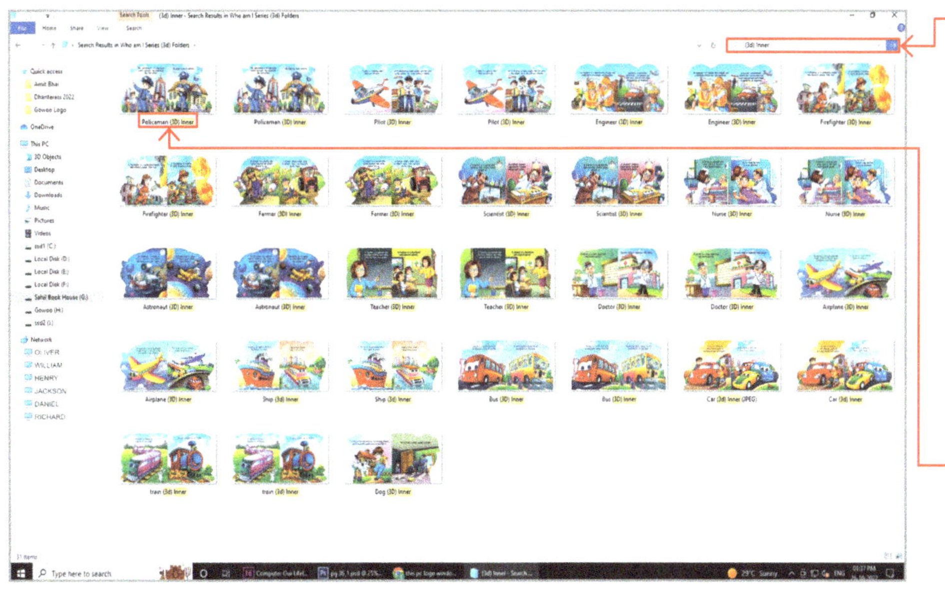

3. Type your search text and press enter.

Windows 10 displays the folders and documents in the current folder with names, contents or keywords that match your search text keep.

4. If you see the folder or document you want, double-click to open it.

SAVE YOUR SEARCH

You can save the search which you run frequently.

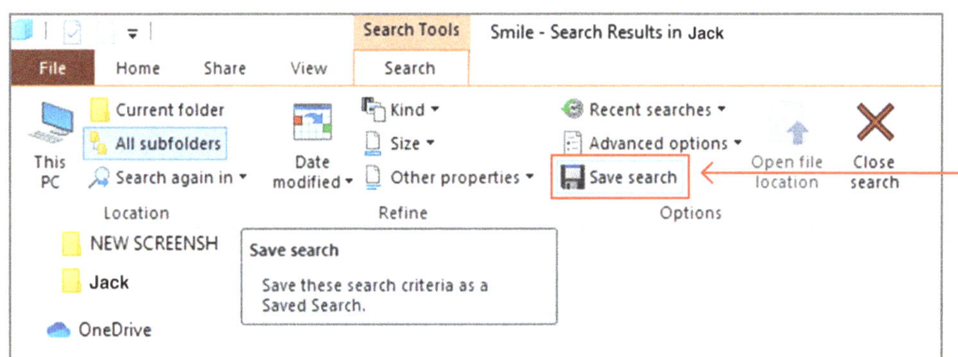

Click on Save search button under Search Tab.

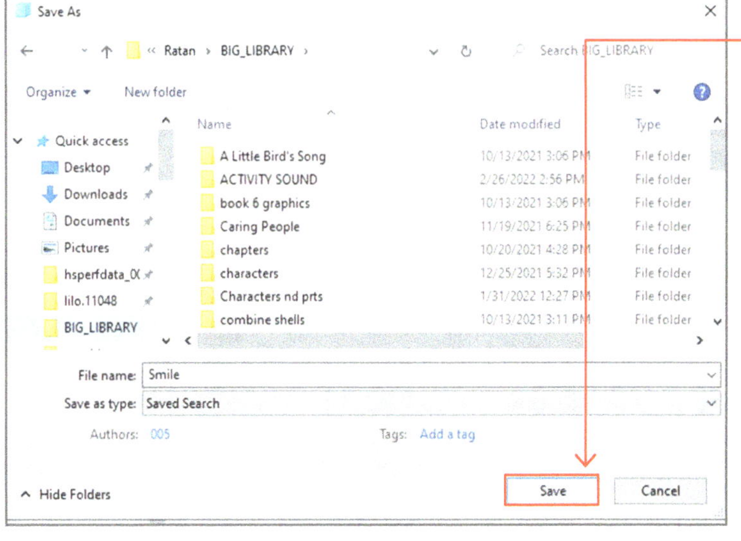

Save as dialog box appears.

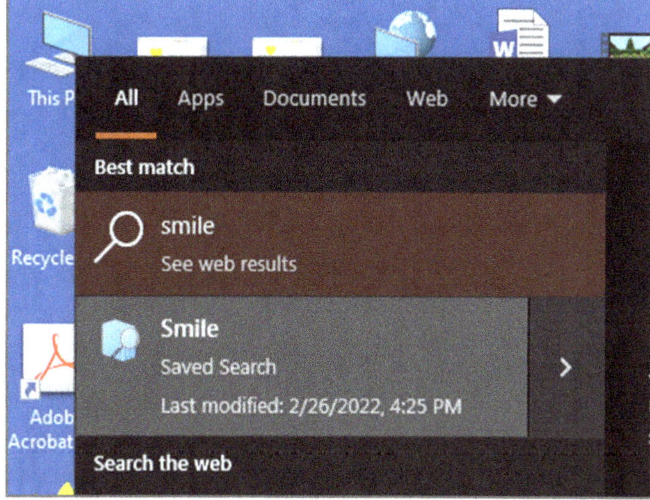

Windows 10 saves the search in the Selected location. Double-click that folder to re-run your search.

LET'S HAVE A LOOK

- A file is a collection of information, like a program, a set of data used by a program, or a user-created document.
- A folder is an object that contains multiple files.
- A folder inside a folder is called a sub-folder.
- Files and folders can be organised in the common folders provided by Windows.
- Windows provides various ways to create, rename, move, copy and delete files/folders.
- To work with a files/folder, first you have to select that file/folder.
- Windows also offers various ways to find files and folders.

BRAIN TEASER

1. Answer each of the following in one word or line:

a. Name several types of files used in the computer.

b. What is a sub-folder?

c. Where are sound files stored by default?

d. Where does the deleted file go by default?

e. Which option is used to change the name of a file?

2. Answer the following in brief:

a. Define files and folders.

b. Which are the common folders provided in Windows?

c. Differentiate between moving and copying files/folders.

d. What is the use of selecting files?

e. What is Recycle Bin?

3. Fill in the blanks:

a. _______________________ folder is used to save image file.

b. A _______________________ is a collection of information.

c. A folder within a folder is called a _______________________ .

d. _______________________ view gives you the detailed information about files.

e. The selected text appears _______________________ on the screen.

f. The file/folder deleted goes into the _______________________ .

4. Multiple Choice Questions

Tick (✓) the correct answer:

a. A collection of information:

   i. Folder ☐   ii. File ☐   iii. Sub-folder ☐

b. The location on a storage medium that contains related documents:

   i. File ☐   ii. Folder ☐   iii. Documents ☐

c. The location where deleted files go:

   i. Documents ☐   ii. Computer ☐   iii. Recycle bin ☐

d. Changing the name of a file/folder is:

   i. Creating ☐   ii. Renaming ☐   iii. Deleting ☐

5. **Name the types of files saved in:**

   a.   Document ____

   b.   Pictures ____

   c.   Music ____

   d.   Video ____

6. **Write 'T' for true or 'F' for false in the boxes:**

   a.   Files and folders are represented with the same icon.

   b.   Data in computer is organized into folders and files.

   c.   Icon view is used to view the detailed information about files.

   d.   It is not necessary to name a file or folder.

   e.   A file can have any number of folders in it.

   f.   Data once stored in a file cannot be changed.

   g.   A folder can store only one type of file.

   h.   Deleted files stored in Recycle Bin cannot be restored.

   i.   We cannot create another folder in a folder.

LAB ACTIVITY

Go to your Computer Lab and perform the following actions on the computer:

- Open Documents Using This PC > Documents option.

- Click on View button, select 'Large Icon' view and observe the effect.

- Click on View button, select 'Details' view and observe the change

- Select any folder from the displayed list. Click Organise > Rename option.

- The current folder name will get highlighted. Type a new name for the folder and then press the Enter key. The name gets changed.

- Rename the folder back to its original name by using the above option.

4 Learning to Type

Hello friends! As we all know, most of the time we type on the keyboard to give commands to the computer system. Do you know there are basic rules for typing that are if followed, save much time in typing and avoid the boredom as well? In this chapter, we will learn to type properly on the keyboard.

 TYPING

Typing is the process of inputting text into a device, such as a typewriter, computer keyboard or a mobile keypad. Typing by visually searching for individual letters and hitting the keys with one or two fingers is extremely boring, wasting hours on the computer every day. A user who uses his all 10 fingers can do more work in fewer hours, giving his/her extra time to other tasks.

Typing with all the 10 fingers is a skill, like riding a bicycle. The more you do, the faster and better you get. Two-finger typing is like riding with your feet on the ground. There is no learnt skill and it leaves you frustrated when the others ride away!

Typing with one or two fingers

This chapter includes the basics of typing which are very essential in today's world.

Some of these are as follows:

⇒ Avoid looking at the keyboard while typing.

⇒ Place your forearms slightly above the keyboard.

⇒ Press the keys softly.

⇒ Your fingers must be placed on the keyboard.

Typing with all ten fingers

HOME KEYS

It is important to position your hands on the keyboard correctly. Your fingers must be in the middle row of your keyboard which are known as 'home keys'.

Starting with your left hand, place your little finger on key A, ring finger on S, middle finger on D and index finger on F. Your thumb must rest on the Spacebar. With your right hand, place your index finger on J, middle finger on K, ring finger on L and your little finger on the next key (;). Use the little finger of your right hand for Pressing the Enter key.

Always put your fingers back on the 'Home Keys' after pressing any key.

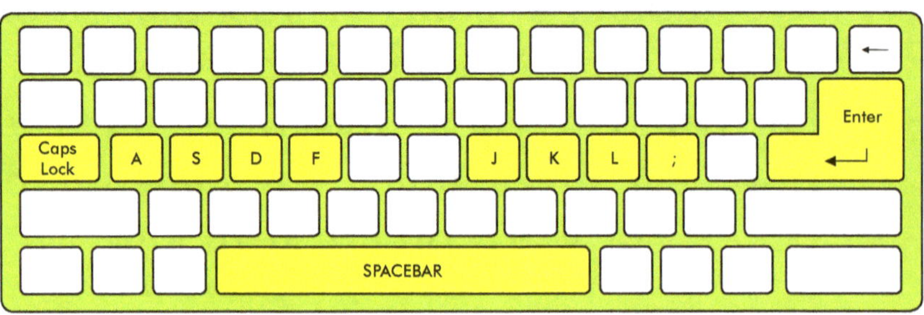

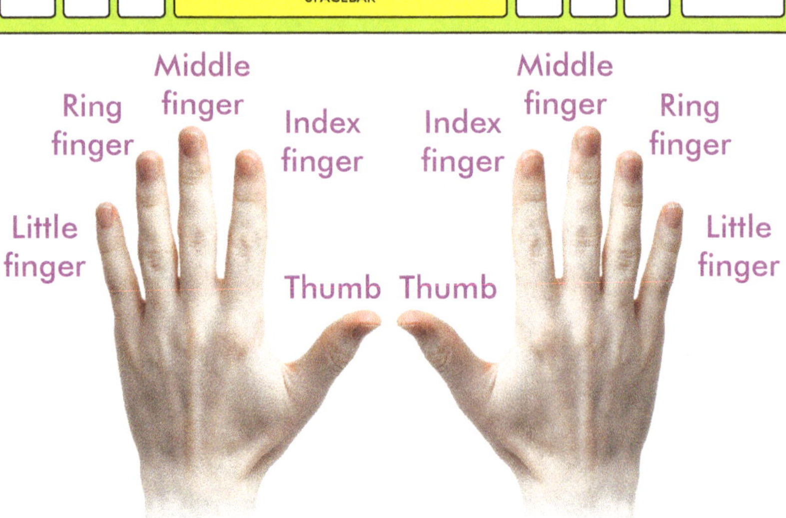

Part 1

Press CAPS LOCK key to turn it ON so that you can write in capital letters. You can press the SPACEBAR with your thumb to make a gap between two letters.

Press the ENTER key at the end of every line with the little finger of your right hand. Position your fingers back on the Home Keys after pressing any key.

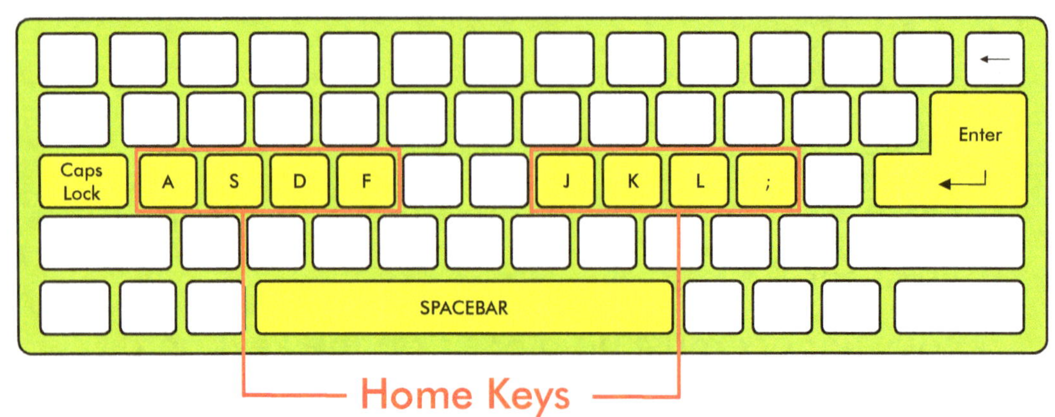

Part 2

In this part, we add two new keys: G and H. Press G with the index finger of your left hand and H with the index finger of the right hand. Once the key is pressed, remember to put your fingers back on the home keys.

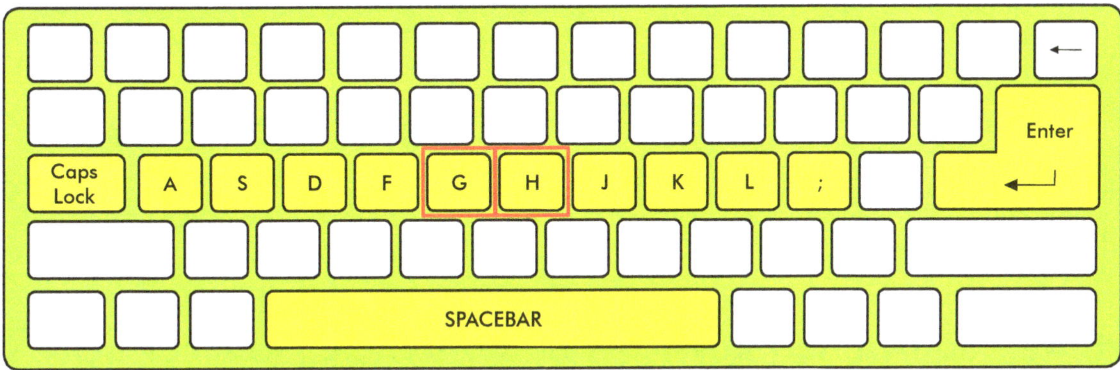

Part 3

In this part, we add two new keys: E and I. To type them correctly, you should slide your middle finger to the upper row. Type E moving the middle finger of your left hand from D and type I with the middle finger of your right hand from K. Once a key is pressed, your fingers must go back on the home keys.

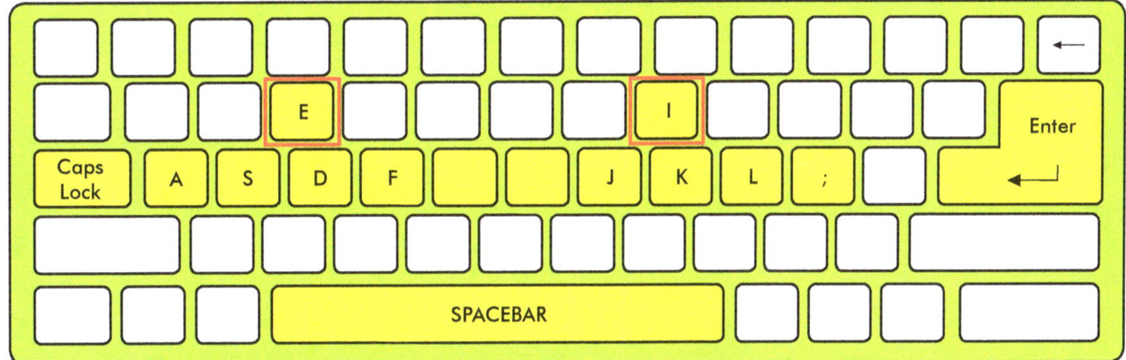

Part 4

In this part, we add two new keys: R and U. To type them correctly, slide your index finger to the upper row from F and J respectively.

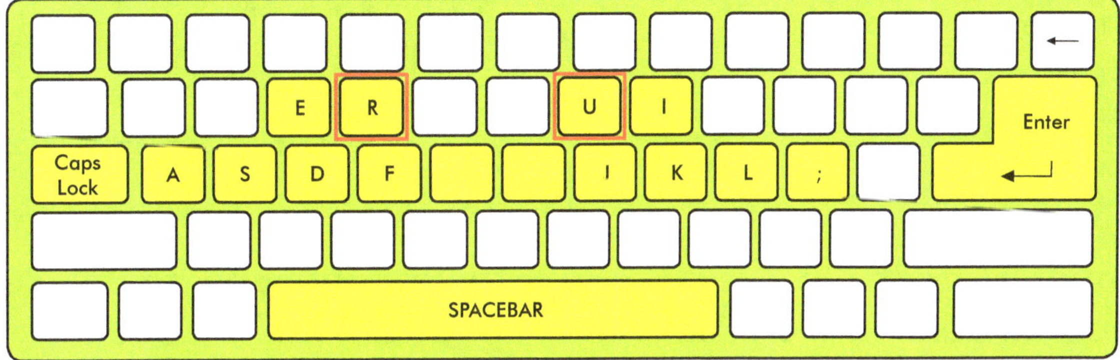

Part 5

In this part, we add two new keys: T and Y. To type them correctly, slide your index finger to the upper row from F and J respectively.

Part 6

In this part, we add two new keys: W and O. To type them correctly, slide your ring finger to the upper row from S and L respectively.

Part 7

In this part, we add two new keys: Q and P. To type them correctly, slide the little fingers of both hands to the upper row.

Part 8

After learning the middle and upper rows, now it is time for the keys of the third row. In this part, we add two new keys: 'C' and 'comma' (,). Press C with the middle finger of your left hand from

D. Press comma (,) with the middle finger of your right hand from K. Remember to place your fingers back on the home keys after every keystroke.

Part 9

In this part, we add two new keys: V and M. To type them correctly, slide your index finger to the upper row from F and J respectively.

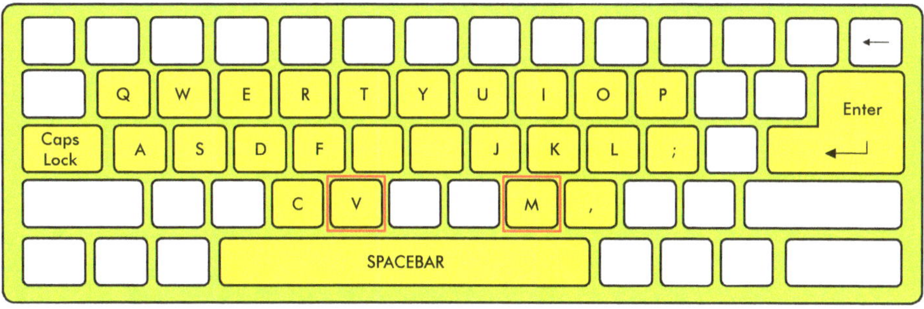

Part 10

In this part, we add two new keys: B and N. Both are pressed with the index fingers. Press B with the index finger of your left hand, and N with the index finger of your right hand.

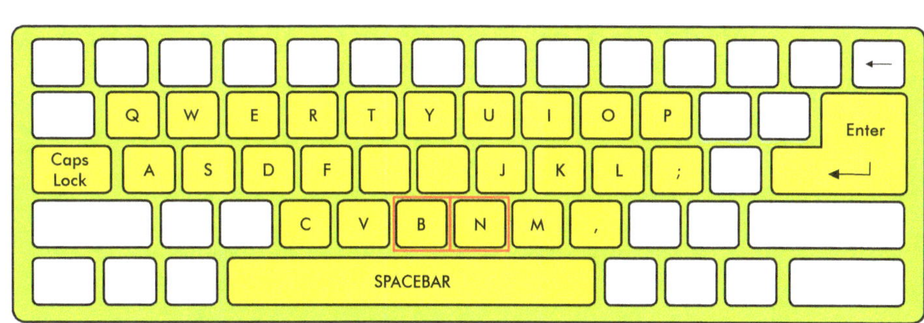

Part 11

In this part, we add two new keys: X and the full stop key (.). Press X with the ring finger of your left hand, and press the full stop key with the ring finger of your right hand.

Part 12

In this part, we add two new keys: Z and (/). Press both keys with the little fingers of both hands.

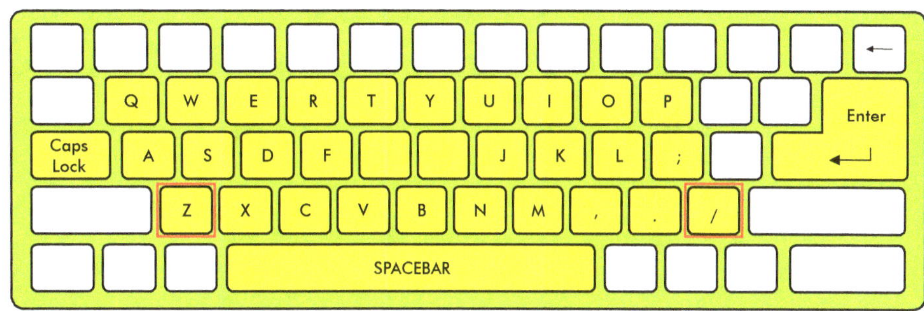

LET'S HAVE A LOOK

- Typing is a process wherein text is input into a device.
- Avoid looking at the keyboard while typing.
- Press the keyboard keys softly.
- Sit straight while typing.

1. Answer the following questions:

a. What is typing?

b. Write the names of four things which we keep in mind while typing.

c. What do you mean by Home Keys?

2. Fill in the blanks:

a. You can press the Spacebar with your ______________ .

b. Avoid looking at the ______________ while typing.

c. Our fingers must be ______________ on the keyboard.

d. Position your fingers back on the ______________ after pressing any key.

3. Write 'T' for true or 'F' for false in the boxes:

a. The typist should not avoid looking at the keyboard while typing.

b. Place forearms hardly above the keyboard.

c. The ENTER key should be pressed with the little finger of your right hand.

d. Our fingers must be placed on the keyboard.

4. Multiple Choice Questions
Tick (✓) the correct answer:

a. Which finger is used to produce the characters S, W and X?

   i. Index finger ☐   ii. Ring finger ☐   iii. Middle finger ☐

b. Which finger is used to produce the characters A, Q, and Z?

   i. Index finger ☐   ii. Little finger ☐   iii. Middle finger ☐

c. Which finger is used to produce the characters F, G, R, T and V?

   i. Index finger ☐   ii. Little finger ☐   iii. Middle finger ☐

d. Your fingers must be in the middle row of your keyboard known as:

   i. Home keys ☐   ii. Keyboard ☐   iii. Typing ☐

LAB ACTIVITY

In the computer lab, open MS-Word and practise the following keys:

JH FG KH DG LH SG H; AG KH DG LH SG H; AG LH SG H; AH LH SG KH DG FG JH DG KH
SG LH AG H; DG KH SG LH AG H; SG LH AG H; SG LH DG KH JF KF LF F; AJ SJ DJ FJ AH
SH DH DH FH G; LG KG JG GH G; HG AH GL GH HG GA H; GS HL GD HK GF HJ GH HG
G; HA GL HS GK HD GJ HF GH HG

SAD; HAD; GAS; HAS; JAS; LAS; DAS; KAD; FAL; HAJ; JAF; LAF; HAK;

SAD; HAD; GAS; HAS; JAS; LAS; DAS; KAD; FAL; HAJ; JAF; LAF; HAK;

DEDE KIKI DEDE KIKI KIKE DEDI EDIK IKED IEIE DILE KELA KILE

DEDE KIKI DEDE KIKI KIKE DEDI EDIK IKED IEIE DILE KELA KILE

HILL DEAL FEEL DIED HEAL HIFI DIAL DEED LIES GILL HEAD KALE

HILL DEAL FEEL DIED HEAL HIFI DIAL DEED LIES GILL HEAD KALE

DEED LIES GILL HEAD KALE HILL DEAL FEEL DIED HEAL LIES GILL

FRFR JUJU RFRF UJUJ JIKU FEDR HUGR KUDR DERE KIUI JURA RAUL RIDE FREE LEAD FUEL
FEAR LIAR DEAR USED LEAF HUGE LEAK HIDE ALL RARE GALA GEAR HEIGH GRASS HILL
FEEL RAIL HELD HIGH GREED LAKE HAS DEAD HAD LIFE ARISE DIALER FEARS HUGE DEAR
HIDE DADS FRFR JUJU RFRF UJUJ JIKU FEDR HUGR KUDR DERE KIUI JURA RAUL RIDE FREE
LEAD FUEL FEAR LIAR DEAR USED LEAF HUGE LEAK HIDE I SEE A HUGE LAKE; I LIKE JULIA;
HE FEARS HER; SHE IS FAR;

SSXX LL.. DDCC KK,, FFVV JJMM XCVB .,MN BVVC NM,. XX.. X.X.

EXIT. EXPECT. EXIST. TEXT. EXAM. EXACTLY. EXALTED. EXPLAIN.

EXCELLENT. EXPANSION. XYLOPHONE. EXTRA. EXALTED. EXPLAIN.

EXIT. EXPECT. EXIST. TEXT. EXAM. EXACTLY. EXALTED. EXPLAIN.

EXCELLENT. EXPANSION. XYLOPHONE. EXTRA. EXALTED. EXPLAIN.

ZZZZ //// ZZZZ //// ZZ// ZZ// Z/Z/ AAZZ ;;// AZAZ ;/;/
ZERO/ZIGZAG/ZINC/ZOO/ZIP/ZOOM/ZONE/ZODIAC/ZEAL/ZANY/ZIPPY
ZZZZ //// ZZZZ //// ZZ// ZZ// Z/Z/ AAZZ ;;// AZAZ ;/;/
ZERO/ZIGZAG/ZINC/ZOO/ZIP/ZOOM/ZONE/ZODIAC/ZEAL/ZANY/ZIPPY
ZZZZ //// ZZZZ //// ZZ// ZZ// Z/Z/ AAZZ ;;// AZAZ ;/;/
ZERO/ZIGZAG/ZINC/ZOO/ZIP/ZOOM/ZONE/ZODIAC/ZEAL/ZANY/ZIPPY

Formative Assessment-2
(Chapters 3-4)

1.   By looking at these folder icons label the following:

2.   Label the Home Keys in the keyboard:

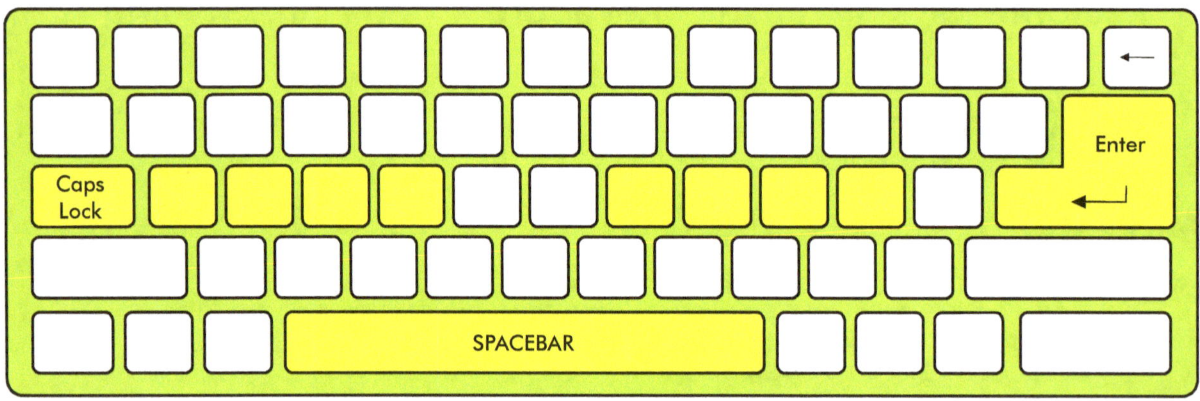

3.   Label the fingers:

Summative Assessment-1
(Chapters 1-4)

1. Fill in the blanks:

a. The First-Generation Computers used ________________.

b. The inventors of integrated circuits were ________________ and ________________.

c. The machine language is also called ________________.

d. An ________________ translates one line at a time.

2. Write 'T' for true or 'F' for false in the boxes.

a. The typist should avoid looking at the keyboard while typing.

b. A, Q, Z characters are produced using the right ring finger.

c. ENIAC is the example of the Second generation Computers.

d. The Third Generation Computers used Integrated Circuits.

e. The computer understands the machine language only.

3. Answer the following questions:

a. Write the two features of the 2nd and 3rd generation languages.

b. What is the significance of the Fifth Generation language?

c. What is the difference between the Machine language and The Assembly language?

d. Explain the following:
   i. Compiler   ii. RAM   iii. IC   iv. Interpreter

e. What is the difference between a file and a folder?

4. Match the following:

a.	Binary Language	(i)	An object-oriented program
b.	Integrated Circuit	(ii)	Left index finger
c.	C++	(iii)	Collection of files
d.	Folder	(iv)	Jack St. Clair Kibly and Robert Noyce
e.	Recycle Bin	(v)	Deleted files
f.	Machine Language	(vi)	1st-Generation Language
g.	F, G, R, T, V	(vii)	0 and 1

5 More In Ms-Word 2016

Dear friends, in the previous class, you learnt about various editing and formatting commands arranged in different groups under each tab on the ribbon. Let's learn about some more tools of editing and formatting in MS-Word.

MS-WORD 2016

You already know that Microsoft Word 2016 is a word processing program used to type text on the computer. It provides many different features that are helpful in creating a document very easily and quickly.

The different features like inserting and deleting text, spell check, thesaurus, find and replace, bullets and numbering and many more are provided in MS-Word.

ADDING OR REMOVING TEXT IN DOCUMENT

The text can be added or removed within or from the document at any time in between.

Adding the text

You can insert a new word or phrase by simply positioning the insertion point where you want to add text and the Word automatically moves the existing text to make room (space) for the new text.

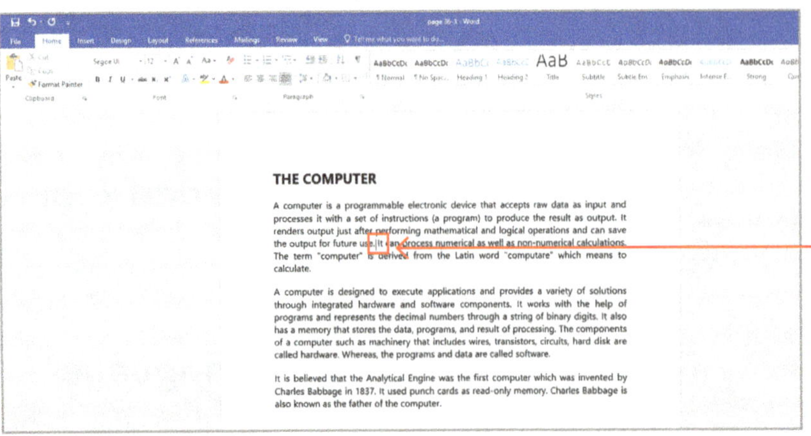

1. Click on the location in your document where you want to insert the new text.

The text you type will appear where the insertion point flashes on the screen.

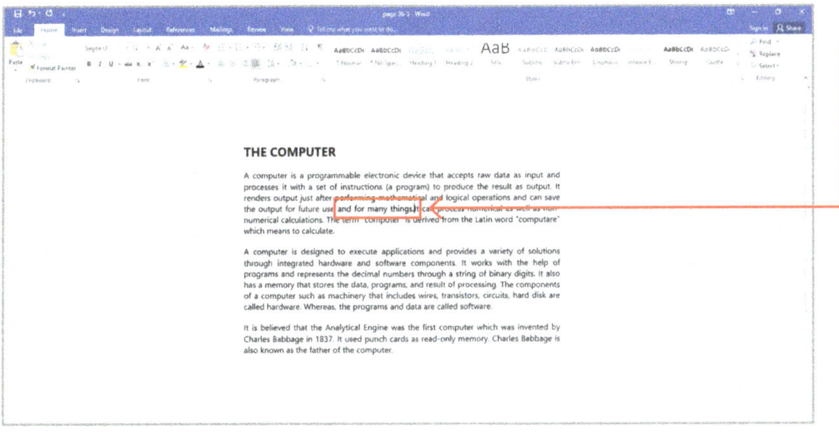

2. Type the text you want to insert.

To insert a blank space, press the Spacebar on the keyboard.

The words to the right of the new text move forward.

Removing the text

You can remove the text within the document that is not required.

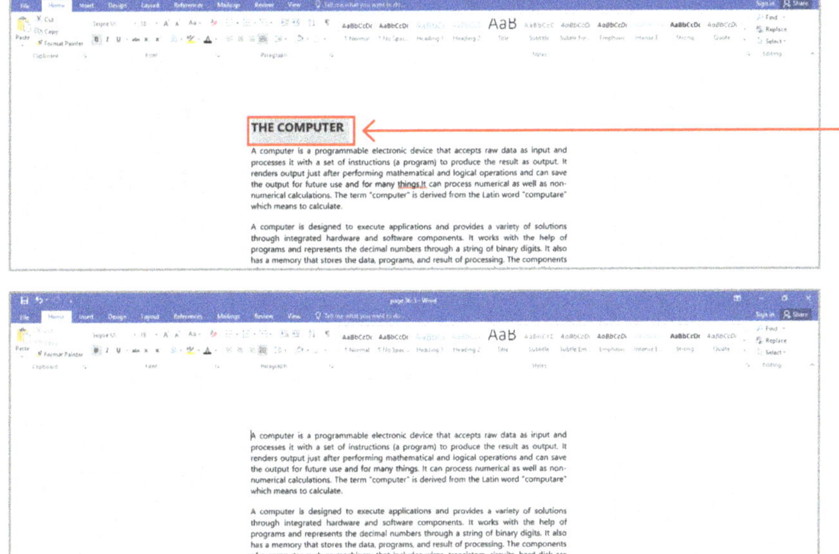

1. Select the text you want to delete.

2. Press the Delete or Backspace key from the keyboard to remove the text.

The text disappears. The remaining text in the line or paragraph moves to fill the empty space.

Undo and Redo

The UNDO feature is used to repeat the last action that is made while typing the text document. This feature is useful when something is deleted by mistake and you want to recover it. The Undo feature can be used in two ways:

⇒ Press Ctrl+Z keys from the keyboard.

OR

⇒ Click the Undo button on the Quick Access Toolbar. 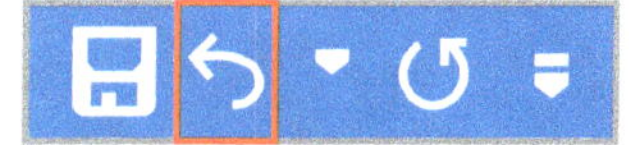

The REDO feature is used to redo the most recent action that you did. The Redo command can be used by:

⇒ Pressing Ctrl+Y keys from the keyboard.

OR

⇒ Clicking the Redo button on the Quick Access Toolbar.

Spelling and Grammar Check

With the Spell Check feature provided by MS-Word you can find and correct all the spellings and grammatical errors in your document. Word compares every word in your document to words in its dictionary. If a word does not exist in the dictionary, the word is considered mis-spelt.

Word automatically places a red squiggly underline beneath spelling errors and a blue squiggly underline beneath grammatical errors.

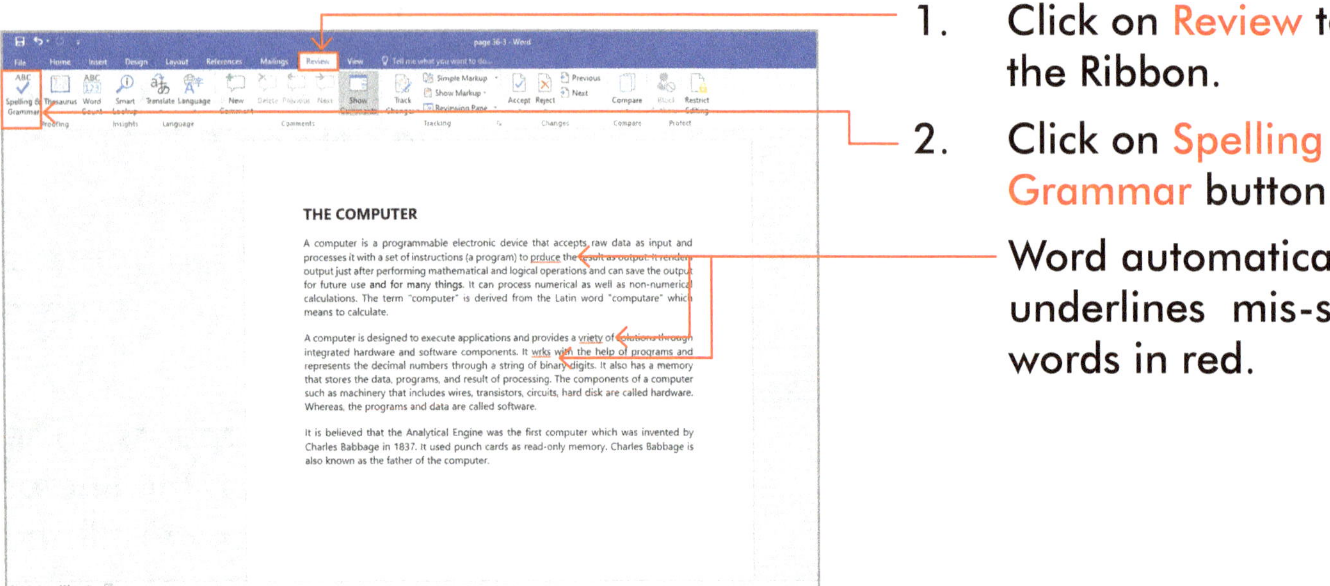

1. Click on Review tab on the Ribbon.

2. Click on Spelling and Grammar button.

Word automatically underlines mis-spelt words in red.

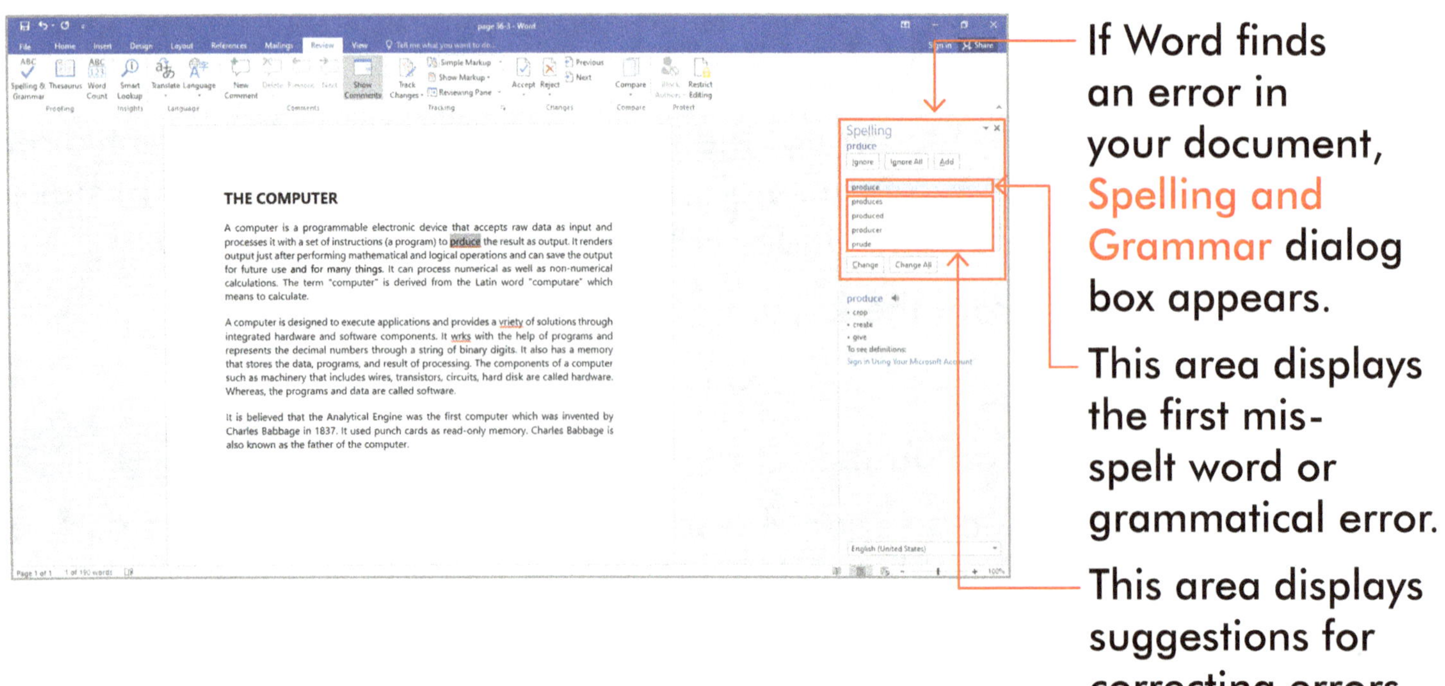

If Word finds an error in your document, Spelling and Grammar dialog box appears.

This area displays the first mis-spelt word or grammatical error.

This area displays suggestions for correcting errors.

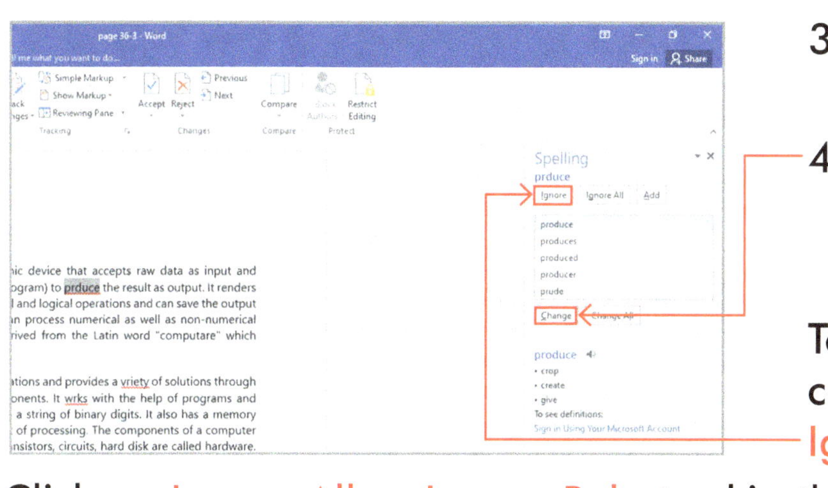

3. Click on the Suggestion you want to use to correct errors.

4. Click on Change to correct the error in your document.

To skip the error and continue checking your document, click on Ignore.

Click on Ignore All or Ignore Rule to skip the error and all other occurrences of errors in your document.

The name of the button depends on whether the error is a mis-spelt word or a grammatical error.

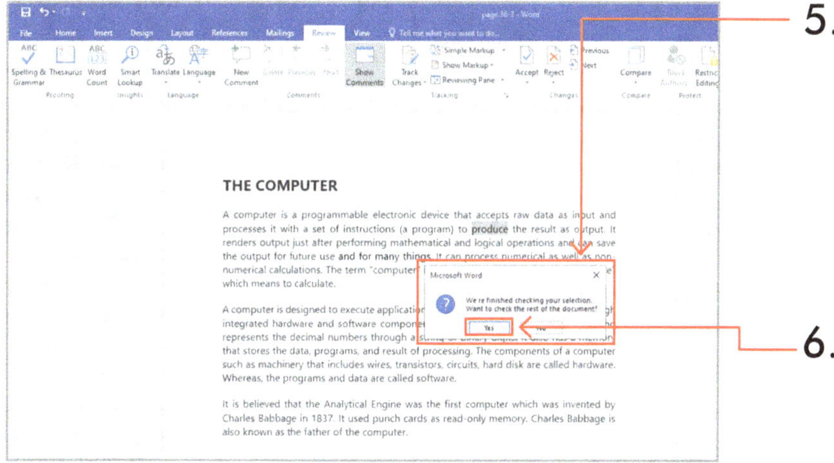

5. Correct or ignore mis-spelt words and grammatical errors until this dialog box appears, telling you that the spelling and grammar check is complete.

6. Click on OK to close the dialog box.

Correct a Mistake by Right-Clicking

The mis-spelt words can also be corrected by right-clicking the word and selecting the desired spelling.

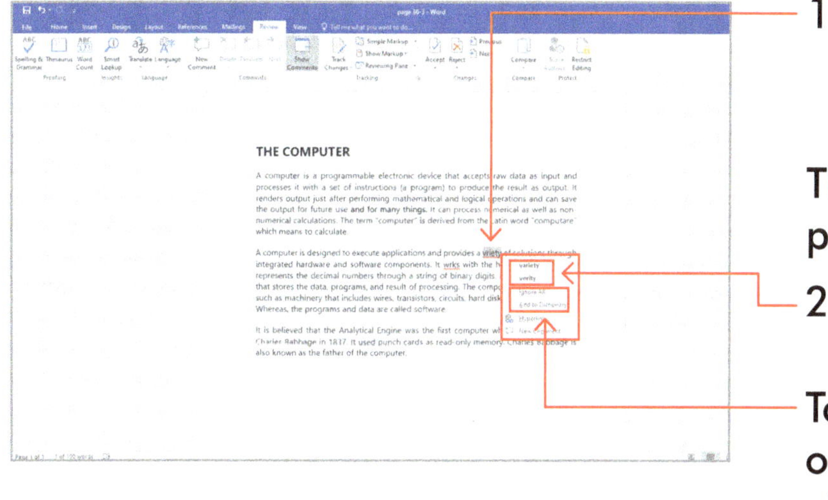

1. When you find a spelling or grammatical problem, right-click on the underlined text.

The menu that appears shows possible corrections.

2. Click on correction from the menu.

To ignore the error, you can click on Ignore or click on Ignore All for all instances of the error.

Using Thesaurus in MS-Word

Thesaurus is a type of dictionary that shows you synonyms, antonyms, word substitutes and alternative spellings of a selected word within the document. It can help you to increase your vocabulary skills.

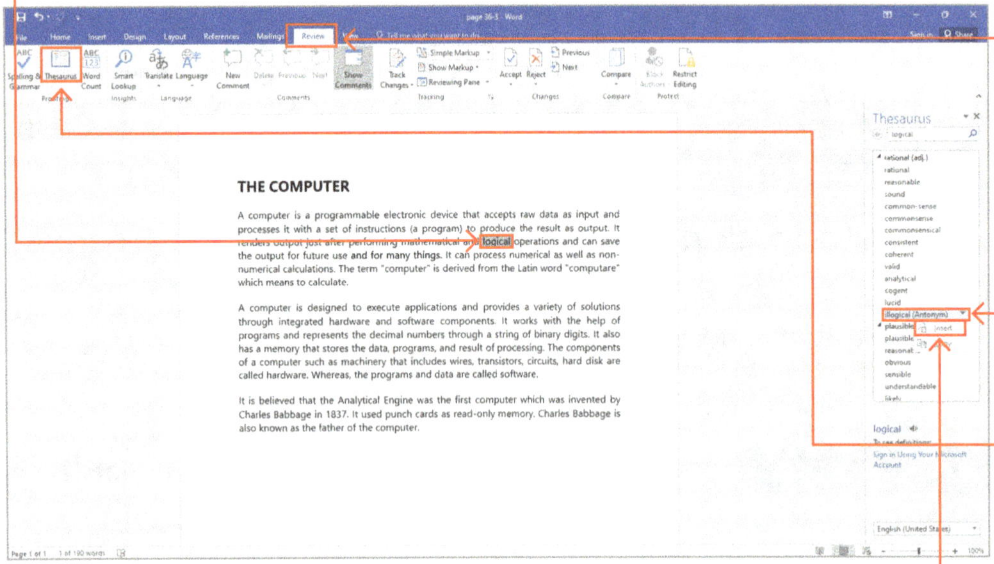

1. Select the word for which you need Thesaurus.

2. Click on the Review tab on the Ribbon.

3. Click on the Thesaurus button.

The Research task pane opens and displays suggested replacements for the word.

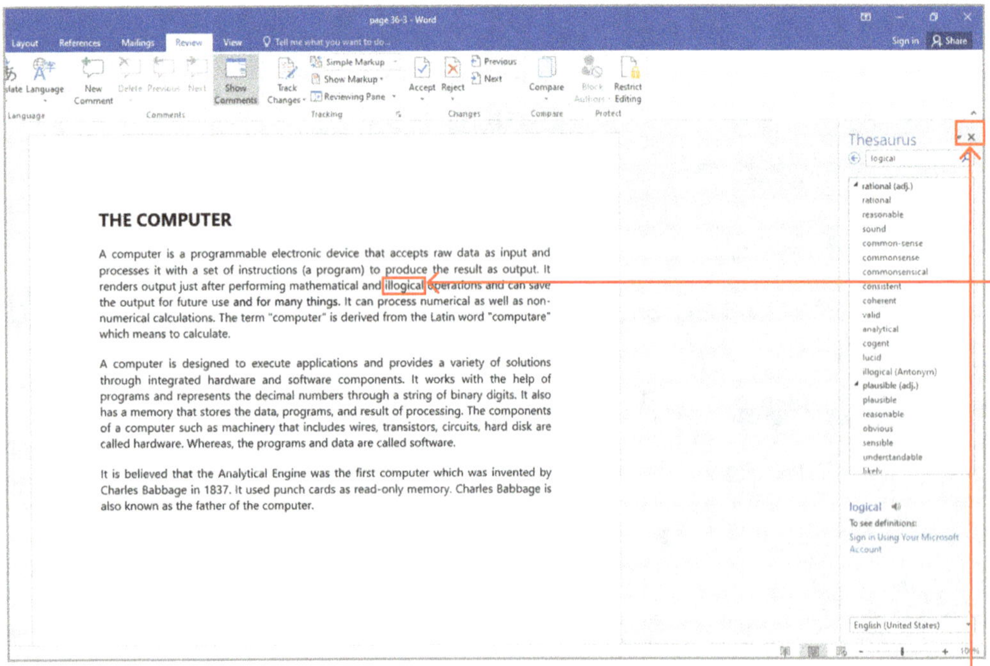

4. Click on the suitable word. A pop-up menu will appear.

5. Click on Insert.

The Word from the Thesaurus replaces the selected word in the document.

6. Click on Close button to close the task pane.

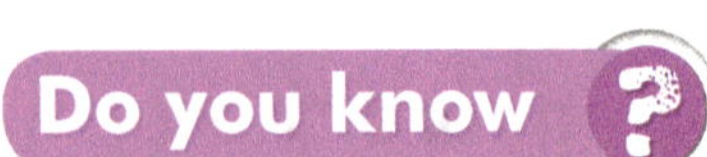

You can press Shift+F7 keys to use Thesaurus.

Finding and Replacing Text

To find out a piece of particular text in your document MS-Word provides you with a **Find** feature. To replace a particular text with another text, MS-Word provides you a **Replace** feature. For example, if you want to replace the word 'e-mail' with 'electronic mail', the Find feature will search for the word wherever within the document and Replace feature will replace it with the new word given.

1. Click at the beginning of your document.

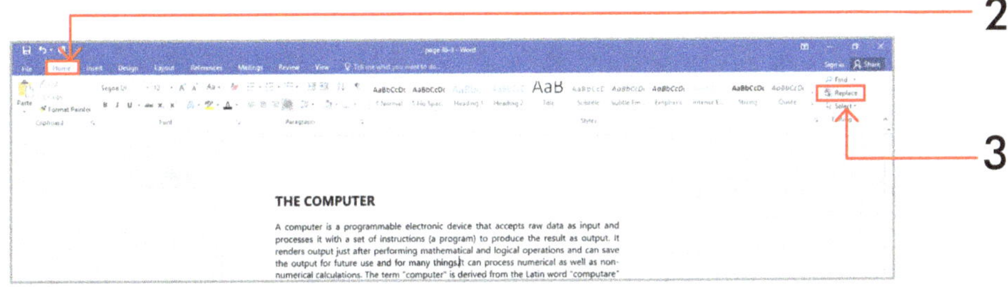

2. Click on **Home** tab on the Ribbon.

3. Click on **Replace** button.

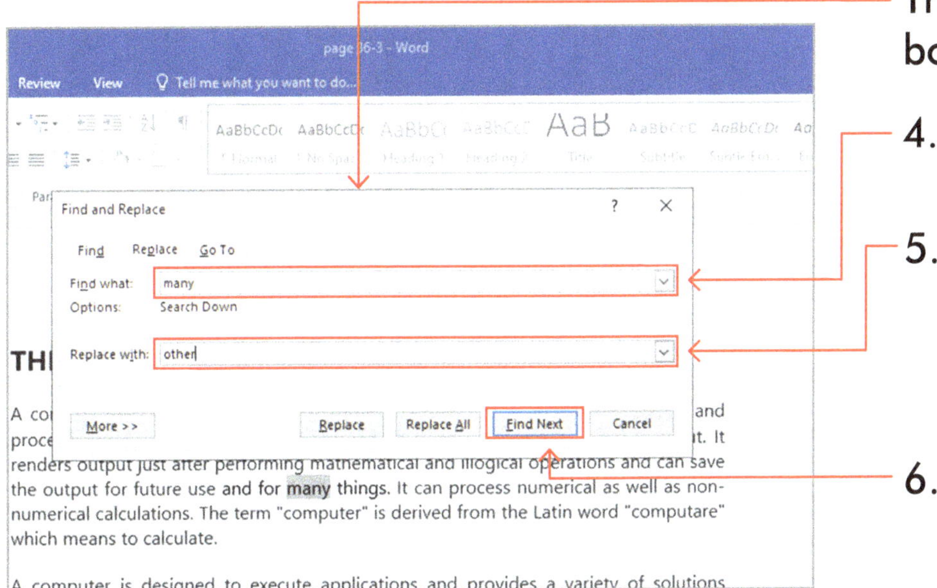

The **Find and Replace** dialog box appears.

4. Type the text you want to find.

5. Click on this area and type the text you want to use in place of the text you typed in step 4.

6. Click on **Find Next** to start search.

Word highlights the first matching word it finds.

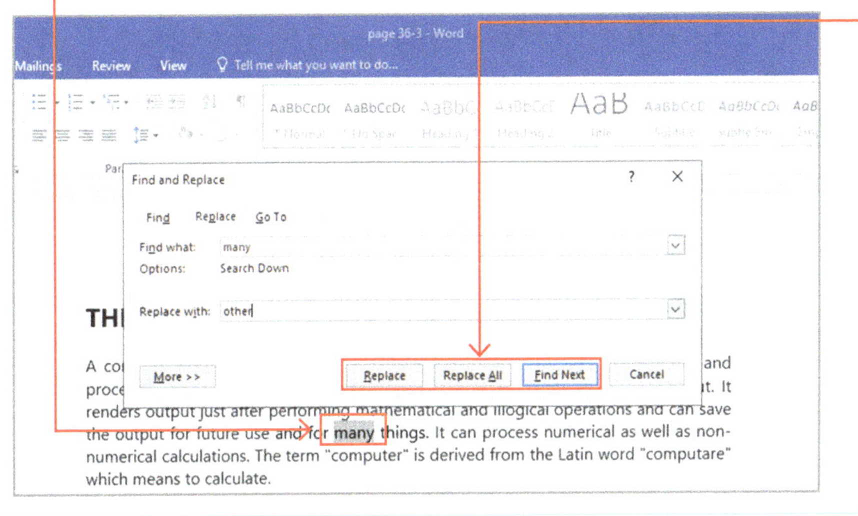

7. Click on any one option:

⇒ **Replace** - Replace the word.

⇒ **Replace All** - Replace the word and all other matching words.

⇒ **Find Next** - find the word.

The word gets replaced.

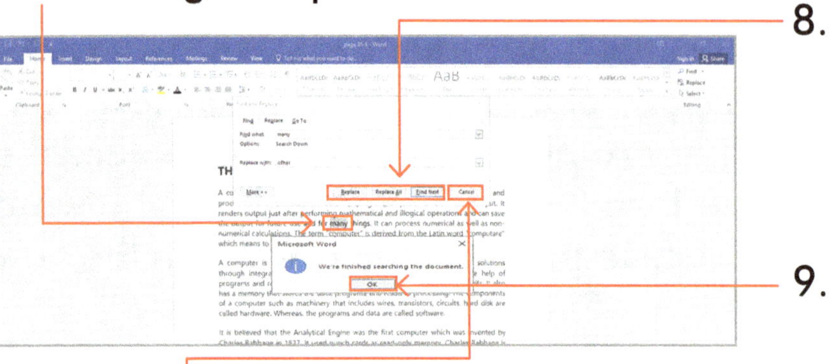

8. Replace or ignore the matching words until a dialog box appears, informing you that the search is complete.

9. Click **OK** to close the dialog box.

10. Click on **Cancel** to close the Find and Replace dialog box.

Changing Text Case

MS-Word provides you with a feature called Change Case through which you can change the case of the text in the document as per the requirement. For example, if you typed a piece of text in small letters and you want to make it into capital letters, you can do it to the whole document at once using this feature. Word offers five case styles.

⇒ **Sentence case**: In this case the text will be in the form of a sentence *i.e.* the first character of the sentence will be in capital letters (uppercase) and the rest will be in small letters (lowercase).

⇒ **lowercase**: In this case, the text will be changed into small letters by using this option.

⇒ **UPPERCASE**: In this case, the text will be changed into capital letters.

⇒ **Capitalize Each Word**: In this case, the first character of each word will be capitalised in the text.

⇒ **tOGGLE cASE**: In this case, the first character of the word will be in small letters and the rest in capital letters.

1. Select the text that you want to change to a new case style.

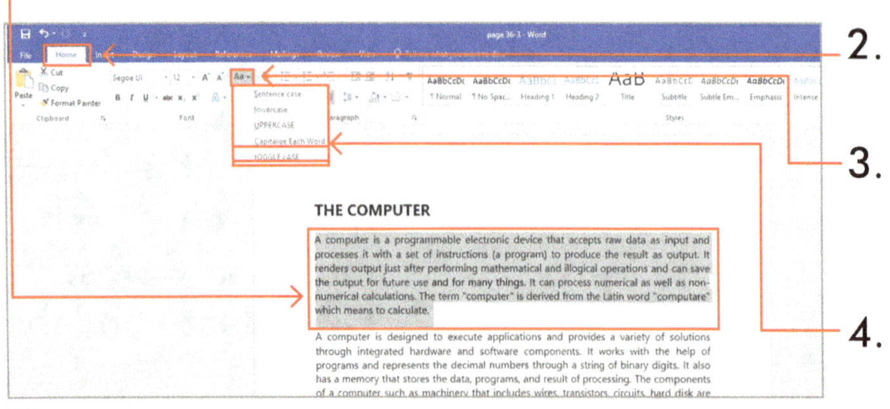

2. Click on **Home** tab on the ribbon.

3. Click on **Change Case** button. The Change Case menu appears.

4. Click on the case style you want to use.

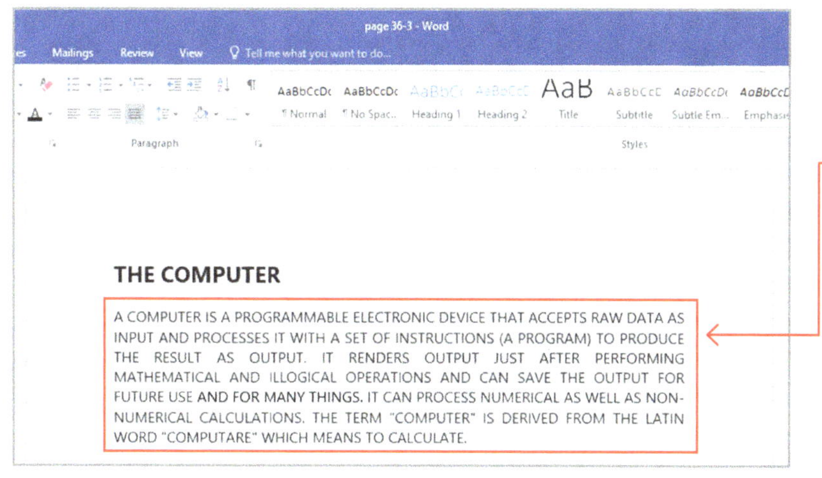

The text you selected changes into the new case style.

To deselect the text, click on outside the selected area.

Bullets and Numbering

A bullet or number is used to make a list of items. This feature is also helpful in typing the point-wise description.

The Bullets are the symbols, such as dots, diamonds, etc. Numbering uses numbers instead of symbols to represent. To apply bullets or numbers to your text, the steps are:

Set Quick Lists

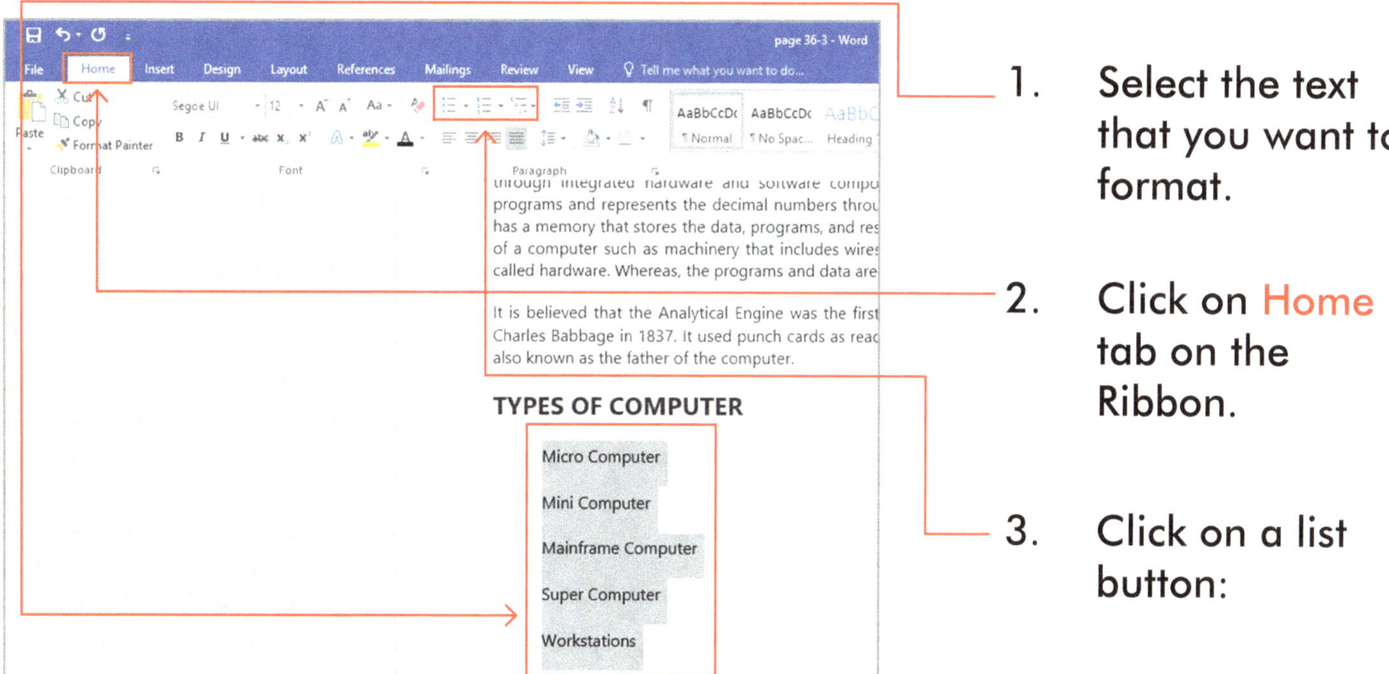

1. Select the text that you want to format.

2. Click on Home tab on the Ribbon.

3. Click on a list button:

⇒ You can click the Bullets button ( ) to create a bulleted list.

⇒ You can click the Numbering button ( ) to create a numbered list.

⇒ You can click the Multilevel button ( ) to create a multi-level list.

⇒ Word applies the formatting to the list.

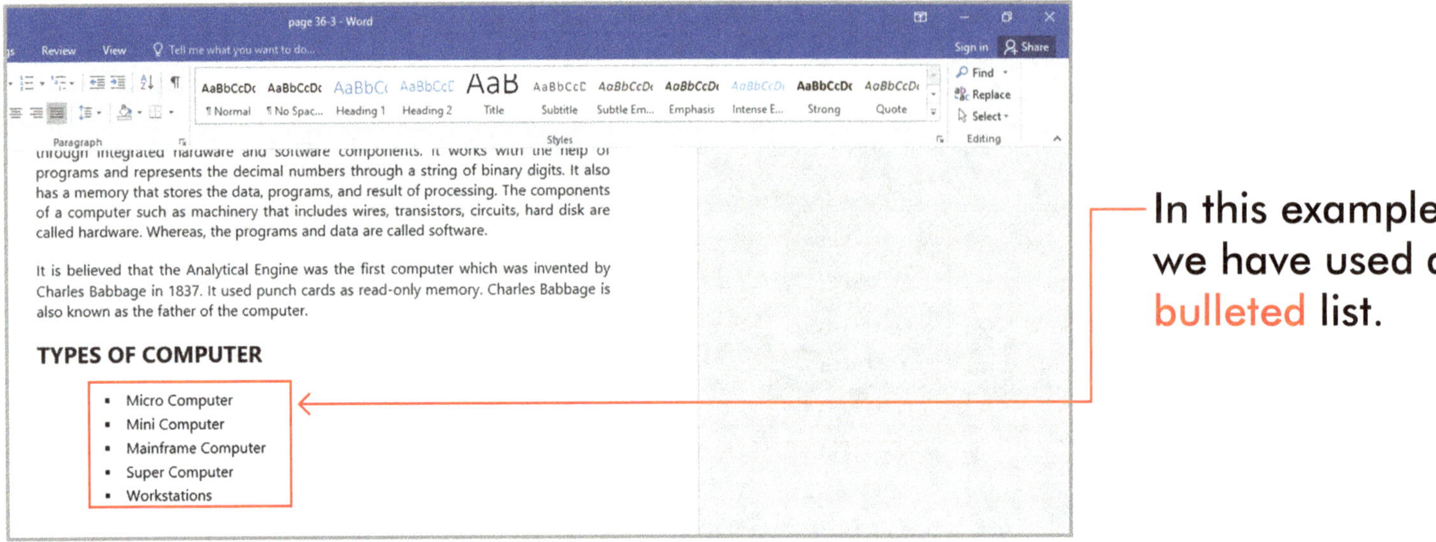

To add more text to the list, you can click at the end of the line and press the **Enter** key; Word immediately starts a new line in the list with a bullet or number.

To turn off a bulleted or numbered list, you can press the **Enter** key twice after the last item in the list.

Change Bullet or Number Styles

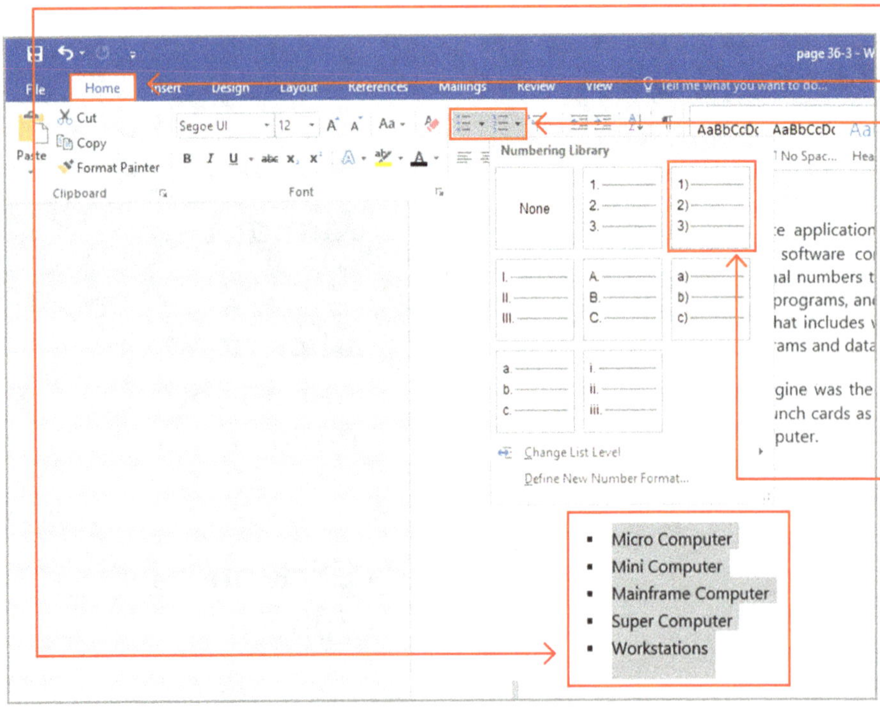

1. Select the text that you want to format.

2. Click on **Home** tab on the Ribbon.

3. Click on the down arrow of either the **Bullets** or **Numbering**.

4. Click on a style.

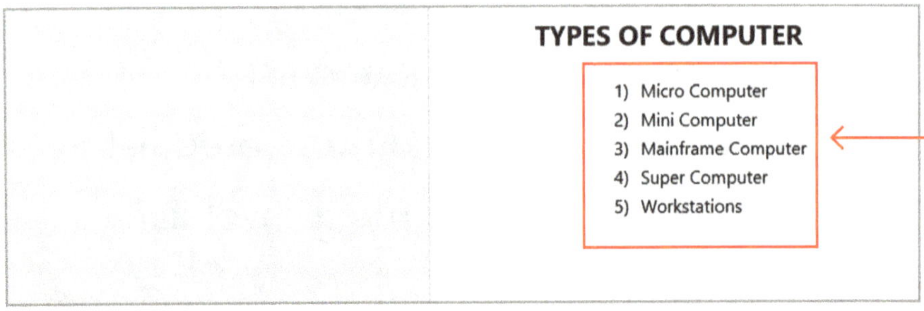

TYPES OF COMPUTER

1) Micro Computer
2) Mini Computer
3) Mainframe Computer
4) Super Computer
5) Workstations

Word applies the new style.

Changing the Line Spacing

The gap between two lines in the document can be adjusted accordingly. You can increase the line spacing to make your document easier to review and edit.

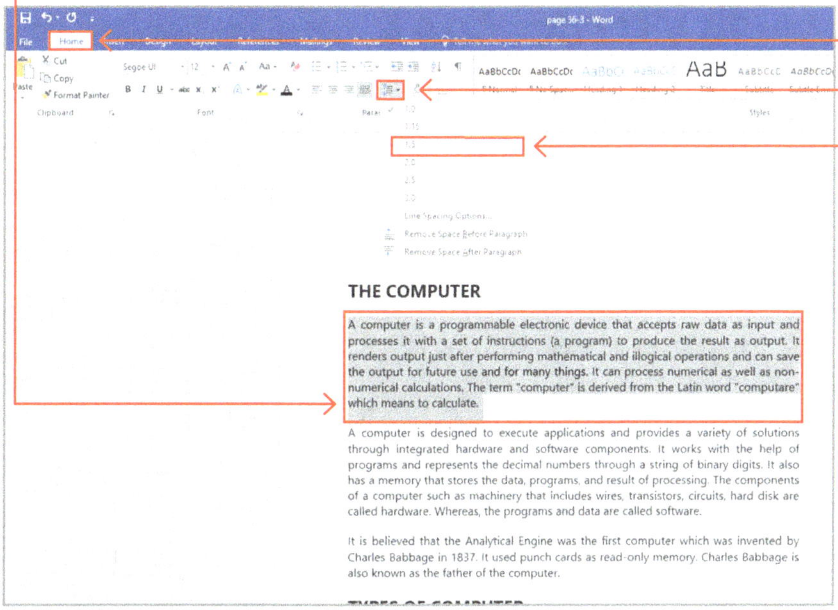

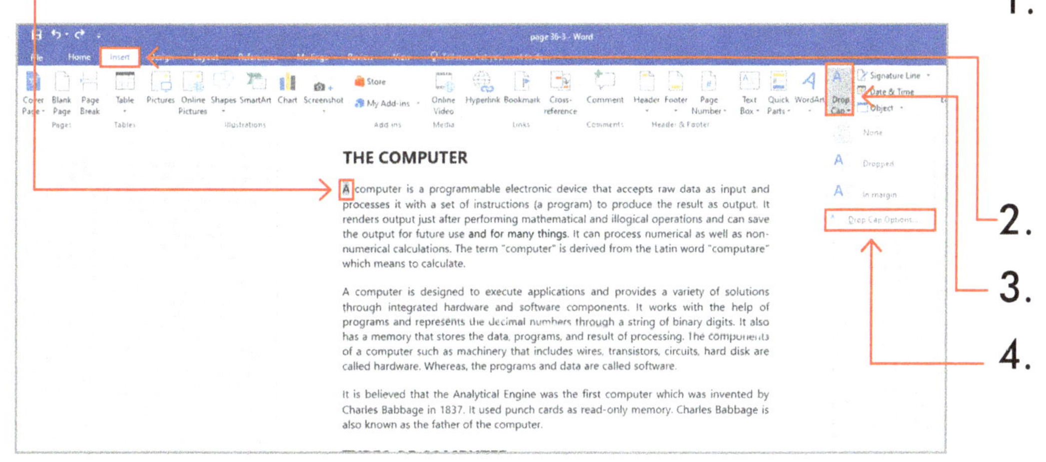

1. Select the text you want to use a different line spacing.

2. Click on Home tab.

3. Click on Line spacing button to display the available line spacing options.

4. Click on the line spacing option you want to use.

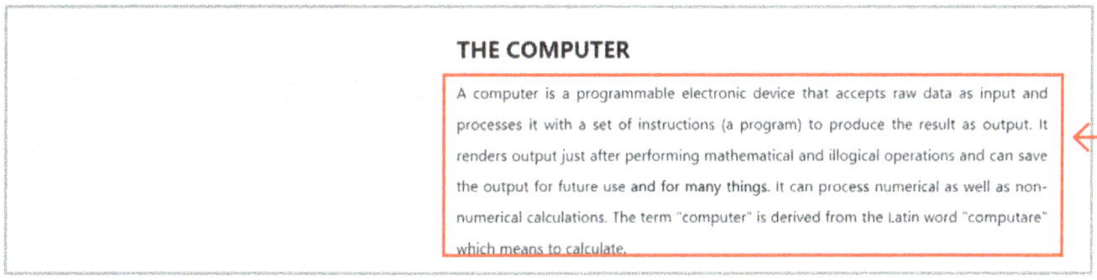

The text appears in the line spacing you selected.

In this example, we apply 1.5 line spacing.

Drop Cap

A drop cap feature allows you to create a large character, usually at the beginning of the paragraph. The letter drops from the top of its own line down several lines below. To insert a drop cap, follow the steps:

1. Click on the paragraph you want to display a drop cap.

2. Click on Insert tab.

3. Click on Drop Cap.

4. Click on Drop Cap Options.

The Drop Cap dialog box appears.

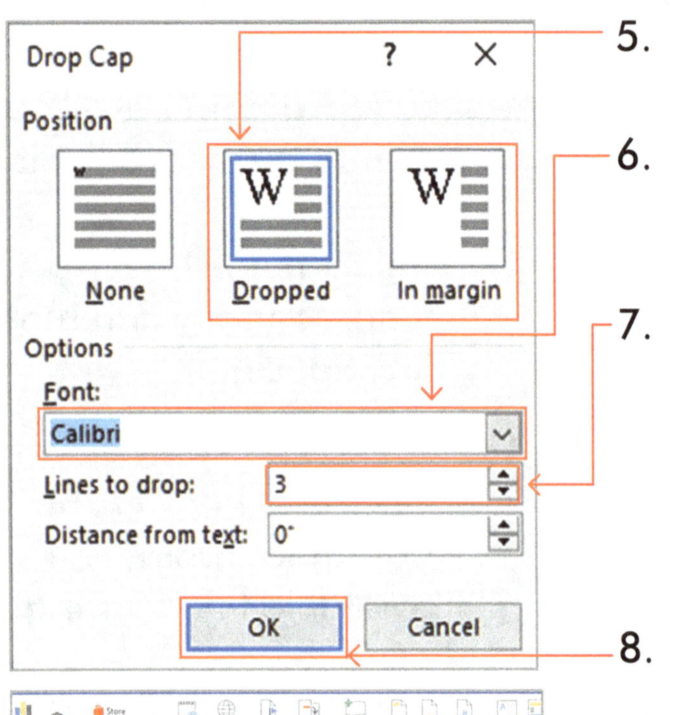

5. Click the type of drop cap you want to create.

6. This area displays the font the drop cap will display. Click the font you want the drop cap to display.

7. This area displays the number of lines that the drop cap will extend down from the first line of the paragraph. To change the number of lines, double-click the number in this area and then type a new number.

8. Click on OK to create the drop cap.

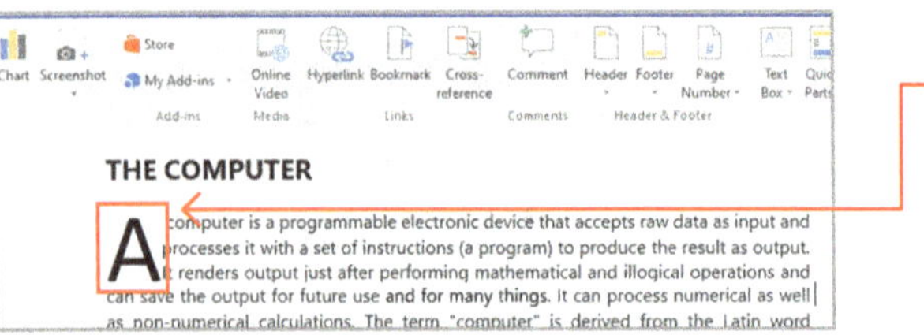

The drop cap appears in your document.

To deselect the drop cap, click outside the drop cap.

To remove a drop cap, repeat steps 1 to 5, selecting None in step 5. Then perform step 8.

Hiding and Displaying Ruler in Document

You can hide or display the rulers on the screen. Ruler is used to indent paragraphs or set tabs within the document. It also helps to identify the position of the insertion point.

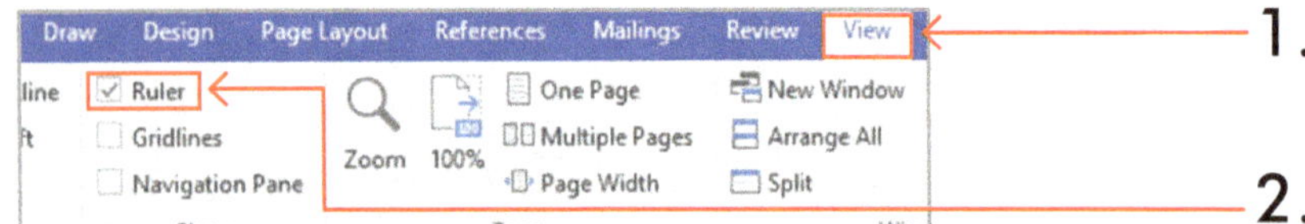

1. Click on View tab.

2. Click in Ruler check box.

3. Click on the Ruler icon to hide or display the ruler.

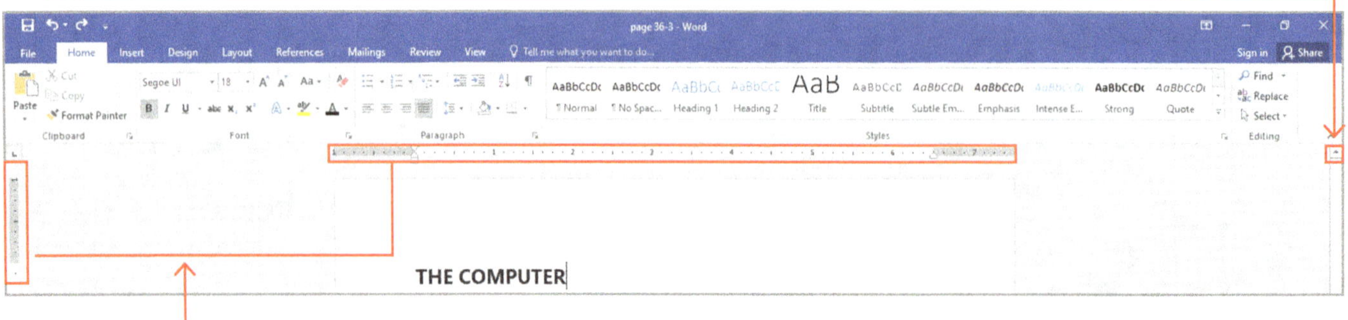

Ruler appears below the Ribbon and on the left side of your document.

Indenting a Paragraph

Indentation determines the distance of the paragraph from the left or right margin of the document. Within the margins, you can increase or decrease the indentation of paragraphs. You also can indent only the first line of a paragraph or all lines except the first line of the paragraph.

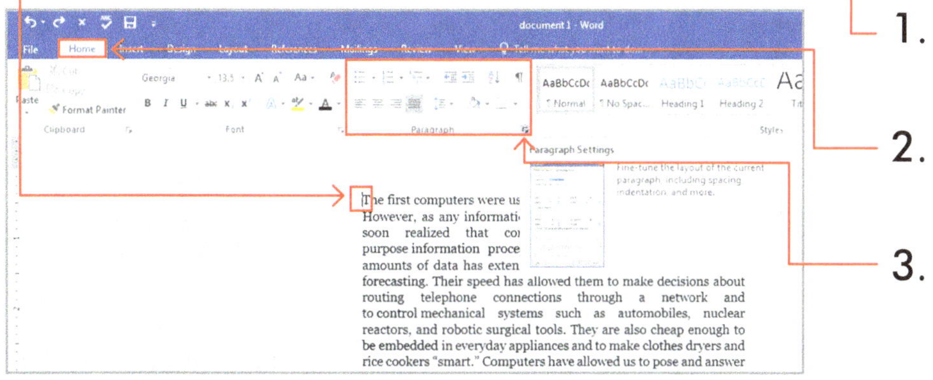

1. Click on the beginning of the passage.

2. Click on Home tab on the Ribbon.

3. Click on Paragraph dialog launcher tab.

The Paragraph dialog box appears.

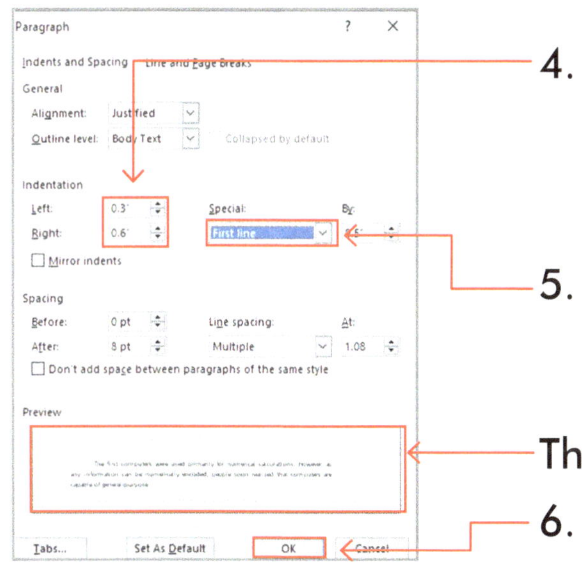

4. Type a specific indentation in the Left or Right indent text boxes. You can also click on up and down arrow to set the indent measurement.

5. Click on the down arrow of Special and set the specific kind of indent. (Here we have taken first line.)

This area shows the sample of indent.

6. Click on OK. Word applies indent to the text.

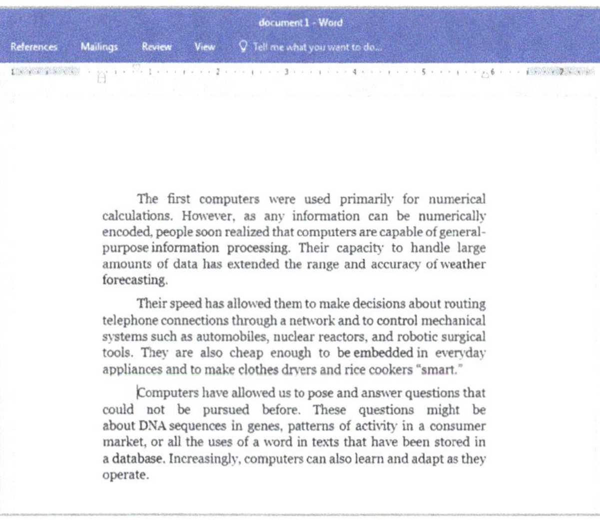

You can make as many paragraphs as you require in your passage by just using the Enter key from the sentence you want to make a new paragraph.

Changing Tab Setting

Tabs control the position of text exactly where you would like it in the document. You can have multiple tabs on a single line. By default tabs are set to every ½ inch. Any tab you set will override the default tab setting. Working with tabs using the ruler is a quick and easy way to set and adjust tabs. The different five types of tabs are:

⇒ **Left Tab (Normal)**: It aligns the following text on the left of the tab stop. The text flows to the right.

⇒ **Right Tab**: It aligns the following text on the right of the tab stop. The text flows to the left.

⇒ **Center Tab**: It aligns text at the middle of the tab stop.

⇒ **Decimal Tab**: The decimal tab is used to align numbers and text with a period.

⇒ **Vertical Line Tab**: It creates a vertical line at the designated tab stop.

To Add A Tab

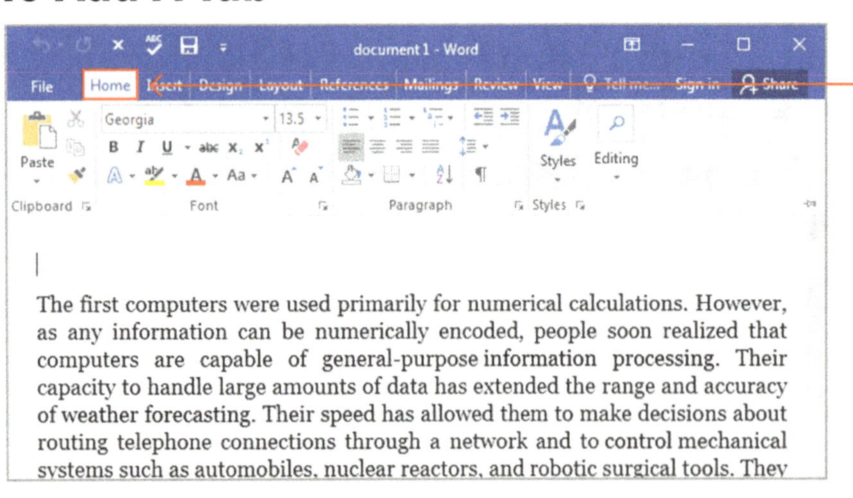

1. Go to Home tab.

2. Click on the Paragraph dialog box launcher.

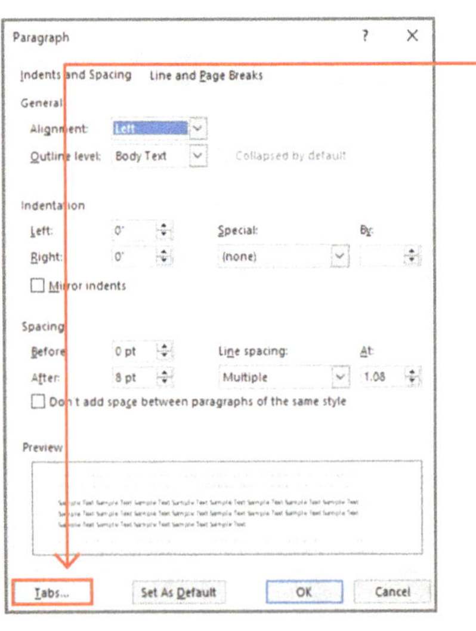

3. Select Tabs.

4. Type a measurement in the Tab stop position field.

5. Select an Alignment.

6. Select a Leader if you want one.

7. Select Set.

8. Select OK.

To Use A Tab

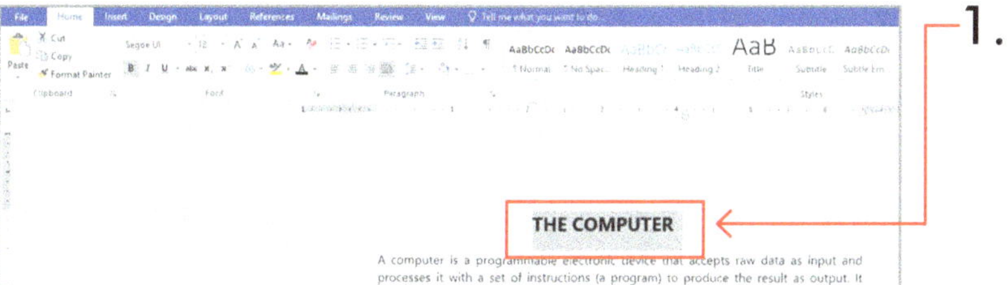

1. Click on the beginning of the line you want to move to the tab. Then, press the Tab key from the keyboard.

The insertion point and the text that follows move to the tab you set.

HEADERS AND FOOTERS

Header and footers are the text or graphics which appear at top and bottom sections of the document respectively. Header and Footer is used for various purposes, such as page numbering, document titles, copyright notices and so on.

Headers and Footer text is displayed as greyed areas.

Create a Header or Footer

To create header or footer, take the following steps:

1. Double-click anywhere on the top or bottom margin of the page.

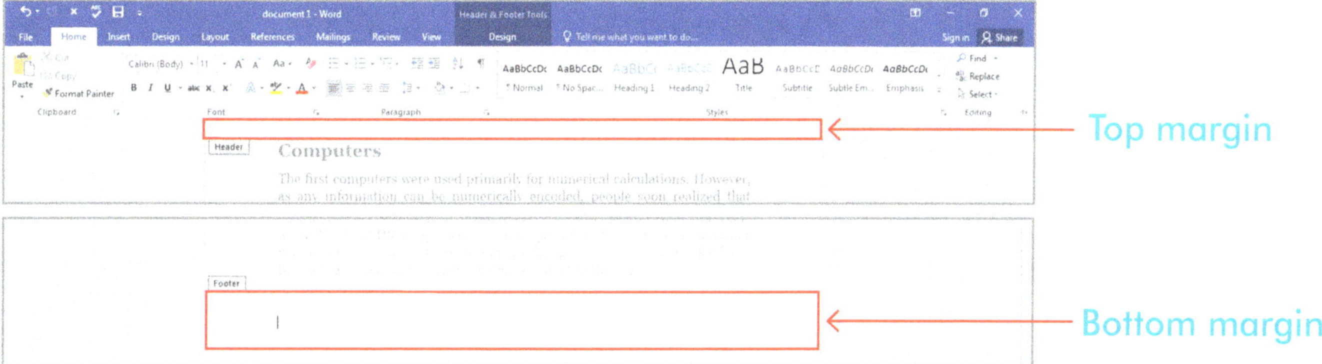

Fox example : Click on the top margin of the page.

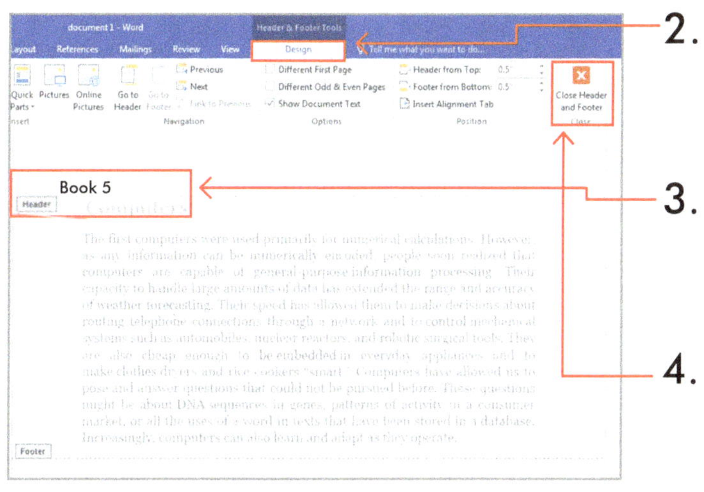

2. The Header and Footer Tools will open, and a Design tab will appear on the right side of the Ribbon.

3. The insertion point will appear in the header. Type the text into the header section.

4. When you have finished, click Close Header and Footer or press the Esc key.

The header or footer text will appear at the top or bottom of every page in the document.

REMOVE THE HEADER AND FOOTER

To remove header or footer from the document, take the following steps:

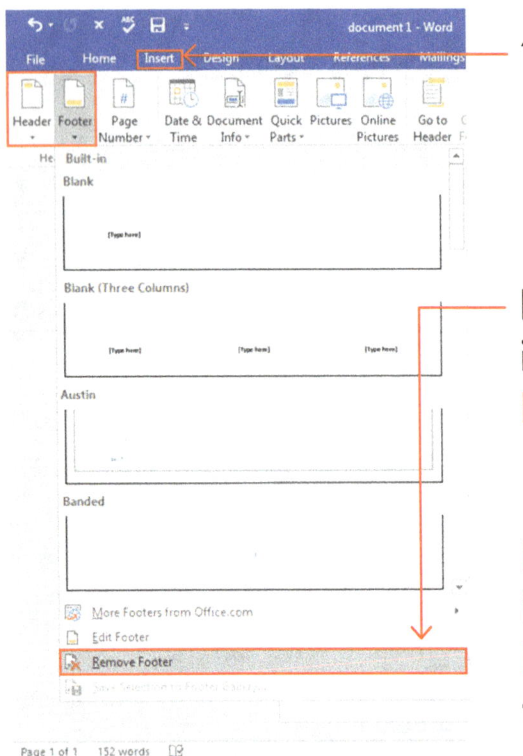

1. On the Insert tab, in the Header and Footer group, click on the Header or Footer drop-down list.

If you want to remove all the information contained in the footer, click the Footer command and select Remove Footer from the menu.

In the same way, if you want to remove all the information contained in the header, click the Header command and select Remove Header from the menu.

ADDING PAGE NUMBER

The page numbers can be added to every page within the document. Adding page numbers is helpful in keeping the pages in order after printing in a longer document.

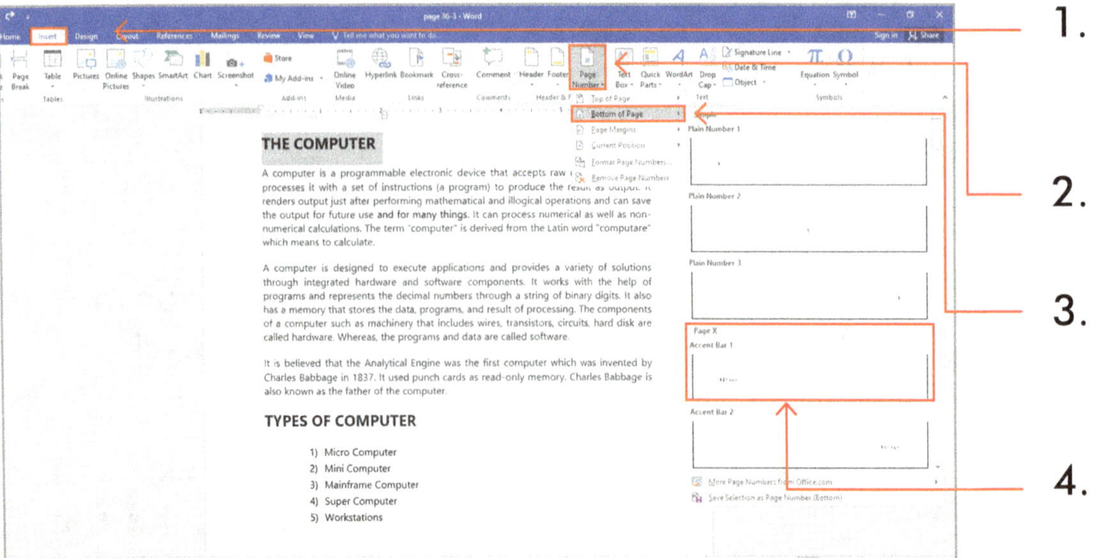

1. Click on Insert tab on the Ribbon.

2. Click on Page Number button.

3. Click on a location for the page numbers.

4. Click on a page number style.

You can use scroll bar to see more styles.

Word assigns page numbers to your document.

5. Desired numbering style appears.

Press Esc key on the keyboard when the work has been done. You can also add page numbers to the header or footer using the following steps:

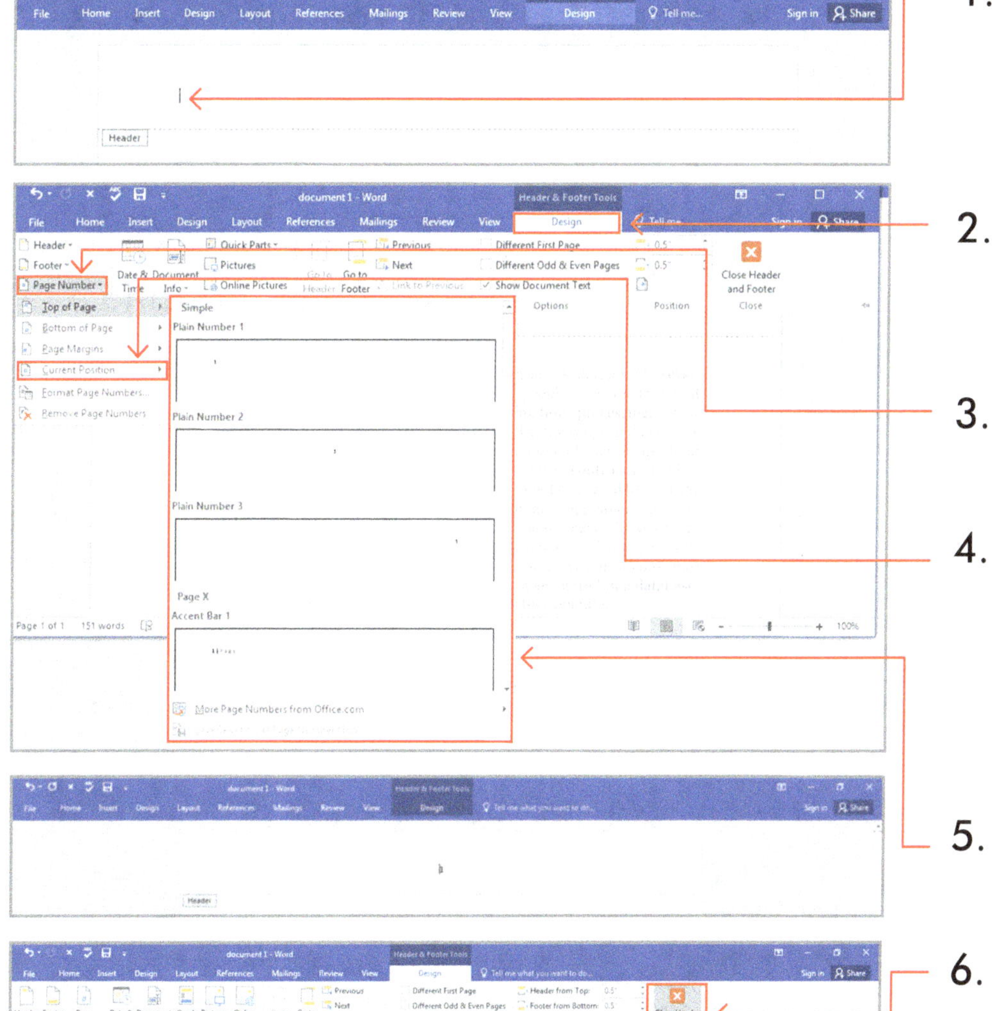

1. Double-click anywhere on the header or footer to unlock it.

2. The Design tab will appear on the right side of the Ribbon.

3. Click the Page Number command.

4. The menu will appear. Click the Current Position and select the desired page numbering style.

5. Desired numbering style appears.

6. Click on Close Header and Footer to exit the header or footer area.

CREATING A NEWSPAPER COLUMN

MS-Word provides a feature that let's you create newspaper style columns where the text flows down the page in a narrow column and thus continues to the next column. The steps to apply the newspaper column are:

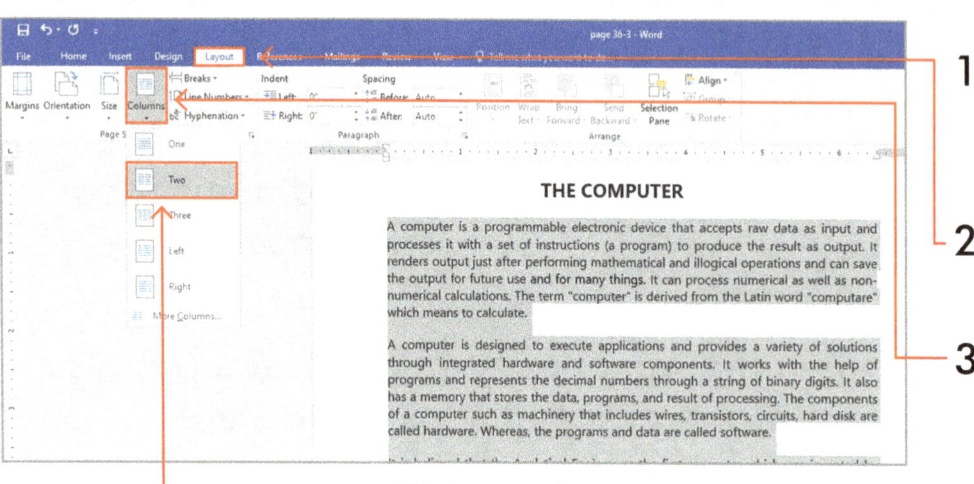

1. Select the text that you want to place into columns.

2. Click on **Layout** tab on the Ribbon.

3. Click on **Columns** button.

4. Click on the number of columns that you want to assign.

THE COMPUTER

A computer is a programmable electronic device that accepts raw data as input and processes it with a set of instructions (a program) to produce the result as output. It renders output just after performing mathematical and illogical operations and can save the output for future use and for many things. It can process numerical as well as non-numerical calculations. The term "computer" is derived from the Latin word "computare" which means to calculate.

A computer is designed to execute applications and provides a variety of solutions through integrated hardware and software components. It works with the help of programs and represents the decimal numbers through a string of binary digits. It also has a memory that stores the data, programs, and result of processing. The components of a computer such as machinery that includes wires, transistors, circuits, hard disk are called hardware. Whereas, the programs and data are called software.

Word will fill one column with text before starting a new column.

To remove newspaper columns, repeat steps **1** to **3**, selecting **one** column in step **3**.

LET'S HAVE A LOOK

- Microsoft Word is a Word processing software used to create a document.
- The text can be added or removed in between the text you have already entered.
- The Undo feature is used to repeat the last action that is made while typing text.
- The Spell check feature lets you find and correct spellings and grammatical errors in your document.
- Thesaurus is a type of dictionary that shows you the synonyms, antonyms, word substitutes and alternative spellings of the selected words within the document.
- The Change Case feature is used to change the case of the text.
- A bullet is a dot or a symbol that is marked at the start of the points. A numbered list gives the points a numerical order.
- Drop cap is a single letter made larger than the other in a paragraph.
- Indentation determines the distance of the paragraph from either the left or the right margin within the margins.
- Tab stops control where on a line, text will be positioned.
- We can add headers and footers to any document.

BRAIN TEASER

1. Answer each of the following in one word or line:

a. Name the feature that is used to repeat the last action.

b. How are spelling errors and grammatical errors indicated in the document?

c. Write the names of the different change case options.

d. Name the feature that is used to break a long sentence into points.

e. What do you mean by Indentation?

f. What is the use of tab stops?

2. Answer the following in brief:

a. What is the use of MS-Word 2016?

b. What is the function of UNDO and REDO feature?

c. What is the function of Spell check provided by MS-Word?

d. What is Thesaurus?

e. What do you mean by Indentation?

f. Explain the different types of tabs.

g. What purposes are header and footer used for?

h. What are the different change cases provided by MS-Word?

i. What is the use of a newspaper column?

3. Multiple Choice Questions

Tick (✓) the correct answer:

a. The feature used to repeat the last action that is made while typing text:

   i. Redo   ii. Change Case   iii. Undo

b. Shortcut key to open Thesaurus:

   i. Alt+F7   ii. Shift+F7   iii. Ctrl+F7

c. The case option that will change the text into capital letters:

   i. Lowercase   ii. Uppercase   iii. Toggle case

d. The feature in which the first letter is made larger:

   i. Indentation ☐   ii. Right Tab ☐   iii. Drop Cap ☐

e. The tab that aligns text on the right:

   i. Center tab ☐   ii. Left Tab ☐   iii. Right Tab ☐

f. Which list gives the point in numerical order?

   i. Bullets ☐   ii. Numbering ☐   iii. Tab setting ☐

4. Fill in the blanks:

a. MS-Word is a _______________ program used to type text on the computer.

b. Word automatically places a _______________ squiggly underline beneath spelling errors.

c. The _______________ command is used to search for a piece of particular text.

d. _______________ can help you to increase your vocabulary skills.

e. In _______________ case, the first character of the word will be in lowercase and the rest in uppercase.

f. The _______________ are the symbols, such as dots, diamonds, etc., and _______________ uses the numbers instead of symbols to represent.

g. _______________ determines the distance of the paragraph from the left or right margin of the document.

LAB ACTIVITY

- Open MS-Word and type a paragraph on 'My favourite Game'. Run Spell check and also use Thesaurus for some words. Find and replace those words with their synonyms.

- Make various paragraphs using the commands.

- Also add header and footer to the document. In the header, add the logo and name of your school. Add class and section in the footer.

6 Ms-PowerPoint 2016

MS-POWERPOINT 2016

Microsoft PowerPoint or MS-PowerPoint is a presentation program developed by Microsoft. It is a part of the Standard Office suite along with Microsoft Word and Excel. PowerPoint is a powerful communication tool to present views and ideas effectively through visual aids, like presentations, diagrams, photos, clipart, sounds, designs and animated special effects.

A single page of a PowerPoint presentation is called a Slide which may contain text, images and other media, such as audio clips and movies. A slide is like a page that displays a brief topic.

The collection of slides on a particular topic arranged in sequential form is called presentation. A presentation is also known as Slide Show.

STARTING POWERPOINT 2016

PowerPoint is a program that allows you to create presentations. To start PowerPoint program, you have to follow the steps as:

1. Click on the Start button.
2. Scroll the menu and click PowerPoint 2016.

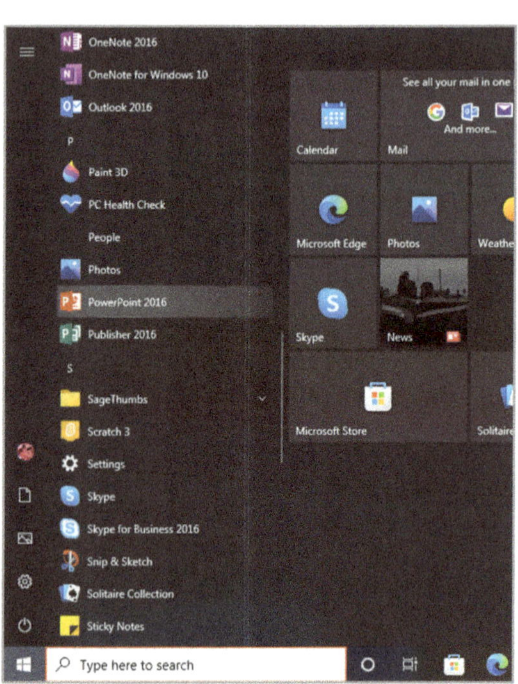

The following screen appears.

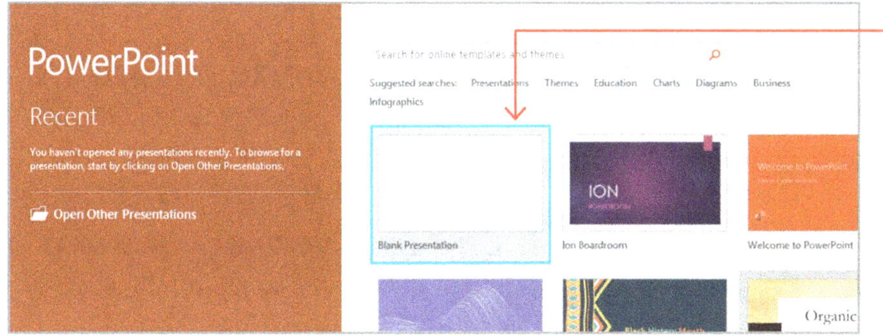

3. Click on Blank Presentation.

A blank presentation titled **Presentation1 - PowerPoint** is displayed in the PowerPoint window.

POWERPOINT WINDOW

Let us look at the various components of the PowerPoint Window.

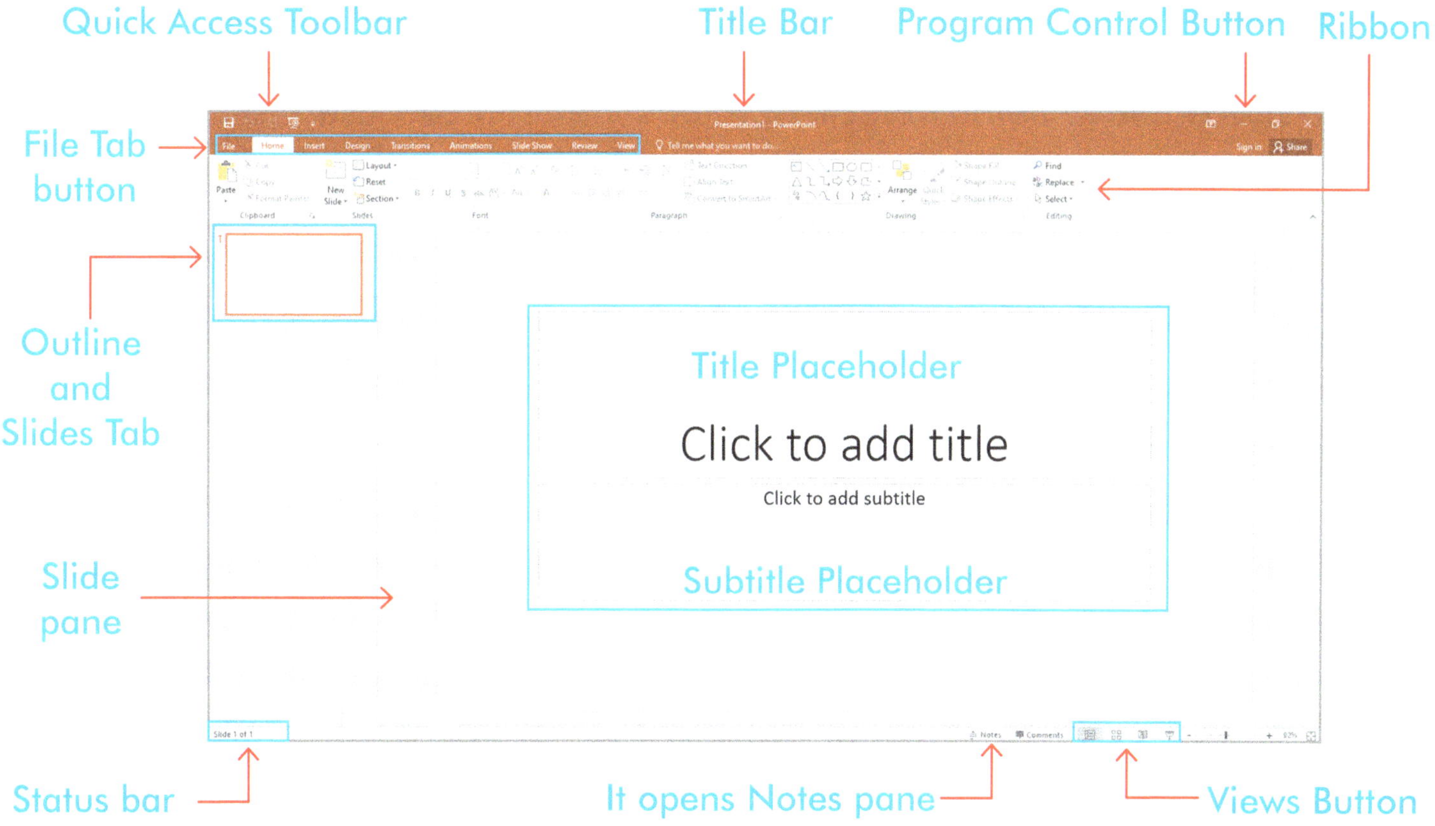

Title Bar: Title bar is on top of the screen. Title bar displays the name of the presentation on which you are currently working. It also contains Minimize, Maximize and Close buttons.

File Tab: A menu button contains the commands like New, Save and Open.

Quick Access Toolbar: Quick access toolbar is present on the left side of title bar. This helps to do common tasks with just one click from the mouse.

Ribbon: Ribbon contains two parts-tabs and groups. Each tab contains commands arranged in different groups.

Program Window Controls: These buttons are used to minimize the program window, restore the window to full size or close the window.

Outline and Slides Tab: It provides you with the two views of the slides of your presentation, *i.e.* the Slide tab shows the thumbnail version of each of the slides in the presentation, and the Outline tab shows a text outline of all the information on the slides.

Slide Pane: It is the main work area of PowerPoint. You can also enter text, graphics and animation effects directly in the slide pane.

Placeholder: It has two boxes with the dotted frames. One is Title Placeholder and the other is Subtitle Placeholder. The Title box contains the title of the slide. Subtitle placeholder holds objects in your slide. You can use a placeholder to hold text, pictures, charts, etc.

Status Bar: This displays the current slide number, total number of slides and view buttons.

View Buttons: Clicking on these buttons will show you the different views of presentation. Normal view, slide sorter view, reading view and slide show view are the four main views of PowerPoint.

Notes Pane: You can display the text notes for any hints or reference for your presentation in the Notes Pane.

CREATING A BLANK PRESENTATION WITH DESIGN THEME

Whenever you open PowerPoint, a blank slide is opened by default. To give the slide an attractive look, a particular design theme can be selected using Design tab on the ribbon. Design themes are built-in designs for creating a presentation. A design theme includes predefined information, layouts, background, text and colours.

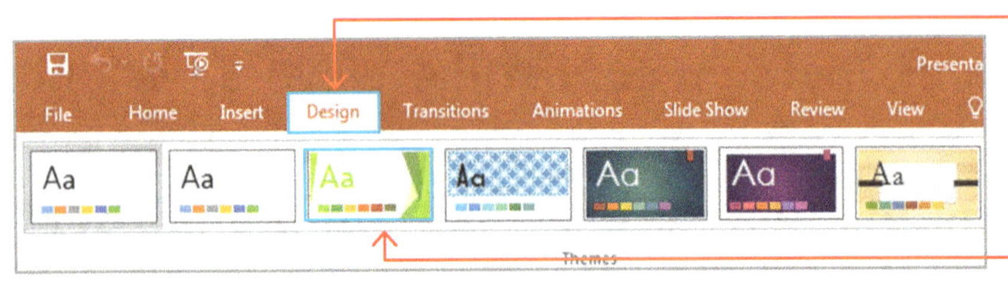

1. Click on the Design tab on the ribbon.

2. Click on one of the themes with your mouse.

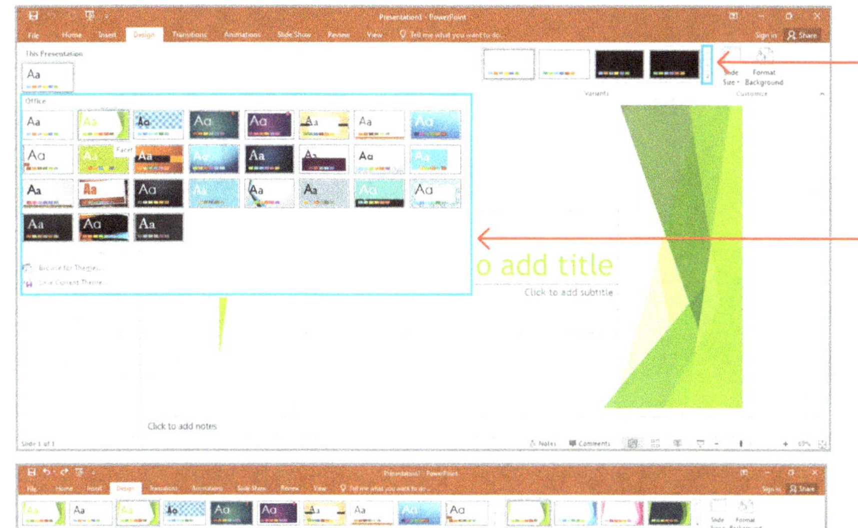

You can click on the down arrow of More button.

You can view the full palette of themes. Click the Theme you want to apply in your slide.

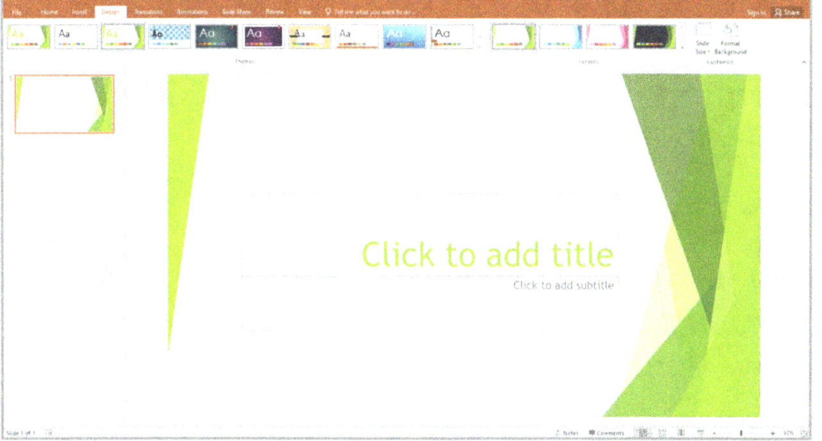

The theme is applied to Slide 1.

When the theme has been applied to the Slide, you can start adding the text.

CREATING THE TITLE SLIDE

Title placeholder is used to add text anywhere on your slide. Any text typed in a new slide becomes title text in the title text placeholder. To insert a title slide the steps are:

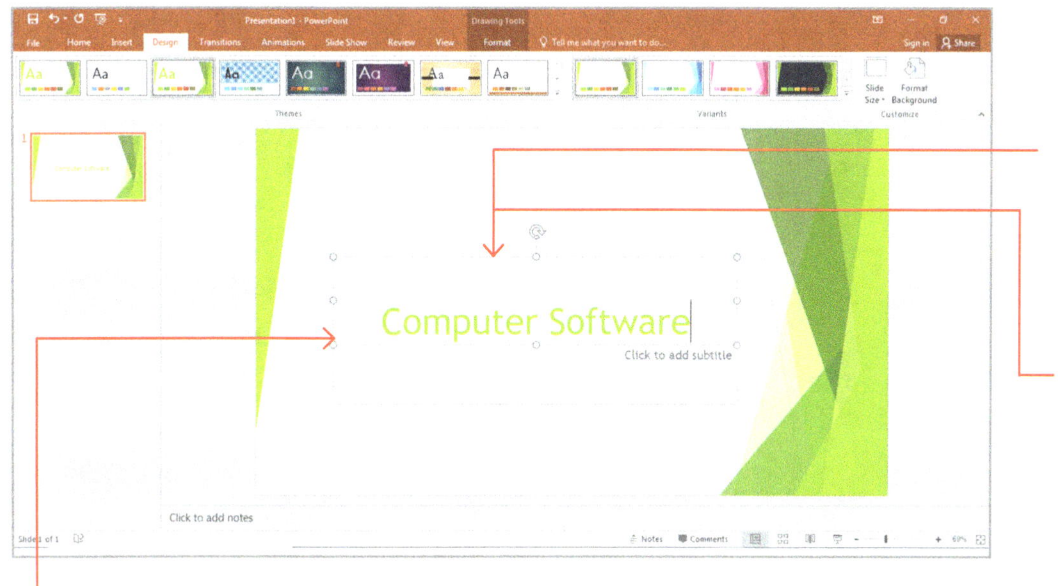

1. Click on the title text placeholder box.

2. Type your text in text placeholder box.

The title text displays in the title text placeholder and in the Slides tab. The insertion point is displayed after the letter 'e' in Software.

Entering Text in Subtitle

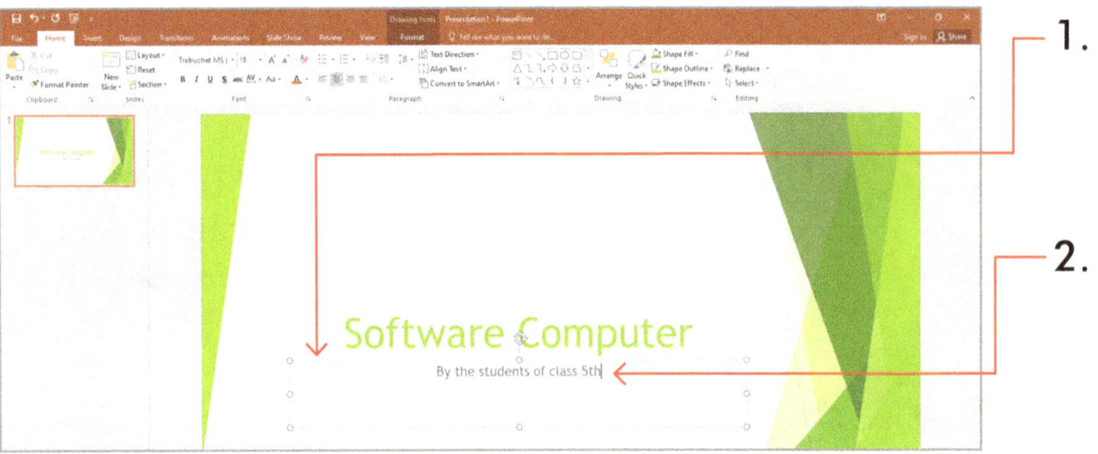

1. Click on the subtitle text placeholder box.

2. Type your text in subtitle text placeholder box.

The subtitle text is displayed in the subtitle text placeholder and the Slides tab. The insertion point is displayed after the letter '5' in class 5.

Note

We can align the text in the centre by selecting it. When we select the text, mini toolbar appears. Click on the alignment button to get the text aligned. You can use other commands also to beautify your text.

ADDING A NEW SLIDE TO A PRESENTATION

A PowerPoint presentation is a combination of many slides. You can create additional slides. These slides, when displayed in sequence, form a presentation. In order to prepare a presentation, we have to add a new slide into the presentation. The new slide can contain text, graphic, charts, etc. To add a new slide, the steps are:

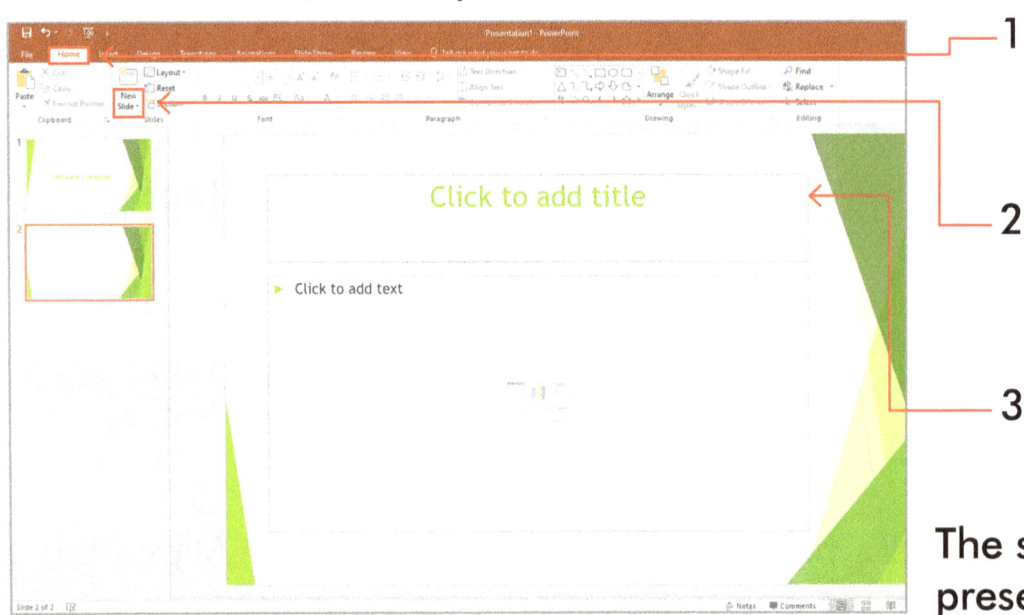

1. Click on Home tab on the ribbon.

2. Click on the New Slide button.

3. Click on Title and Content.

The slide 2 appears in the presentation.

Adding Text to Slide 2

Now type the text in the same way as you typed the text for slide 1.

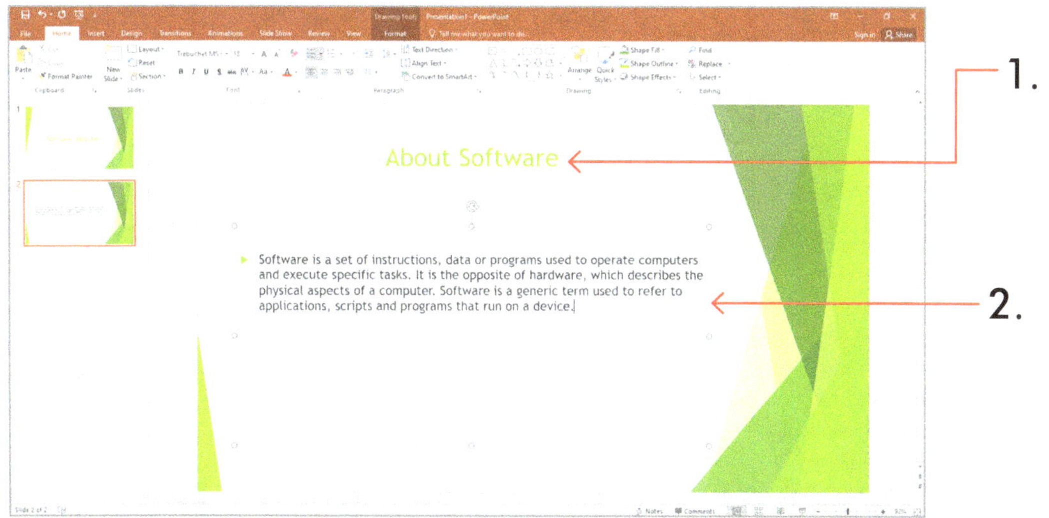

1. Click on the title text placeholder box and type your text.

2. Click on the subtitle text placeholder box, and type your text.

A bullet appears beside your text. If your text takes more than one line, PowerPoint automatically shifts the text to the next line. When you press the Enter key a new bullet appears in the next line.

SELECTING TEXT

Before performing any action to the text within the presentation, the particular text has to be selected. To select the text or a group of text, the steps are:

To Select a Word

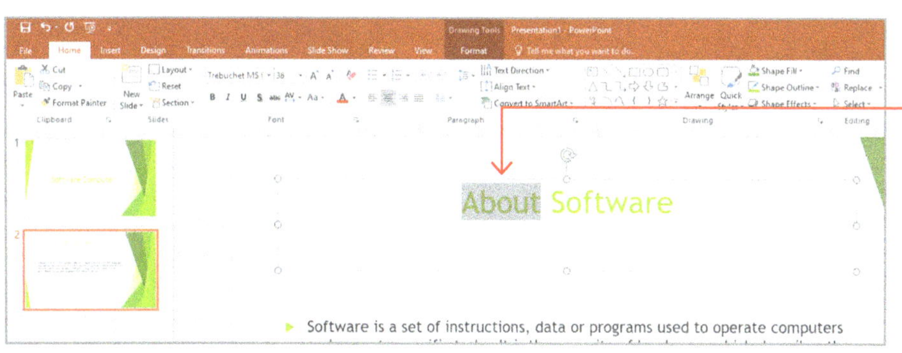

Double-click on the word you want to select.

To deselect the text, click outside the selected area.

To Select a Sentence

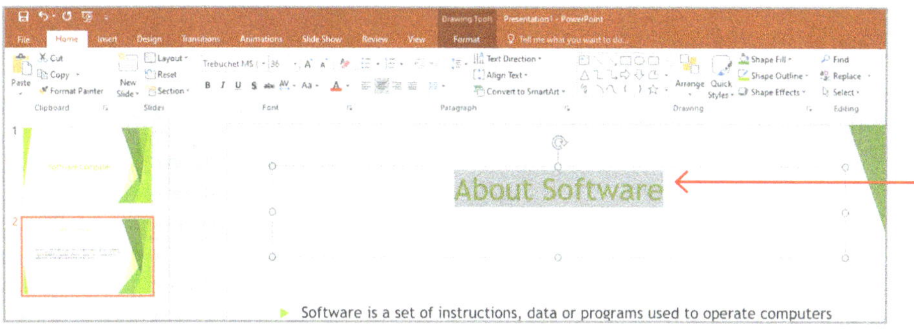

Triple-click on the sentence you want to select.

To Select a Point

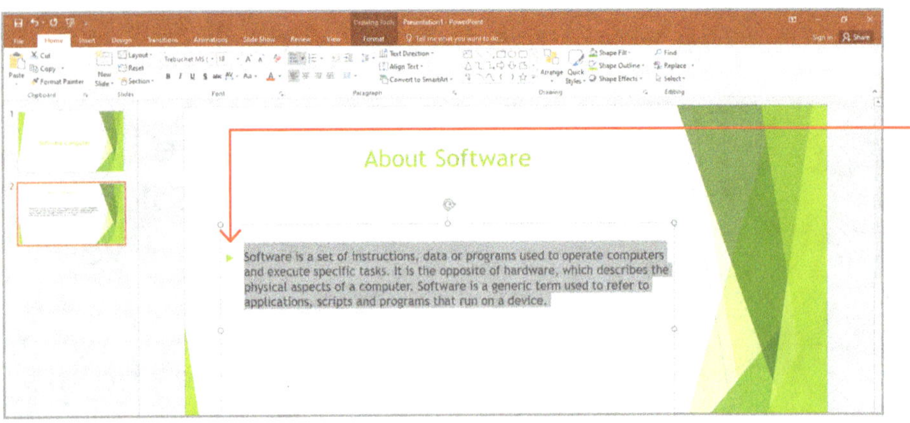

Click on the bullet (▶) beside the point you want to select.

To Select Any Amount of Text

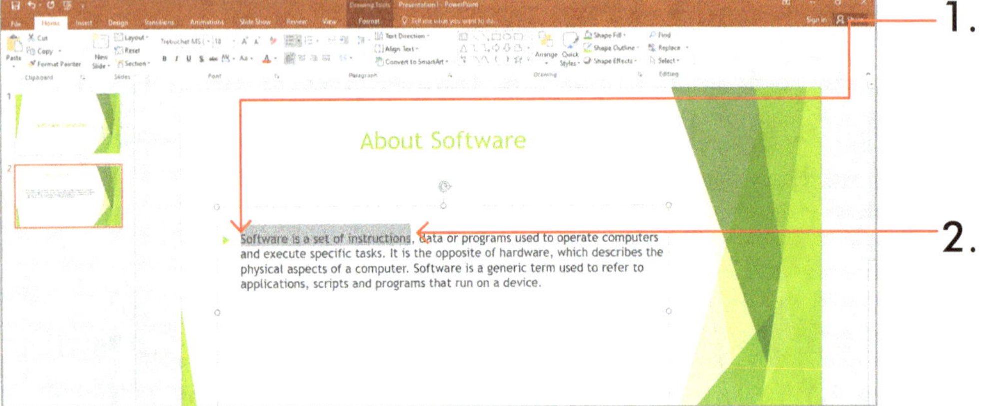

1. Place the mouse pointer (I) over the first word you want to select.

2. Drag the mouse pointer (I) over the text you want to select.

DELETING THE TEXT

The text or information that is required no more in the presentation can be removed or deleted. To delete a particular text, the steps are:

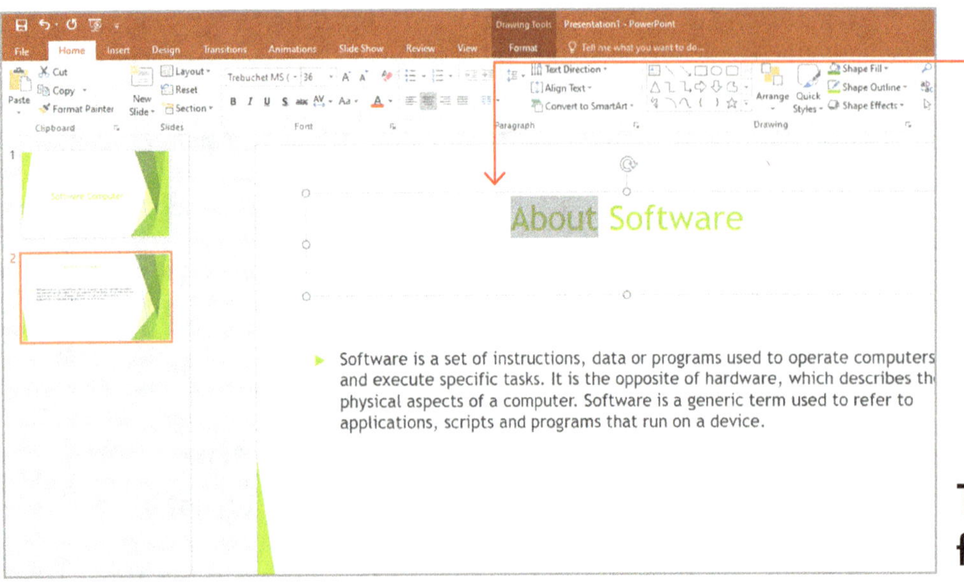

1. Select the text you want to delete.

2. Press the Delete key from the keyboard to remove the text from your presentation.

The text will disappear from the slide.

UNDOING THE CHANGES

The Undo features in a PowerPoint is used to cancel the last changes you made earlier into the presentation.

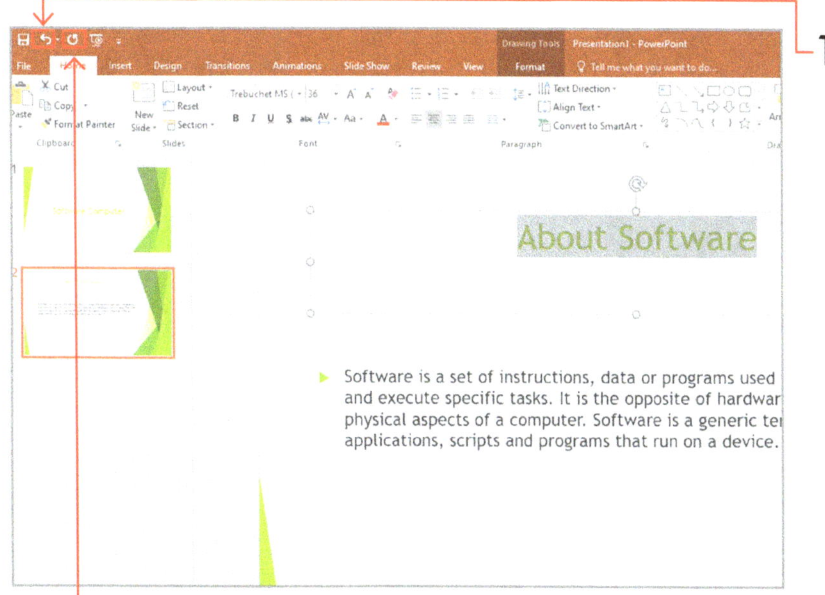

1. Click on Undo clear button (⟲) from Quick Access toolbar to undo the last changes you made to your presentation.

   PowerPoint cancels the last changes you made to your presentation.

   You can repeat step 1 to cancel previous changes you made.

To reverse the results of using the Undo feature, click on Repeat Clear (⟳) from Quick Access toolbar.

CHANGING THE FONT OF THE TEXT

You can change the font of text to change the appearance of your slide text.

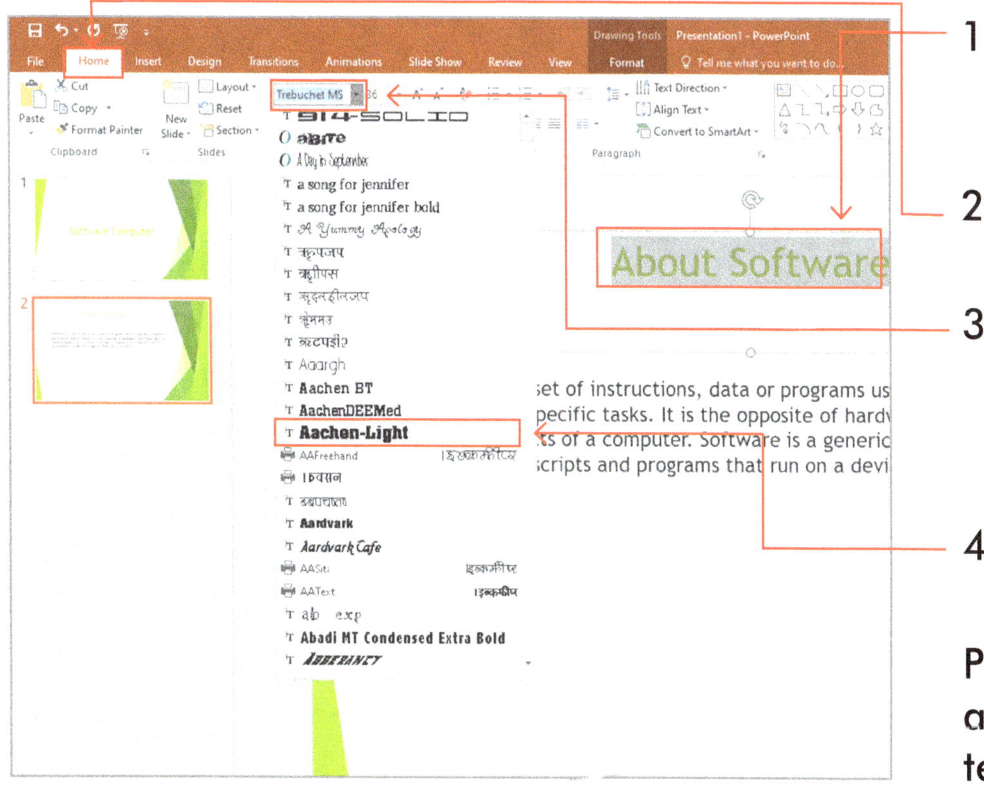

1. Select the text you want to change into a different font.

2. Click on Home tab on the ribbon.

3. Click on down arrow button of Font to display a list of the available fonts.

4. Click on the font you want to use.

PowerPoint immediately applies new font to the text.

CHANGING THE FONT SIZE OF THE TEXT

The size of the text can be increased or decreased in the presentation.

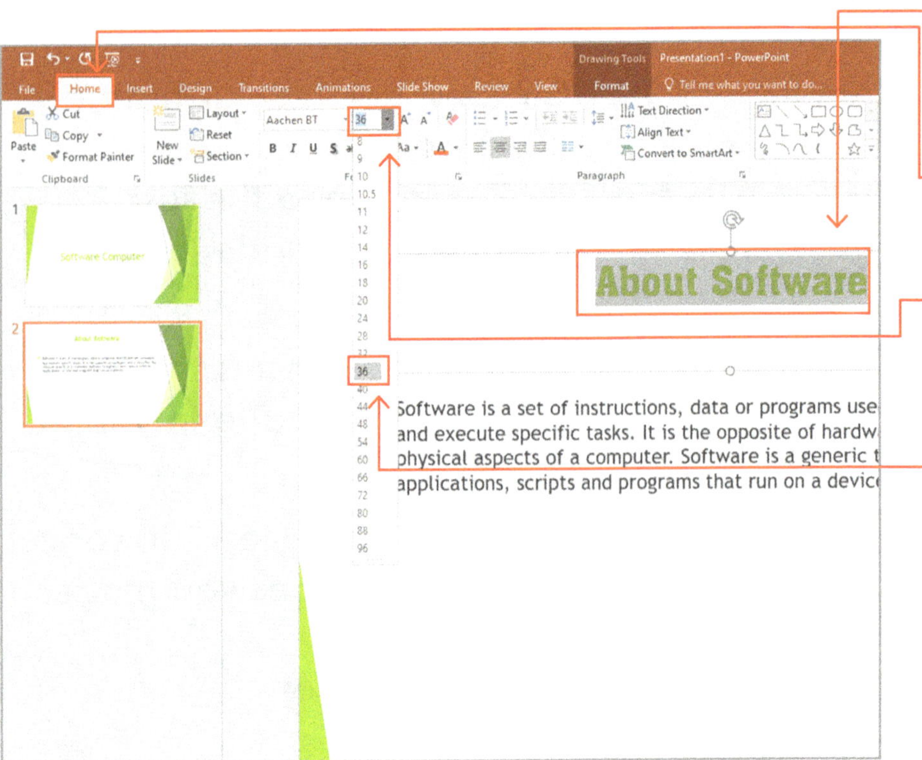

1. Select the text you want to change to a different font size.

2. Click on Home tab on the ribbon.

3. Click on down arrow button of Font Size to display a list of the available sizes.

4. Click on the size you want to use.

PowerPoint immediately applies the new font size to the text.

CHANGING THE COLOUR OF THE TEXT

To give your presentation an attractive look, you can change the colour of the text on a slide.

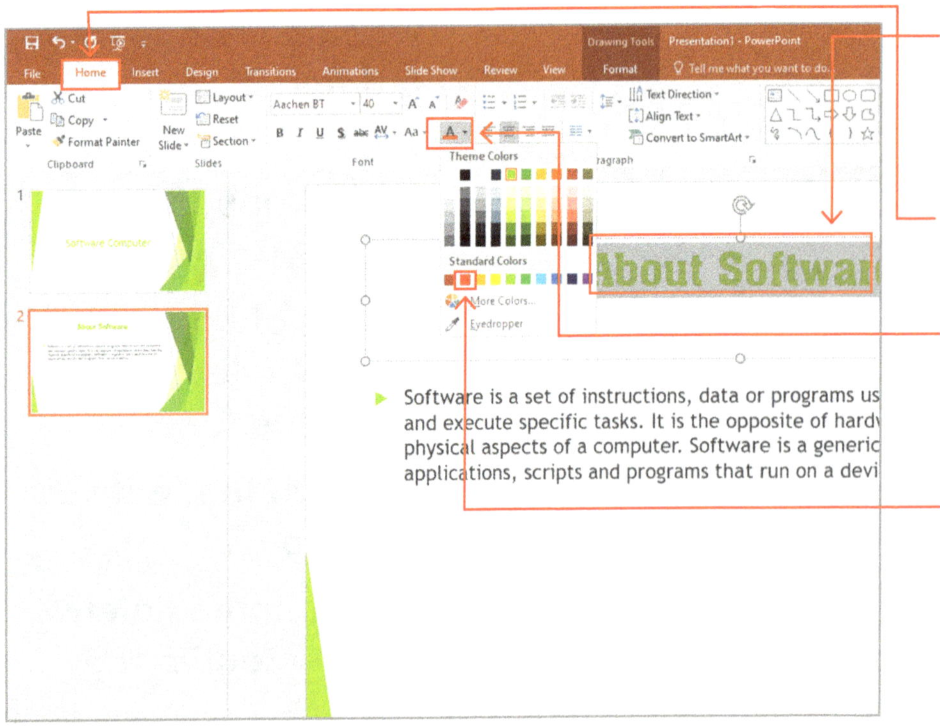

1. Select the text you want to change to a different colour.

2. Click on Home tab on the ribbon.

3. Click on the down arrow of Font Color button.

4. Click on the colour of your choice.

PowerPoint applies colour to the text in the selected text box.

CHANGING THE TEXT STYLE

The appearance of the text can be changed by making the text bold, italic, underline and shadow.

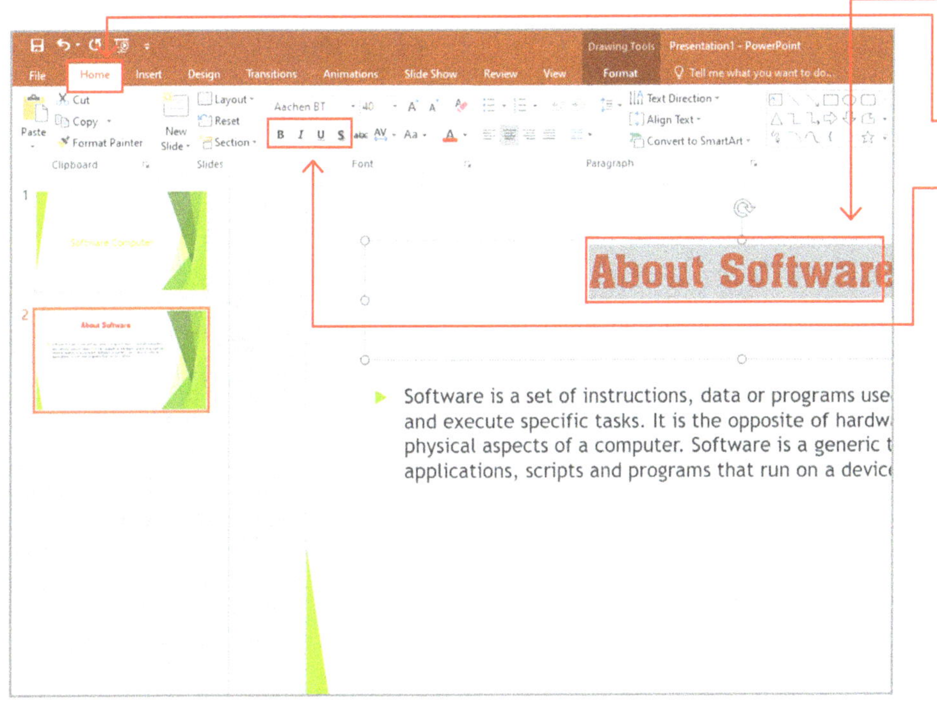

1. Select the text that you want to change.

2. Click on Home tab.

3. Click a style button:

   Bold (B)

   Italic (I)

   Underline (U)

   Shadow (S)

PowerPoint assigns the formatting.

In this example, we use Shadow style.

CHANGING THE TEXT ALIGNMENT

Alignment is the positioning of text in a text box. The different text alignments, such as left, right, centre or justified, can be given to the selected text.

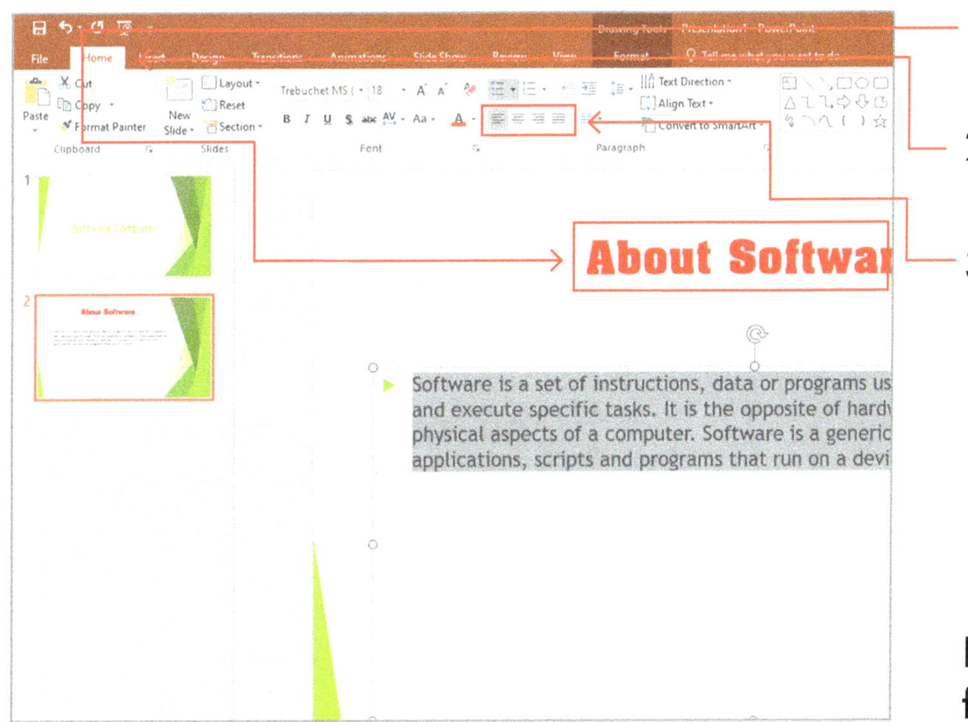

1. Select the text that you want to change.

2. Click on Home tab on the ribbon.

3. Click on an alignment button:

   Left align (≡)

   Center (≡)

   Right align (≡)

   Justify (≡)

PowerPoint assigns formatting.

SETTING THE LINE SPACING

You can set the distance between the gap of two lines in a text box. To change the line spacing, follow the steps:

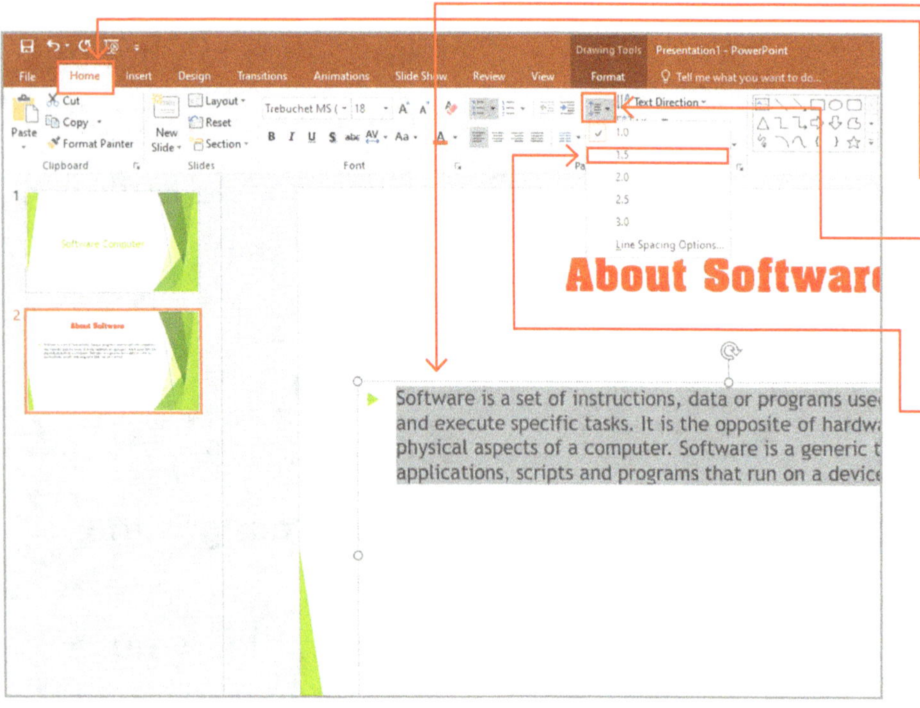

1. Select the text or text box that you want to change.

2. Click on Home tab.

3. Click on the down arrow of Line Spacing button.

4. Click on a line spacing figure.

PowerPoint applies the line spacing.

In this example, we apply 1.5 spacing.

SAVING A PRESENTATION

You can save the presentation for its future use. Once the presentation is saved, you can review and edit any time.

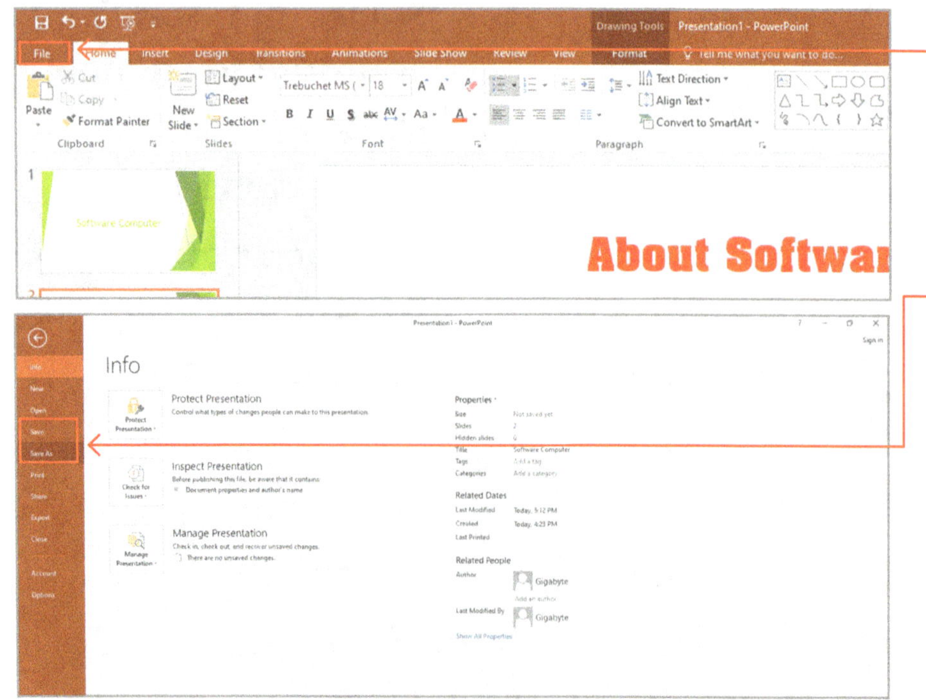

1. Click on File tab.

Backstage view will appear.

2. Click on the Save or Save As button.

You can also click the Save button ( ) on Quick Access toolbar to save the file.

The Save As dialog box appears.

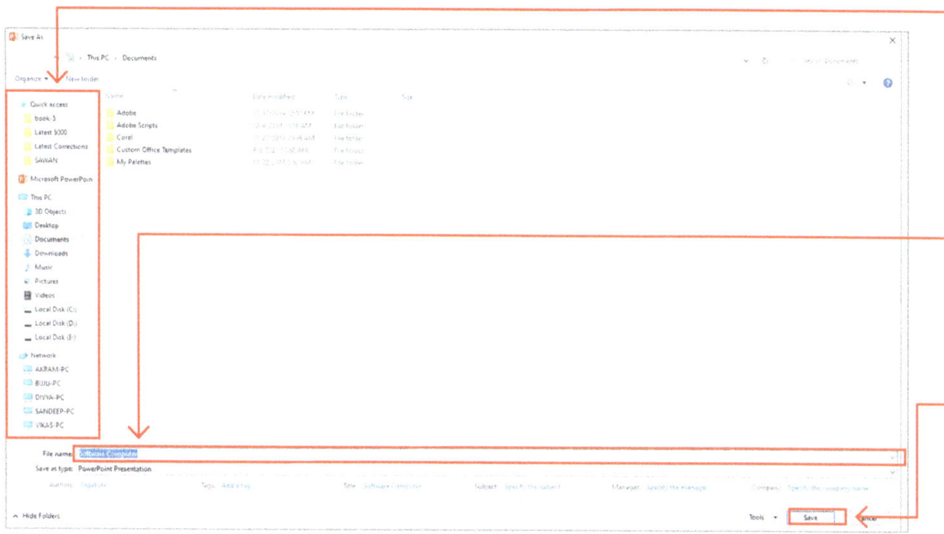

3. Click on these areas to navigate to the folder in which you want to save the file.

4. Click in the **File name** text box and type a name for the file.

5. Click on **Save**.

PowerPoint saves the presentation and the new filename appears on the title bar.

The keyboard shortcut to save a document is Ctrl+S.

CLOSING A PRESENTATION

After finishing your work, you must close the presentation. Closing the presentation will not close the PowerPoint window. To close PowerPoint presentation, the steps are:

1. Click on **File** tab.

Backstage view will appear.

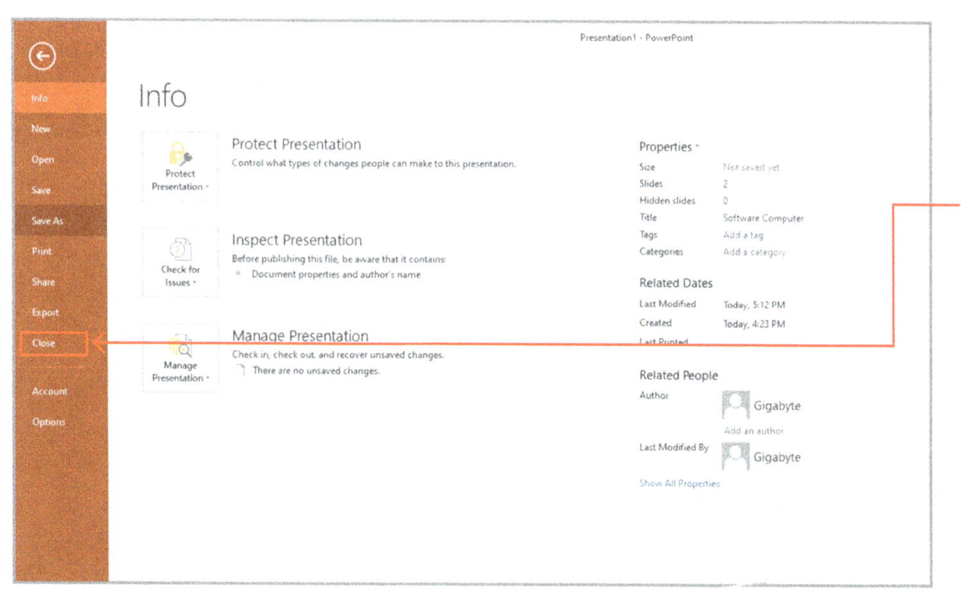

2. Click on the **Close** button.

PowerPoint closes the current open presentation.

LET'S HAVE A LOOK

- MS-PowerPoint is a program that enables you to create and design presentations.
- A presentation is a collection of slides arranged in a sequential manner that can include graphics, movies, sound, etc.
- A single page of a PowerPoint presentation is called a slide.
- The PowerPoint begins the first slide as a Title slide.
- Before performing any action to the text the particular text has to be selected.
- Title bar, File tab, Quick Access Toolbar, Ribbon, etc. are some of the elements of PowerPoint window.

BRAIN TEASER

1. Answer each of the following in one word or line:

a. Which program is used to create a presentation?

b. Write the keyboard shortcut to save the presentation.

c. Name any five components of PowerPoint window.

d. What is the use of Title bar?

e. What is Notes pane?

f. Why do we save the presentation?

2. Answer the following in brief:

a. What is PowerPoint?

b. Mention the steps to open PowerPoint window.

c. Write different ways to select the text.

d. Explain the uses of the following:
   i. Status bar

   ii. Quick Access Toolbar

   iii. Notes Pane

   iv. Ribbon

   v. View Buttons

e. What is the use of Undo and Redo features?

f. What do you mean by Alignment?

3. Multiple Choice Questions

Tick (✓) the correct answer:

a. A presentation software from Microsoft:
   i. MS-Excel   ii. MS-PowerPoint   iii. MS-Word

b.   An individual page of Presentation is:

   i.   Slide ☐   ii. Notes pane ☐   iii. Outline ☐

c.   The bar consists of message area:

   i.   Status Bar ☐   ii. Splitter Bar ☐   iii. Title Bar ☐

d.   The toolbar appears at the top left corner of the PowerPoint screen:

   i.   Status bar ☐   ii. Splitter bar ☐

   iii. Quick Access Toolbar ☐

e.   The keyboard shortcut to save a presentation:

   i.   Ctrl+Z ☐   ii. Alt+S ☐   iii. Ctrl+S ☐

4.   Fill in the blanks:

a.   PowerPoint is a collection of ________ arranged in sequential manner.

b.   PowerPoint is used to create ____________ .

c.   ______________ is the bar at the top of the window.

d.   PowerPoint begins the first slide as a ____________ .

e.   The size of text can also be ____________ or ____________ .

5.   Write 'T' for true or 'F' for false in the boxes:

a.   PowerPoint is a spreadsheet software. ☐

b.   View button is present at the top of the window. ☐

c.   The PowerPoint is opened with a blank presentation. ☐

d.   A single page of PowerPoint is called a slide. ☐

e.   There are four options for text alignment. ☐

LAB ACTIVITY

- Open a PowerPoint to create a presentation on 'computer'. Give the information about the importance of computer and its uses. Format the text using attractive fonts, size, colour, alignment, spacing, etc.

- Save your presentation with the name 'My Computer' and close the PowerPoint.

Formative Assessment-3
(Chapters 5-6)

1. Open your English book and type the first page of the first chapter in MS-Word and do the following:

- Save the document with the filename 'English'.

- Run the Spell check feature to correct the spelling errors and grammatical mistakes in the document.

- Now change the font, font size, style, alignment, border, shading, etc. to make it more beautiful.

- Format the title of the chapter in uppercase, blue colour, bold and underline style, size 18 points and centre-aligned.

- Insert the drop cap in the first paragraph.

- Now save the document once again and close Microsoft Word.

2. Label the following PowerPoint window:

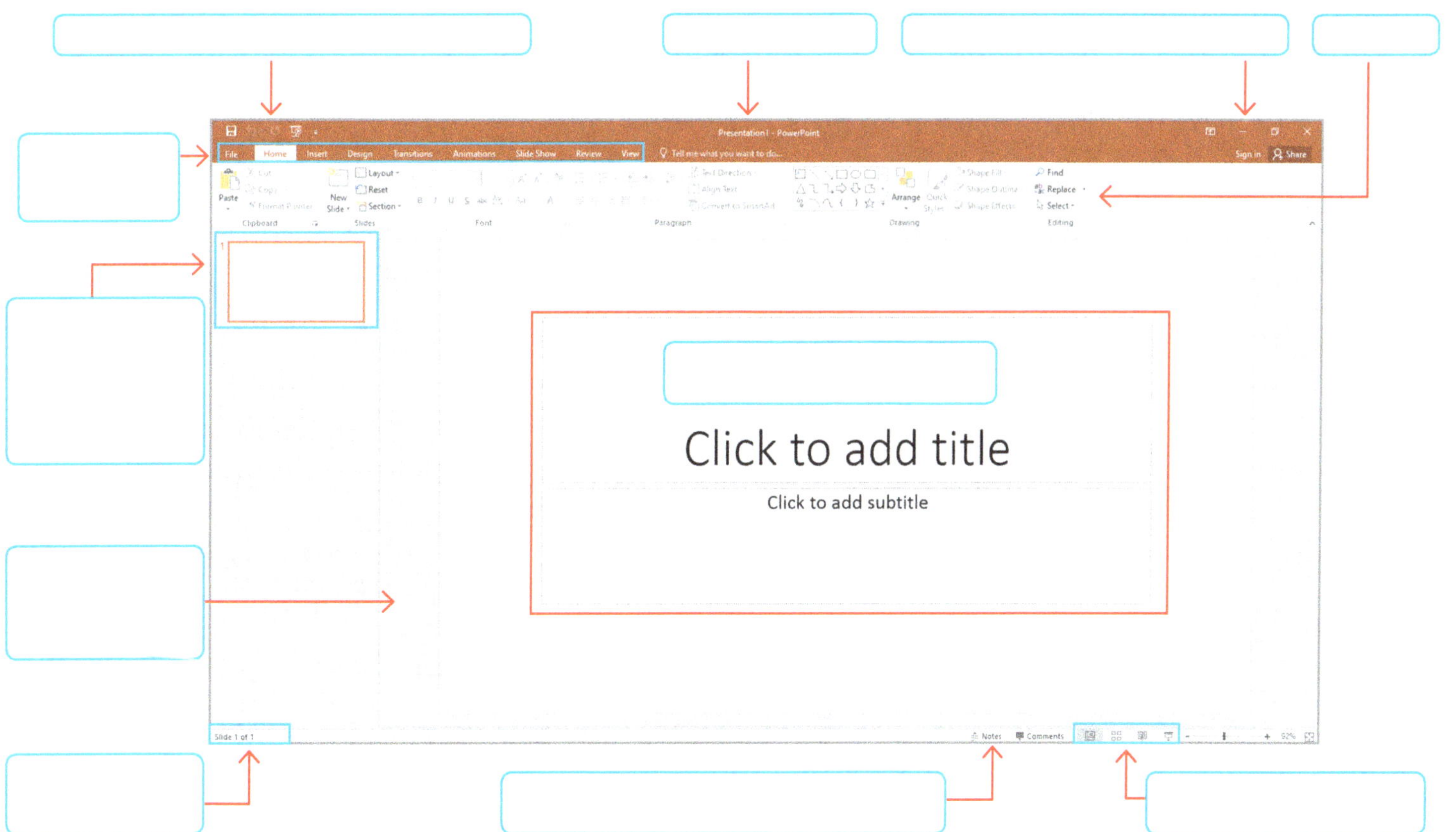

7 More on PowerPoint

Dear children, after creating and saving the slides in PowerPoint, now let's move further and learn some more features in it like adding pictures and applying animation in presentations.

SLIDE LAYOUT

In PowerPoint, slide layout arranges all elements, like Title, subtitle text, images, clipart, chart, autoshapes, sound and movie clips within a slide.

Slide Layouts are related to placeholders, which refer to the containers in layouts that hold such elements. Text placeholders accept only text. Content placeholders accept either text or a graphic element. A content placeholder contains icons that help you insert graphics. You can move placeholders to design slides that suit your particular needs.

PowerPoint 2016 includes nine inbuilt slide layouts, also called standard layouts. You can also create custom layouts that meet your specific needs.

CHANGING THE SLIDE LAYOUT

By using layout, you can quickly change your whole presentation.

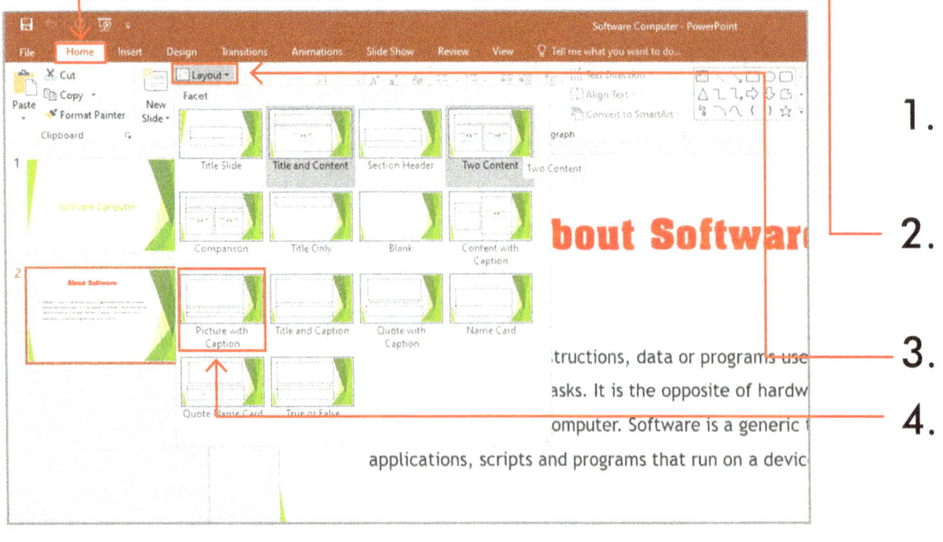

1. Display the slide that you want to change.

2. Click on Home tab on the Ribbon.

3. Click on Layout button.

4. Choose your desired layout.

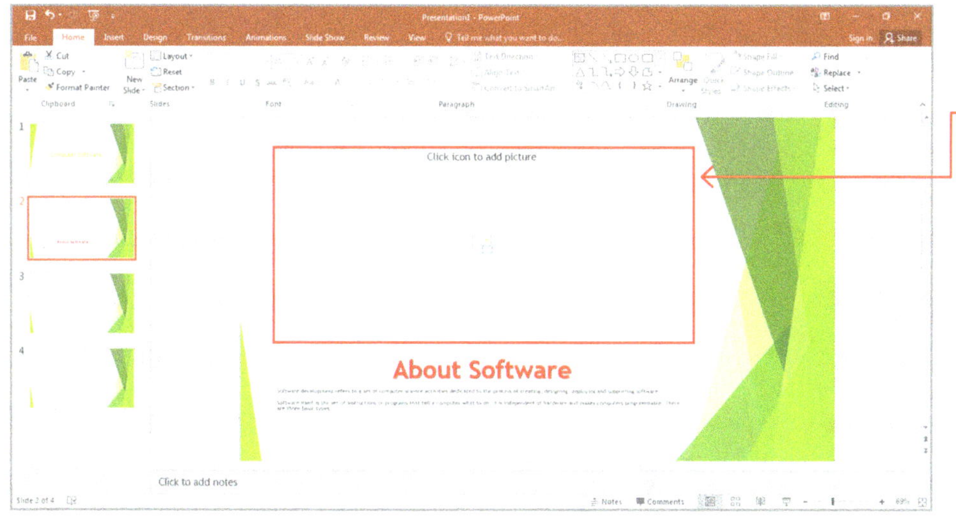

PowerPoint immediately assigns the selected layout to the slide.

The text in the slide will automatically adjust itself to the new layout.

ADDING A CLIPART IMAGE

Images and pictures can be added to the presentation by using Clipart. This helps to create a visually appealing presentation and keep viewers entertained and interested. To insert a clipart in a presentation, the steps are:

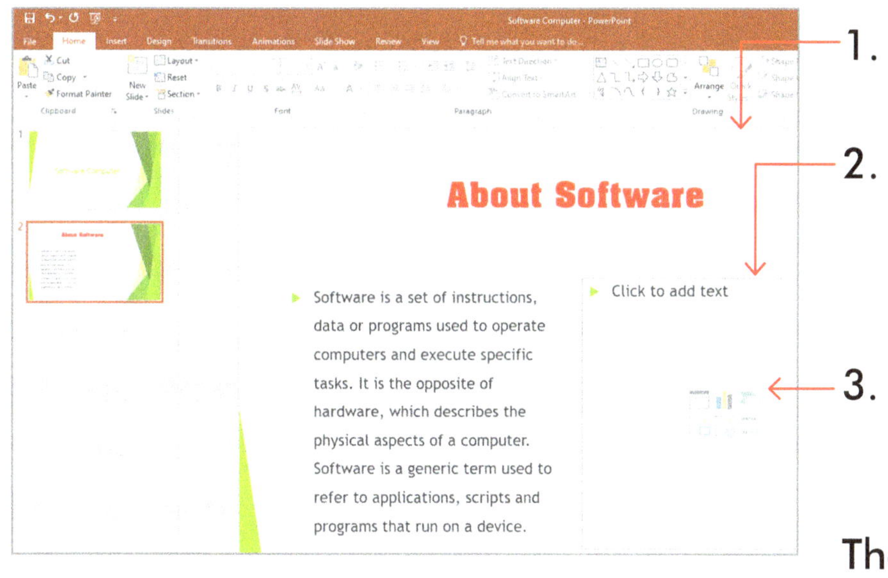

1. Display the slide you want to add a ClipArt image to.

2. Change the layout of the slide to the one that includes a placeholder for a ClipArt image.

3. Click on Online Pictures icon ( ) to add Clipart image.

The Clip Art task pane opens.

4. Type the name of an image in a search box that you want to insert.

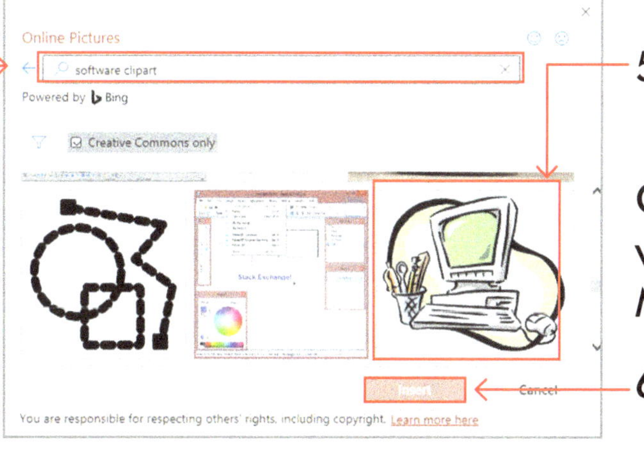

5. Choose the picture that you like to insert.

Click on the checkbox if you want to insert the content from Microsoft Office Website.

6. Click on Insert.

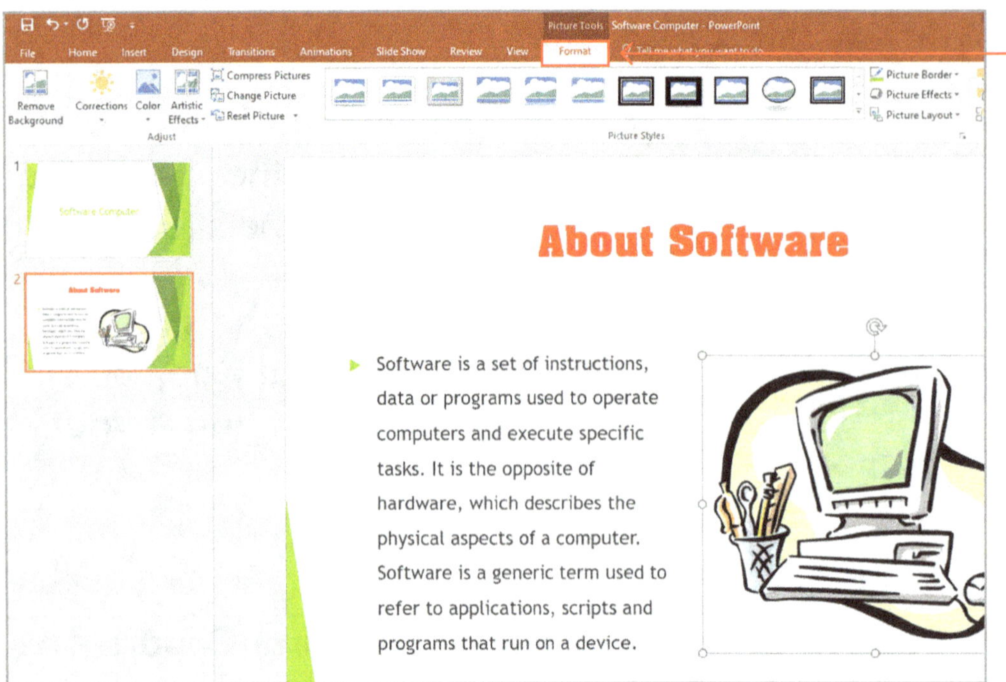

The ClipArt is inserted and the Picture Tools appears on the Format tab.

You can resize or move the ClipArt.

To deselect the ClipArt, click on anywhere else in the work area.

ADDING A PICTURE IMAGE

The pictures or graphics stored in the computer memory can also be inserted in the presentation. To add a picture, the steps are:

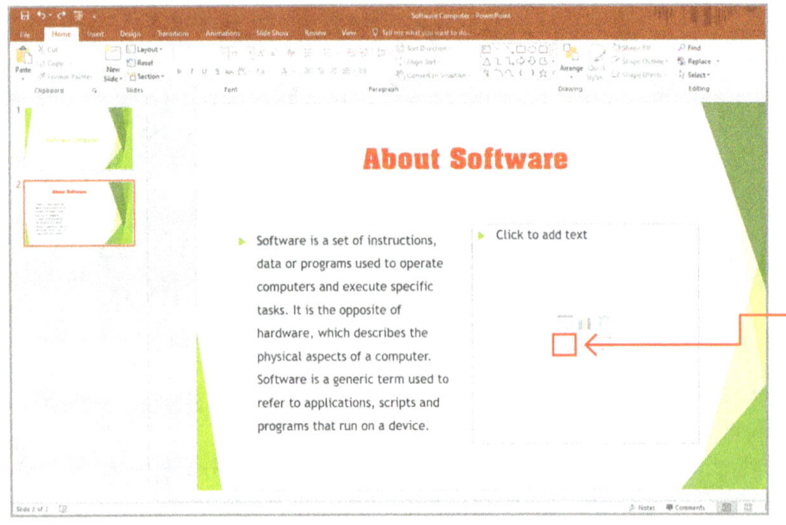

1. Display the slide you want to add a picture to.

2. Change the layout of the slide to the one that includes a placeholder for a picture.

3. Click on picture icon (🖼) to add a picture to the slide.

The Insert Picture dialog box appears.

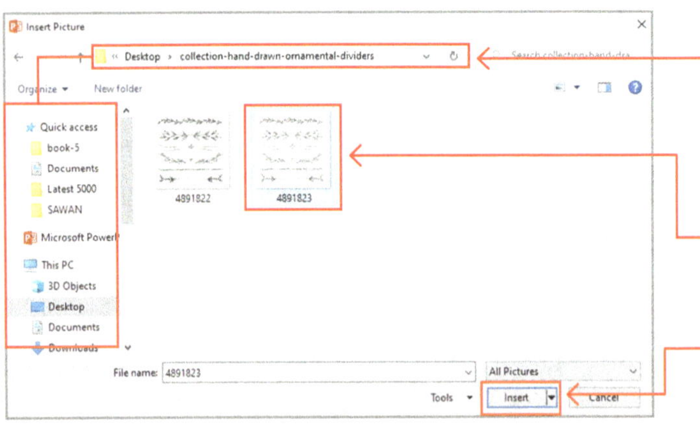

These areas show the location of the displayed pictures. You can click on these areas to change the location.

4. Click on the picture you want to add to the slide.

5. Click on Insert to add a picture to the slide.

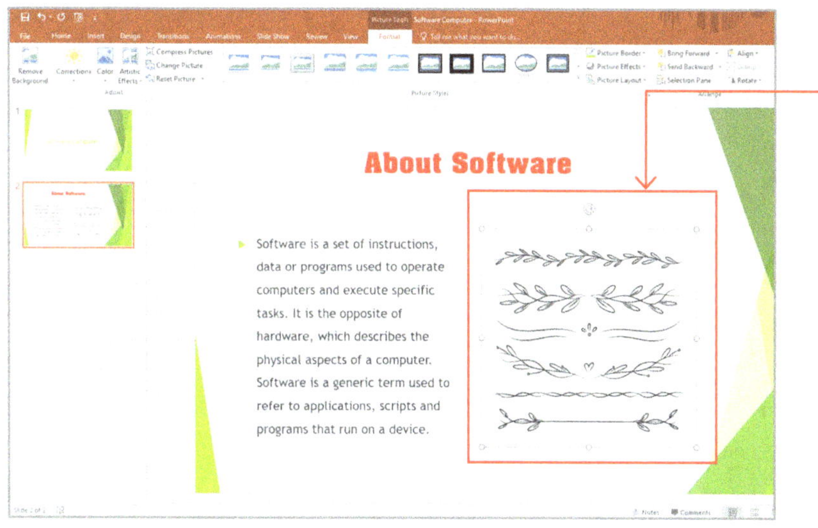

The Picture is inserted and Picture Tools appears on the Format tab.

You can resize or move the picture. To deselect the picture, click on anywhere else in the work area.

You can also insert the picture without using the content placeholder. In place of using steps 1, 2 and 3, click on Insert tab and on Picture. The Insert Picture dialog box will appear. Now use the above-mentioned steps from step 4.

ADDING BACKGROUND

You can change a different background style of a slide by adding colour, gradient, texture or image to it. To change the background, the steps are:

Solid Background Colour

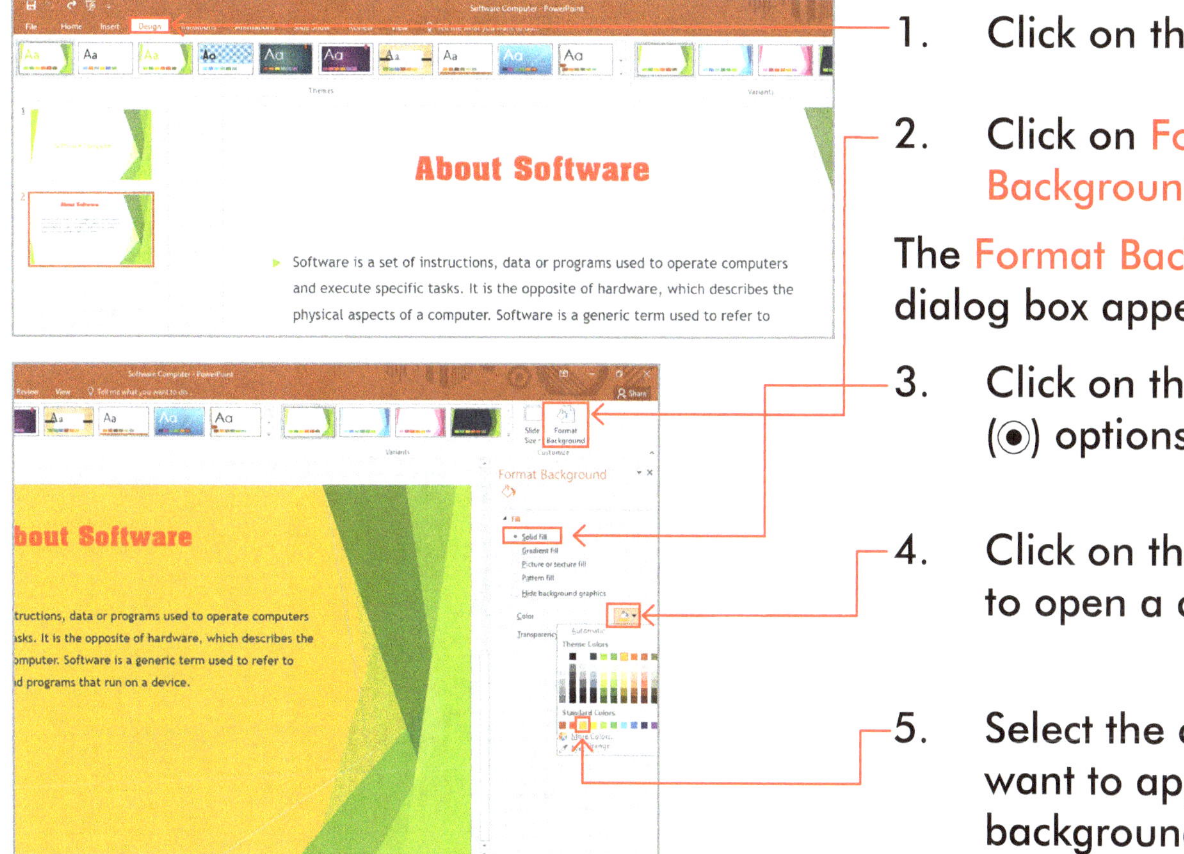

1. Click on the Design tab.

2. Click on Format Background.

The Format Background dialog box appears.

3. Click on the radio button (◉) options of Solid fill.

4. Click on the Color button to open a colour palette.

5. Select the colour you want to apply as a background.

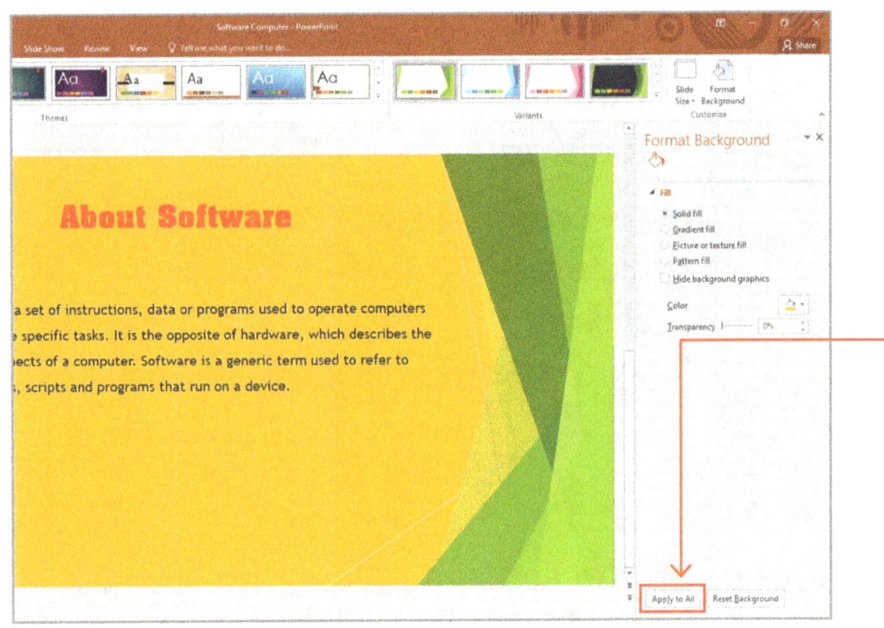

The colour selected by you applies in the current slide.

You can click on Apply to All button to apply solid color on all the slides.

Gradient Color

1. Repeat steps 1 to 3 from the previous section to bring Format Background dialog box.

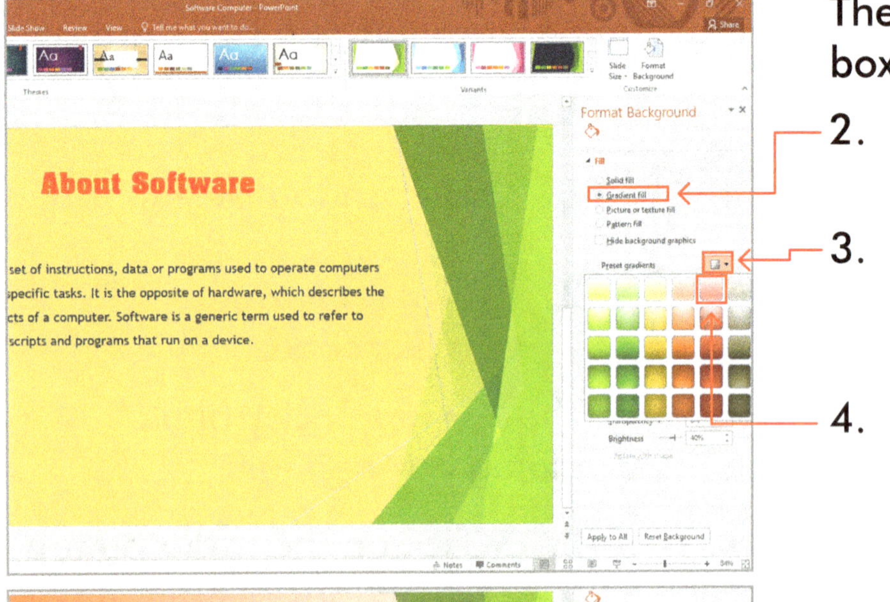

The Format Background dialog box appears.

2. Click on the radio button options of Gradient fill.

3. Click on the Preset gradients button to open gradient pattern.

4. Select the pattern you want to apply as a background.

5. Click on the down arrow button of Type.

6. Select the type of gradient pattern.

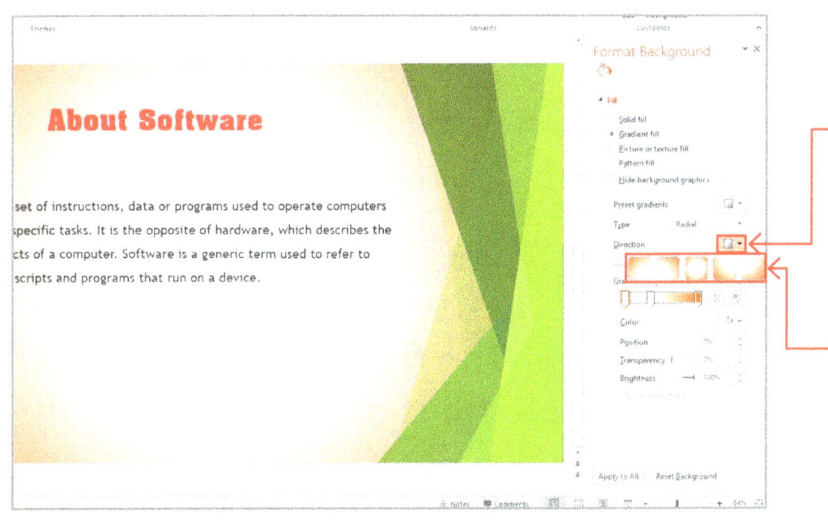

7. Click on the down arrow button of Direction.

8. Select any direction of gradient fill.

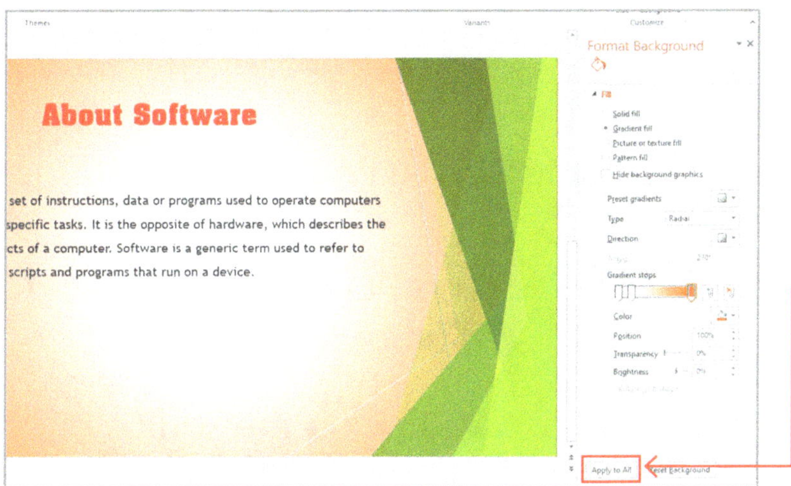

The gradient fill selected by you applies in the current slide.

You can click on Apply to All button to apply gradient fill on all the slides.

Textured Fill Color

1. Repeat steps 1 to 3 from the previous section to bring Format Background dialog box.

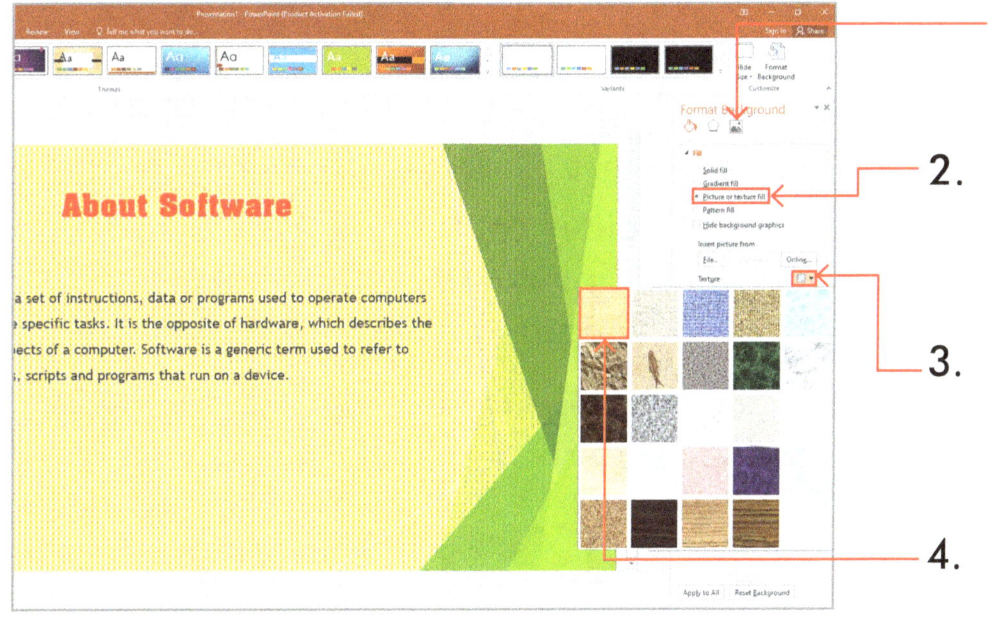

The Format Background dialog box appears.

2. Click on the radio button options of Picture or texture fill.

3. Click on the Texture button to open a list of textures.

4. Select the texture you want to apply.

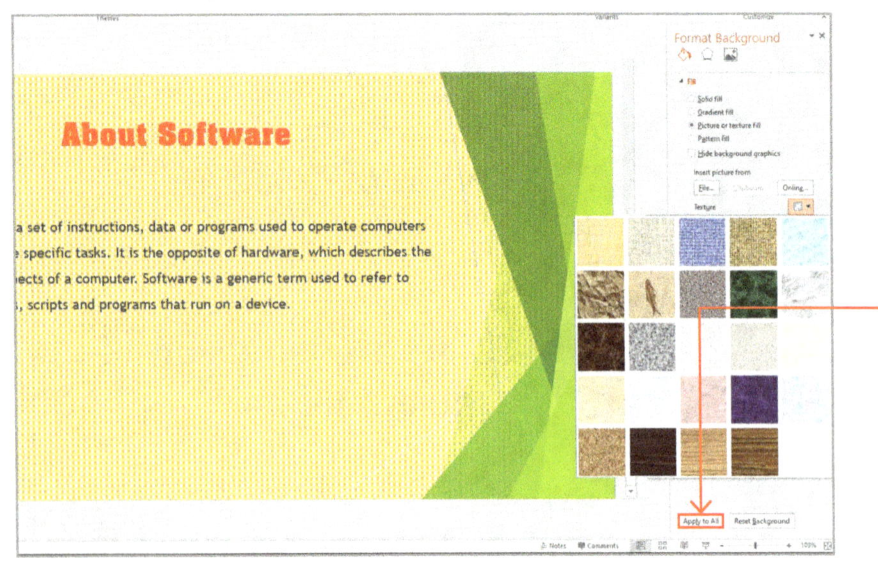

The textured fill selected by you is applied in the current slide.

You can click on Apply to All button to apply texture fill on all the slides.

Custom Image Fill

1. Repeat steps 1 to 3 from the previous section to bring Format Background dialog box.

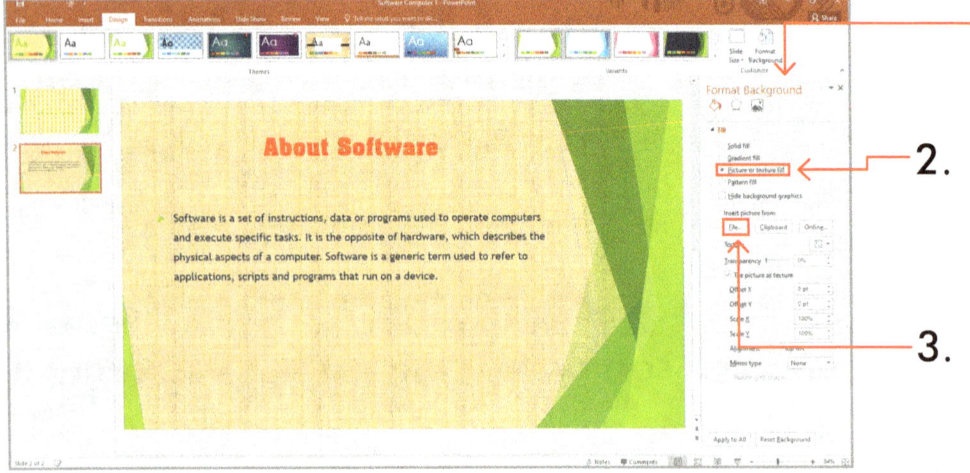

The Format Background dialog box appears.

2. Click on the radio button options of Picture or texture fill.

3. Click on File button to open Insert Picture dialog box.

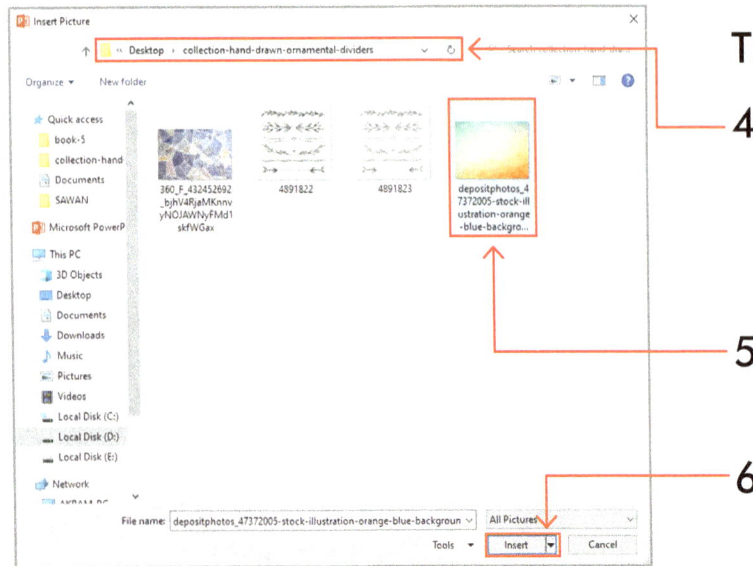

The Insert Picture dialog box appears.

4. Click on this area and locate the folder containing the file you want to use as the background image.

5. Click on the image file you want to use.

6. Click on Insert.

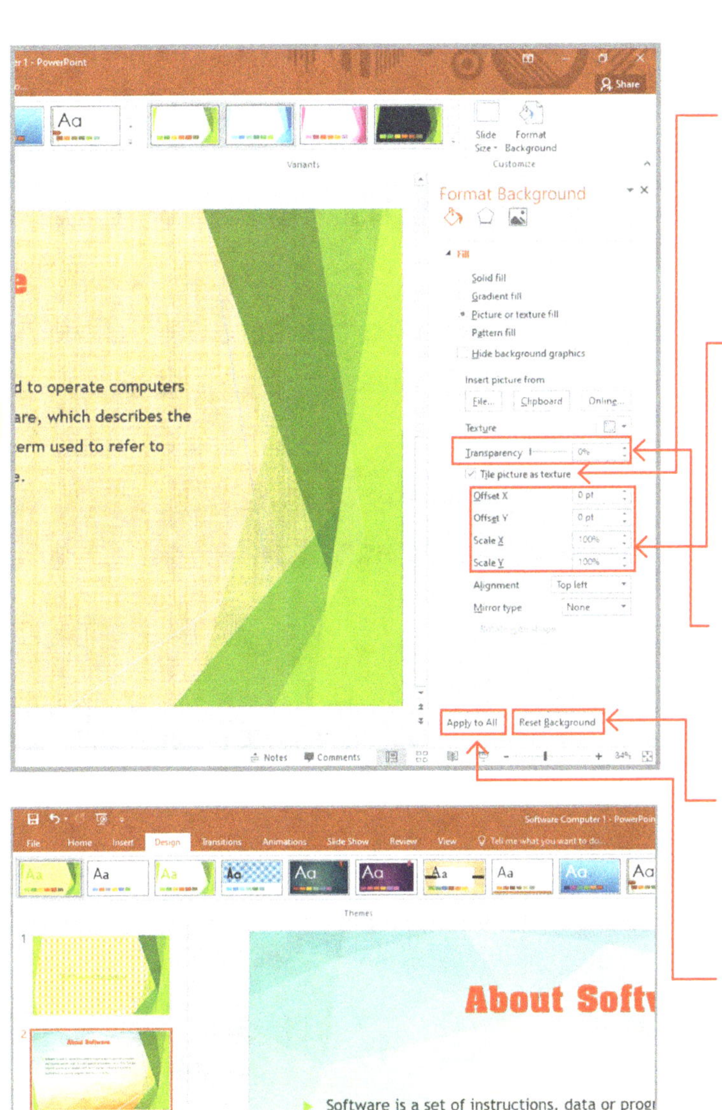

PowerPoint applies the background image to the current slide.

If the image is small, you can click the check box of the Tile picture as texture to repeat the image so that it may cover the entire slide background.

If the image does not properly cover the entire background, increase the values in the Left, Right, Top, and Bottom spin boxes as necessary to stretch the image to the full background size.

If the image is dark or blurry, you can make the slide text easier to read by increasing the Transparency value.

7. Click on Reset Background button to apply Custom Image on the current slide.

You can click on Apply to All button to apply Custom Image on all the slides.

After all the setting is done, the custom image is applied to the current slide.

CHANGING POWERPOINT VIEWS

PowerPoint provides us with different presentation views such as Normal View, Outline View, Notes Page, Slide Sorter, Reading View and Slide Show View. By default, PowerPoint displays our presentation in Normal view.

Normal View : It allows you to work with the three basic components of PowerPoint: the Slides, Outline and the Notes Pane box.

Outline View : It shows the main points of the text without any picture or table. It also shows the appearance of the slide.

Slide Sorter View : It opens up the whole workspace to display all your slides in one area. As it provides an overall view of the whole of the presentation, it is a good view to help you to organize and resequence the slides.

Notes Page : It enables you to see how your presentation will look when printed out with notes.

Reading View : It is used to view a presentation not in full screen but in a window with simple controls that make the presentation easy to review.

Slide Show View : This is the view that is used to deliver your presentation to your audience. It shows the presentation on a full screen.

Using Normal View

Normal View is the default view and displays one slide at a time in the Slide Area.

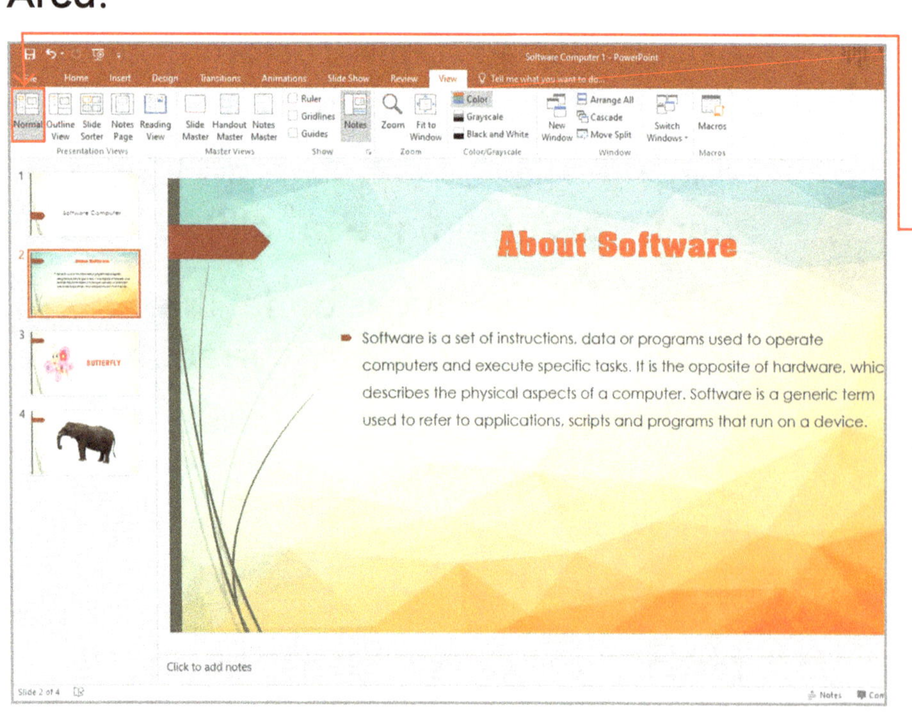

1. Click on Normal View (▣) button.

PowerPoint shows the default view, displaying the current slide in the presentation.

On the View tab you can find the different options of the views of the slides.

To Move Slides in Normal View

Click the Normal View button in the View tab.

Click a slide on the left pane, hold down the left mouse button and drag the slide to its new location.

Using Outline View

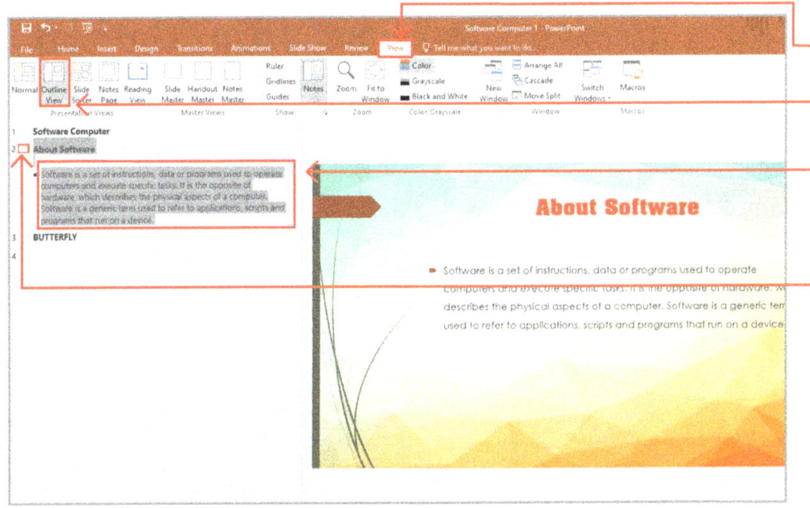

1. Click on **View** group.

2. Click on **Outline view** tab.

An outline view of your slides appears with the text.

You can click on the **small red box** to edit it. Select the slide in the outline and type the changes directly onto the main slide.

Using Slide Sorter View

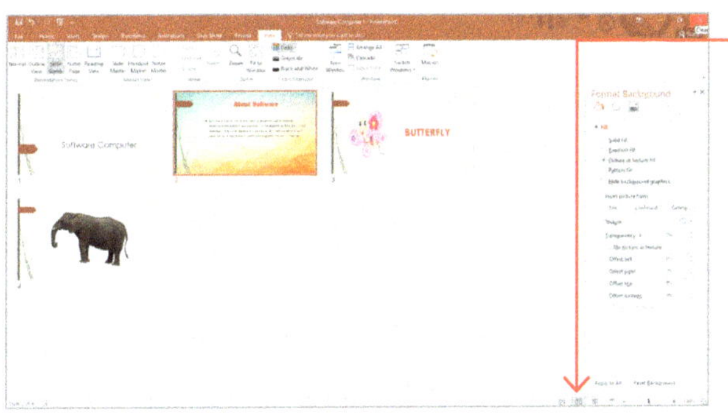

1. Click on **Slide Sorter View** (⊞) button under View Tab.

PowerPoint displays all the slides in the presentation. We can rearrange slides in the Slide Sorter view. We can easily copy, paste, add, and delete the slides in the **Slide Sorter** view.

Using Reading View

Reading view helps us review our presentation before presenting it before the audience.

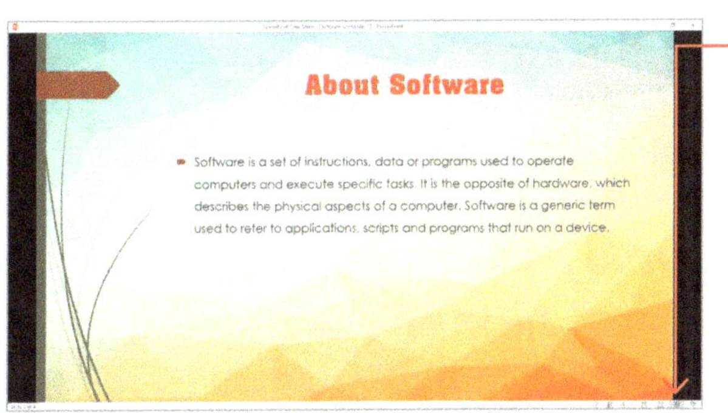

1. Click on **Reading View** (📖) button.

PowerPoint shows the slide in full screen. But with **Title bar** and **Status bar** with simple controls you can use arrow buttons to show next or previous slide in your presentation.

Using Slide Show View

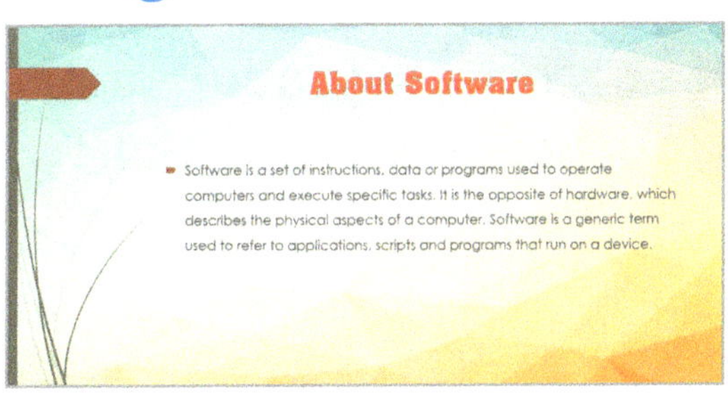

1. Click on **Slide Show** button (🖵).

PowerPoint views your presentation as a slide show. You have to click on each slide to view the next slide. Press **Esc** key to come back to **Normal** view.

ADDING SLIDE TRANSITION

A slide transition is a visual effect that appears when you move from one slide to another. Transition effects include fades, dissolves, wipe, etc. To add a transition to slides, the steps are:

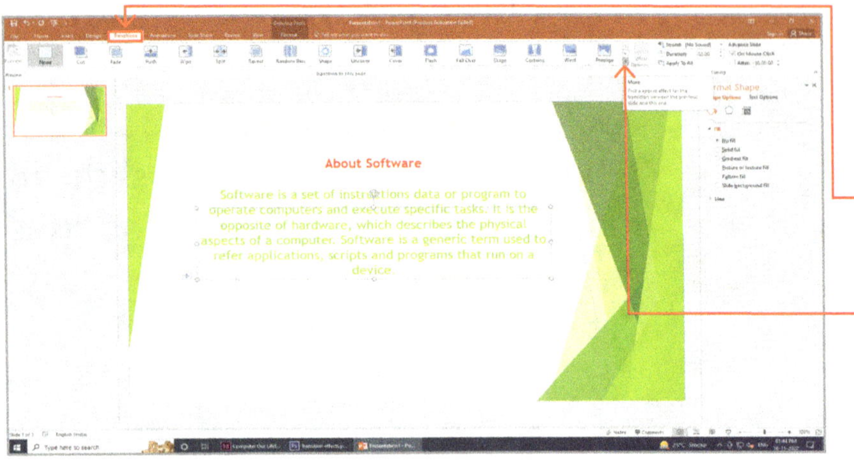

1. Bring the slide in which you want to add a transition.

2. Click on Transition tab on the Ribbon.

   Click on More to see the different types of Transition effects.

3. Click on a transition. PowerPoint immediately displays a preview of the transition effect.

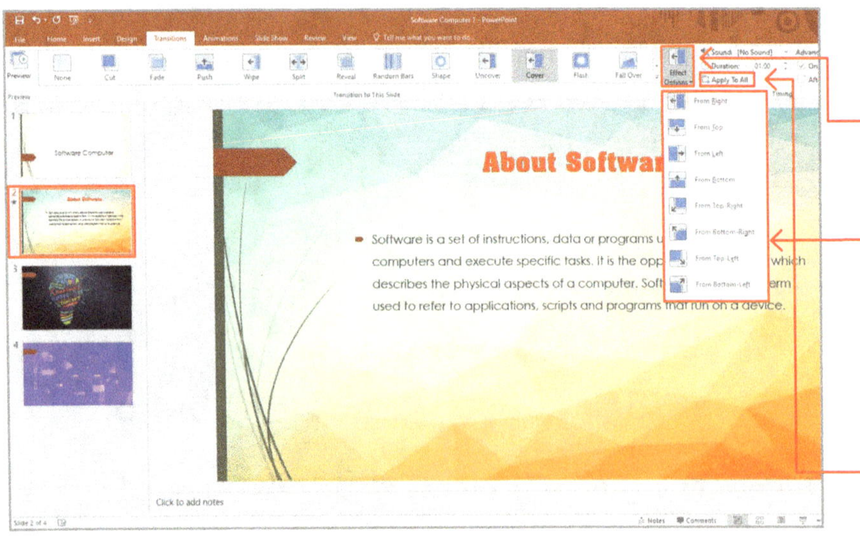

4. Click on the down arrow of Effect Options.

5. Click on the effects setting for transition.

   PowerPoint displays a preview of the transition effect.

6. You can click on Apply to All if you want to apply the same transition effect to the entire slide show.

ADDING ANIMATION EFFECTS

Animation in PowerPoint refers to the way that items, such as text box or images, move onto a slide during a slide show. Animation can certainly add variety and interest to your presentation. It adds finishing touches to a presentation. To add animation effects, the steps are:

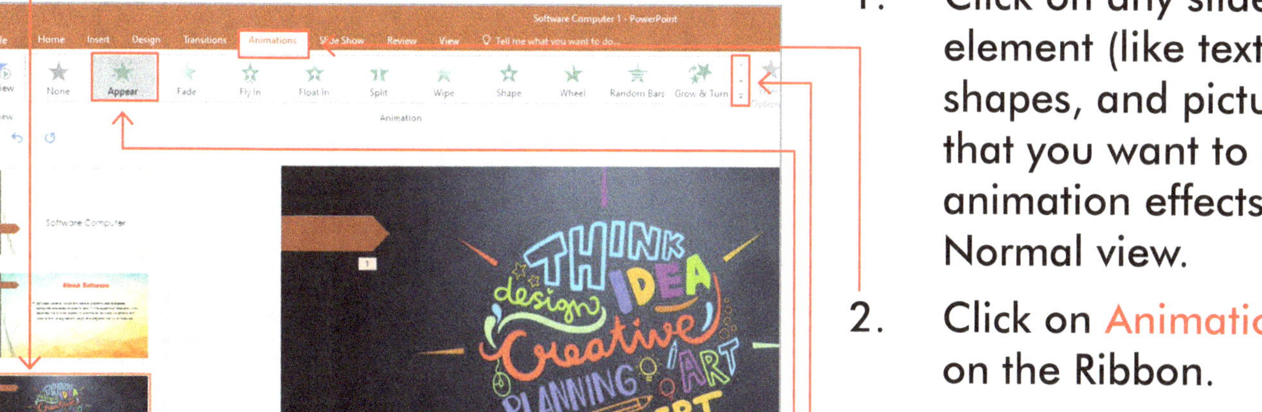
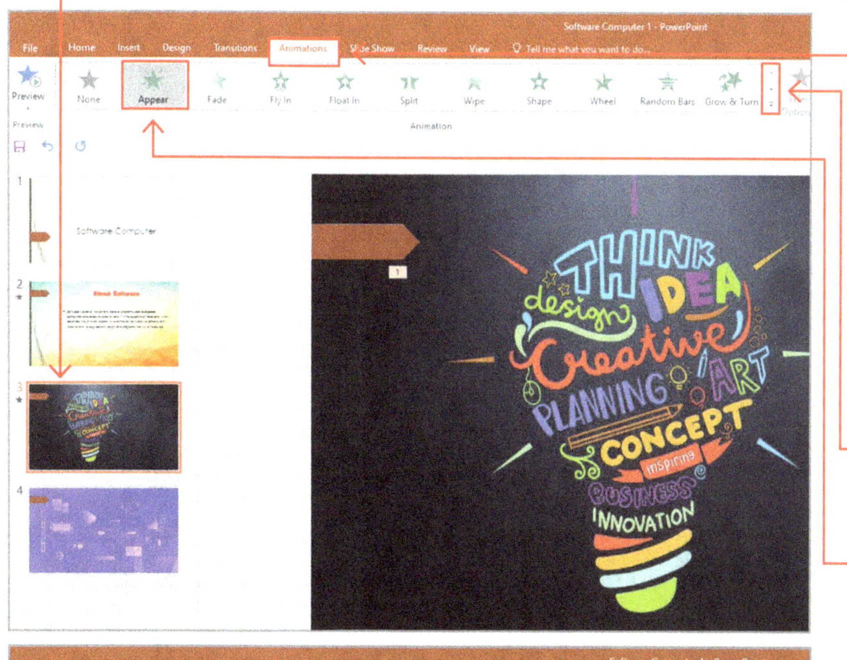

1. Click on any slide element (like text boxes, shapes, and pictures) that you want to add animation effects in Normal view.

2. Click on **Animations** tab on the Ribbon.

You can scroll through the available animation effects.

3. Click on an animation effect, i.e. Appear.

PowerPoint immediately assigns the effect and previews the effect on the slide.

You can click on **Preview** button to preview the effect again.

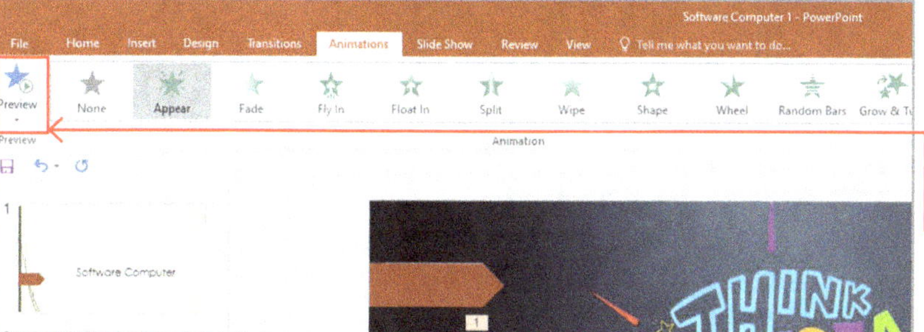

MULTIPLE ANIMATION EFFECTS

You can also set animation effects on the other elements on a slide in the PowerPoint.

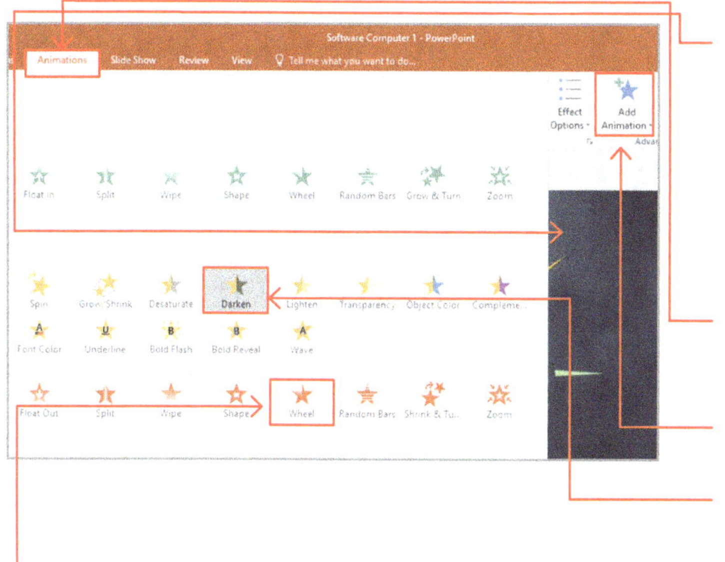

1. Click on the slide element that you want to animate.

You can assign an animation effect to any object on a slide, including text boxes, shapes and pictures.

2. Click on **Animations** tab on the Ribbon.

3. Click on **Add Animation**.

4. Take your mouse pointer over the effect to see its preview.

5. Click on the effect to apply.

The animation effects will happen in the order they are applied.

ANIMATION PANE

You can view a list of the animation effects applied to a slide by opening the Animation Pane.

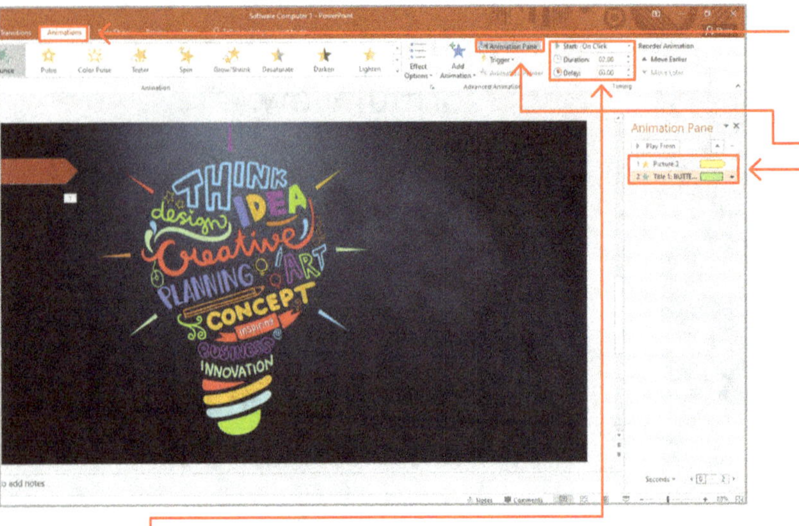

1. Click on Animations tab on the Ribbon.

2. Click on Animation Pane. Animation Pane appears on the right.

You'll see that each animation effect in the animation pane has an assigned number to the left.

Now by clicking the down arrow of the Timing tab you can change the animation timing effects.

CREATING NOTES

Notes can be created with the ideas you want to discuss with each slide in your presentation. You can use your notes as a guide while delivering your presentation.

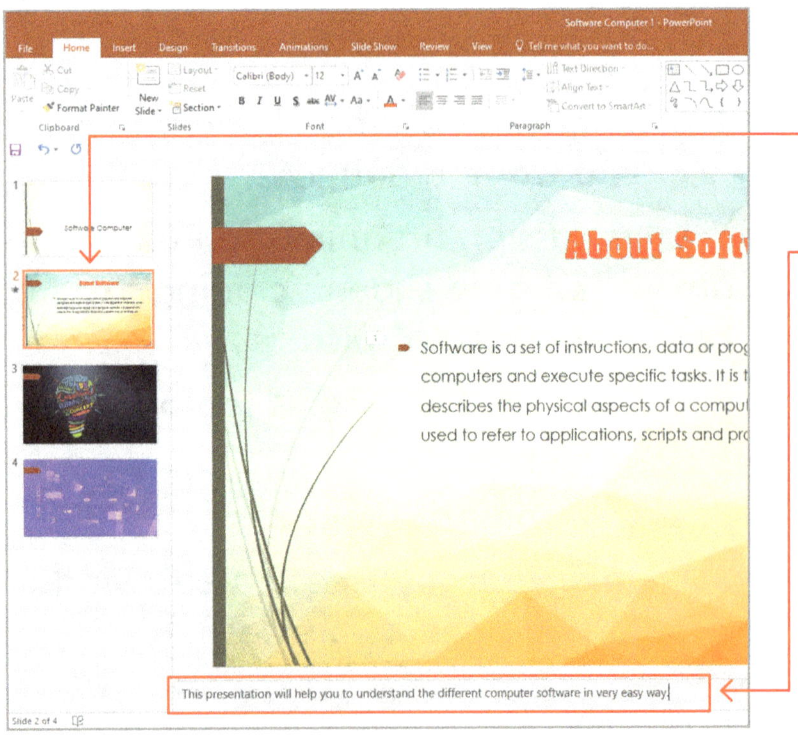

1. Display the slide you want to create notes for.

2. Click this area and then type the notes for the slide.

If you type more than one line of the text, you can use the scroll bar to browse through the text.

To Use the Notes Page

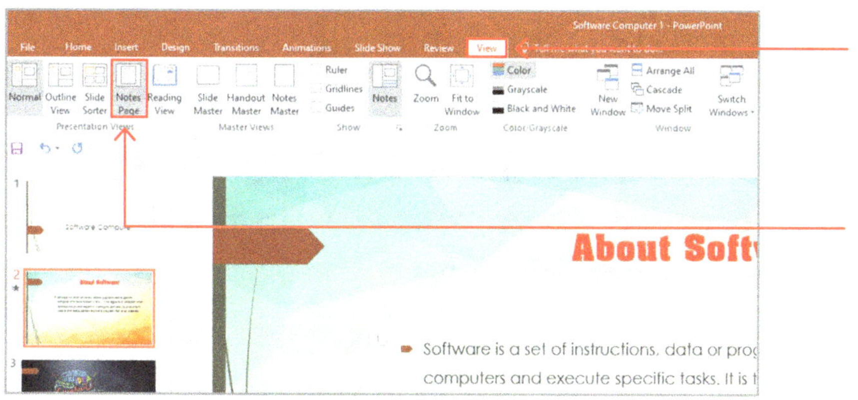

1. Click on View tab on the Ribbon.

2. Click on Notes Page to display the pages of your note.

The notes page for the current slide appears.

You can use the scroll bar to view the notes pages for other slides in the presentation.

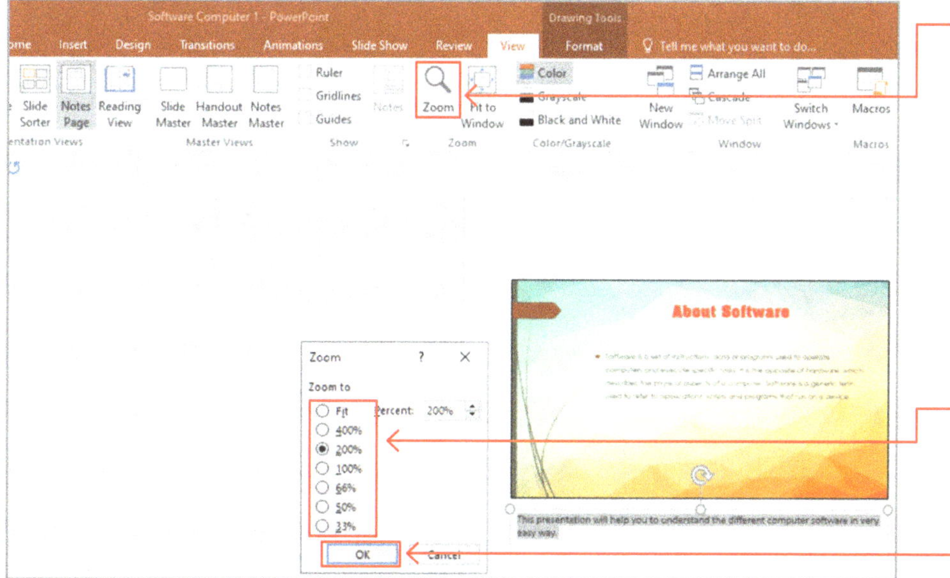

3. To magnify the notes page in order to clearly view the notes, click on Zoom.

Zoom dialog box will appear.

4. Click the magnification you want to use.

5. Click on OK.

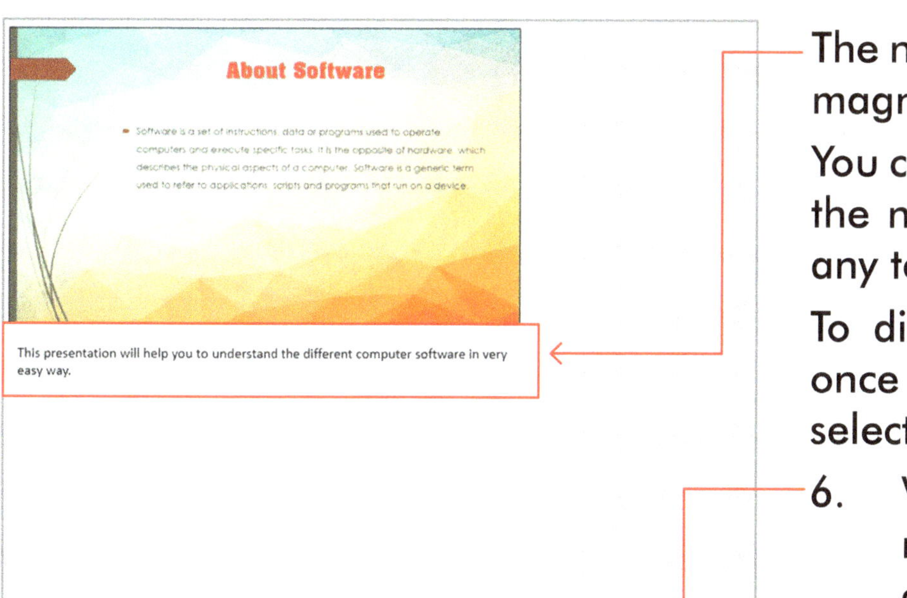

The notes page appears in the new magnification.

You can edit and format the text on the notes page as you can do on any text in your presentation.

To display the entire notes page once again, repeat steps 3 and 4, selecting Fit to Windows in step 4.

6. When you have finished reviewing your notes pages, click (▣) to return to the Normal view.

RUN A SLIDE SHOW

To show your presentation on a full screen, you can run a slide show.

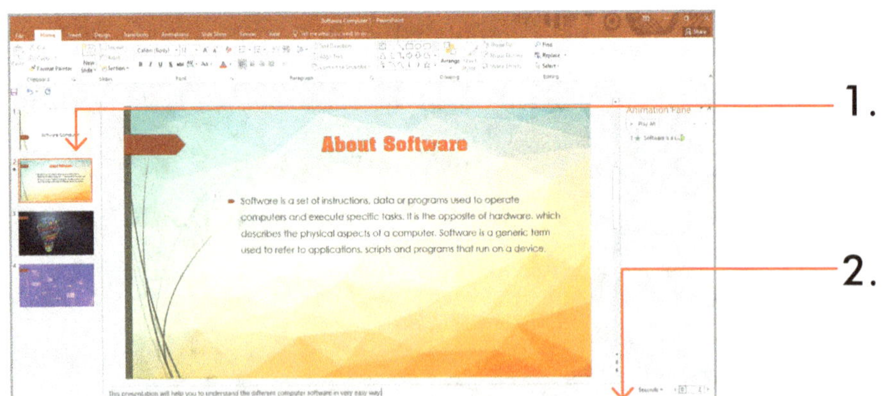

1. Click on the first slide you want to view in the Slide Show.

2. Click on Slide Show (🖳) to start the slide show.

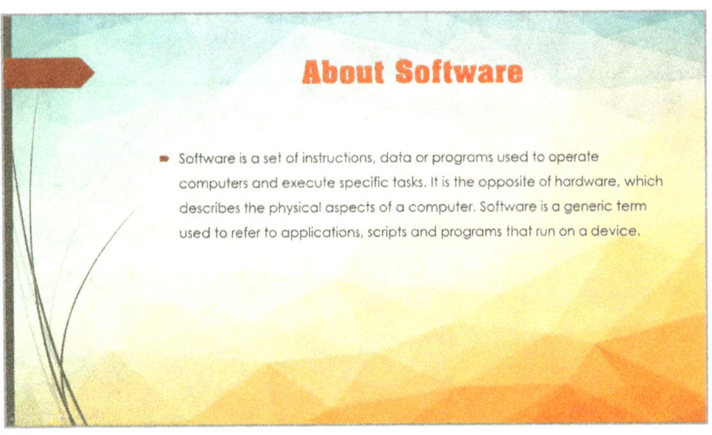

The slide you selected fills your screen.

You can press Esc key to end the slide show any time.

3. To display the next slide, click anywhere on the current slide.

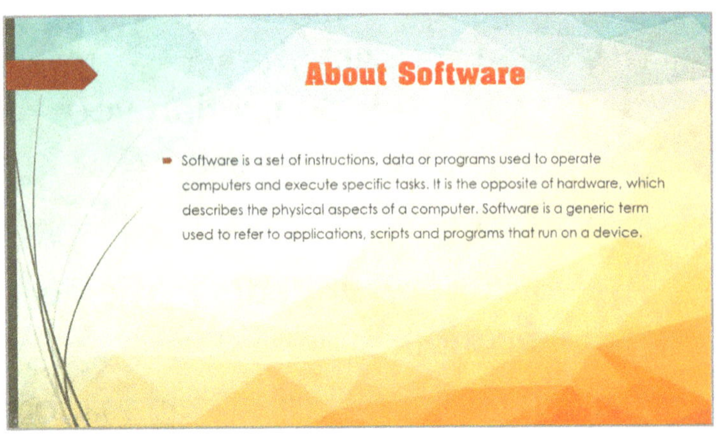

The next slide appears.

To return to the previous slide, press Backspace key.

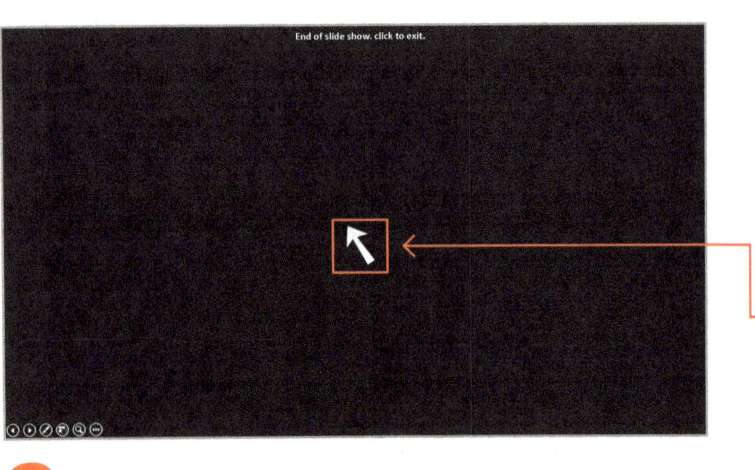

4. Repeat step 3 until this screen appears, indicating that you have reached the end of the slide show.

5. Click on the screen to exit from the slide show.

LET'S HAVE A LOOK

- Slide layout arranges all elements, like title, sub-title, text, list, pictures, tables, charts, autoshapes, sound and movie clips within a slide.
- PowerPoint 2016 has nine built-in slide layouts.
- Images and pictures can be added to the presentation by using ClipArt.
- PowerPoint provides us with different presentation views.
- A slide transition is a visual effect that appears when you move from one slide to another.
- Animation in PowerPoint refers to the way that items move into the slides during slide show.

BRAIN TEASER

1. Answer each of the following in one word or line:

a.   Define Placeholder.

b.   How many inbuilt layouts are there in PowerPoint 2016?

c.   Name the different views available in PowerPoint.

d.   Name the view in which you deliver a presentation to the audience.

e.   How can you make a slide object move on the screen?

f.   Why do we save the presentation?

2. Answer the following in brief:

a.   What is slide layout?

b.   What is ClipArt?

c.   Explain the different views provided in PowerPoint.

d.   What is slide transition?

e.   What is the use of Notes pane?

f.   What is animation in PowerPoint?

3.   **Multiple Choice Questions**
      Tick (✓) the correct answer:

a.   The container in layout that holds contents:
      i. Placeholder ☐   ii. Animation ☐   iii. Slide Layout ☐

b.   Number of built-in slide layouts provided by PowerPoint:
      i. 9 ☐   ii. 14 ☐   iii. 7 ☐

c.   The library of pictures and graphics:
      i. ClipArt ☐   ii. Transition ☐   iii. Placeholder ☐

d.   Visual effect that appears when you move from one slide to another:
      i. Transition ☐   ii. Animation ☐   iii. Layout ☐

e.   It adds finishing touches to a presentation:
      i. Transition ☐   ii. Animation ☐   iii. Layout ☐

f. The view that opens up the whole workplace to display all of your slides in one area:

    i. Outline view   ii. Normal View

    iii. Slide Sorter View

4. Write 'T' for true or 'F' for false in the boxes:

a. Slide layout is used to animate the object in a slide.

b. You can use gradient effect as a background in the slide.

c. There are fourteen in-built slide layouts in PowerPoint.

d. Ctrl+s is the shortcut to save the presentation.

e. Transition is used to run the slide in full screen.

5. Fill in the blanks:

a. The normal view contains three panes ____________ , ____________ and ____________ .

b. In ____________ view, you can see the outline view of your slides with the text.

c. There are ____________ in-built slide layouts in PowerPoint.

d. A ____________ is a visual effect that appears while moving from one slide to another.

e. ____________ shows you one slide at a time in full screen.

6. Write the steps for applying slide transition:

____

____

____

LAB ACTIVITY

• Open the PowerPoint and create a presentation on the topic 'Generations of Computers'. A presentation should contain at least 5 slides and use different layouts, background, images, etc. Give animation and transition as well to your presentation.

8 Algorithm and Flowchart

Dear children, as you know being a machine a computer needs instructions to do any particular task or solve any problem. These instructions are given in a step-by-step manner in the form of programs, which are written sequentially to get the accurate results. Here we will study about Algorithm and Flowchart that help to write a computer program easily and efficiently.

INTRODUCTION

Children, in our day-to-day life we perform many types of different tasks. In computer terminology these tasks can be considered as problems. Every problem can be solved by following a procedure. This procedure can be broken into a planned set of steps.

To understand this, let us take an example of a task that you perform every day, *i.e.* brushing your teeth in the morning.

Step 1.   Get up in the morning.

Step 2.   Go to the bathroom.

Step 3.   Pick up your toothbrush from the stand.

Step 4.   Pick up the toothpaste.

Step 5.   Open the cap of the tube.

Step 6.   Apply the toothpaste on the brush.

Step 7.   Put the cap on the tube.

Step 8.   Brush your teeth.

Step 9.   Wash your mouth with water.

Step 10. Wash your toothbrush.

Step 11. Keep your toothbrush back on the stand.

Step 12. Wipe your face.

Step 13. Come out of the bathroom.

Here you saw that to complete a task, you had to follow a number of steps. These steps have to be followed in a particular order. For example, you cannot brush your teeth first and apply paste on the brush later. The steps involved to carry out a task have to be executed in a planned systematic manner.

Similarly, to carry out a task, a computer also has to carry out a number of steps in a planned order. A computer being a machine needs instructions to carry out each step. It has to be clearly instructed to carry out each step involved in solving a problem.

A set of instructions given to the computer in a step-by-step manner to perform a specific task is called a computer program.

ALGORITHM

An Algorithm is defined as a formal set of instructions. When different sets of instructions are put together, they form a computer program.

In computing, a set of instructions is implemented by a computer to perform a specific task, such as solving a logical or mathematical problem.

It will be easier to code a program after we have well prepared an algorithm and a flowchart. For example, if you want to find the sum of two numbers, you take the first number, then the second number, and add them to get addition as their result. An algorithm is written in a simple language.

Let's write an algorithm for buying a birthday card for your friend:

Step 1.   Start

Step 2.   Go to the market.

Step 3.   Go to the stationery shop.

Step 4.   Select the birthday card for friend.

Step 5.   Pay the money.

Step 6.   Take the birthday card.

Step 7.   Come back home.

Step 8.   Stop

FLOWCHART

A flowchart is a visual representation of a problem-solving process, in which steps are laid out in logical order. It is called a flowchart since it charts the flow of a program.

The program flowchart can be likened to the blueprint (map) of a building. As we know, a designer draws a map before starting the construction of a building; similarly, a programmer prefers to draw a flowchart prior to writing a computer program.

Once the flowchart is drawn, it becomes easy to write the program in any high-level language. To make a flowchart, you need some geometrical shapes, arrows and symbols prescribed by the American National Standards Institute, Inc. Each symbol represents a specific type of activity.

Different Symbols of flowchart and their purposes are as follows:

Purpose	Name & Symbol
Start / End Terminal Box - Start / End Used to represent the Start and the End of the steps. A flowchart can have only one Start and Stop box.	Oval Start/End
Input / Output Describes data to be read into the program and gives or displays output by the program.	Parallelogram Input/Output
Process / Instruction Used to describe arithmetic or data-manipulation operations.	Rectangle Process
Decision Box Used for logic or comparison operations. The outflow path depends on the answer to the Yes/No question asked.	Diamond Decision
Flow lines Connect symbols and show the flow of the algorithm logic.	Flow Lines

| **Connector**
Connects different flow lines. | Circle

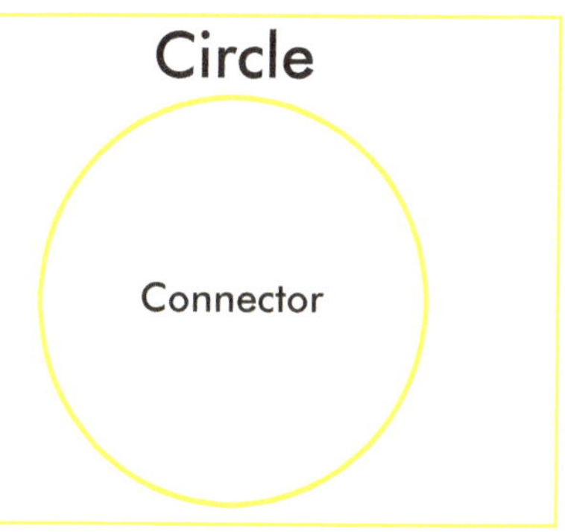 |

Advantages of Flowchart

1. Flowcharts are better way of communicating the logic of a system.

2. With the help of a flowchart, a problem can be analyzed in more effective way.

3. A flowchart acts as a guide or blueprint during the system analysis and program development phase.

4. The flowchart helps find out errors.

Disadvantages of Flowchart

1. Sometimes, the program logic is quite long. In that case, a flowchart becomes complex.

2. If alterations are required, the flowchart may need redrawing completely.

Rules for Drawing a Flowchart

1. The direction of a flowchart generally flows from top to bottom and left to right.

2. The flowchart should be clear, neat and easy to follow.

3. Arrow heads indicate the flow and sequence of information.

4. You can use connector if your flowchart is too long to adjust in one sheet.

5. Only one flow line should come out from a process symbol.

6. Ensure that the flowchart has a logical start and finish.

Note

The flowchart should be clear, tidy, and easy to understand. There should be no space for misunderstanding when it comes to interpreting the flowchart.

Write an algorithm and draw a flowchart to find the area of a square.

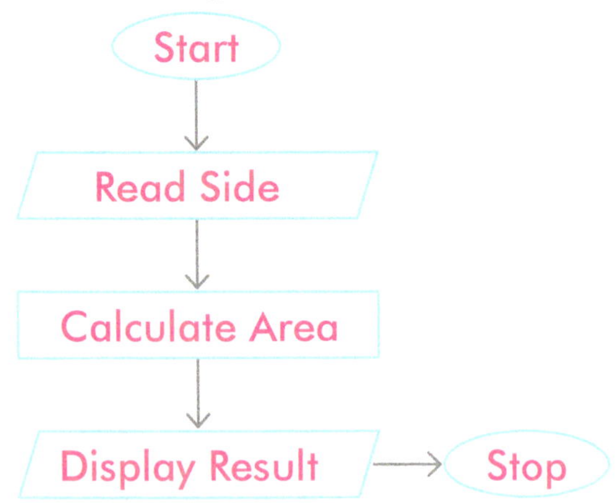

Step 1. Input Side

Step 2. Calculate Area = Side*Side

Step 3. Display Result

Converting an algorithm into a flowchart for adding two numbers.

ALGORITHM

Step 1. Start

Step 2. Take two numbers

Step 3. Add the two numbers

Step 4. Print the result

Step 5. Stop

FLOWCHART

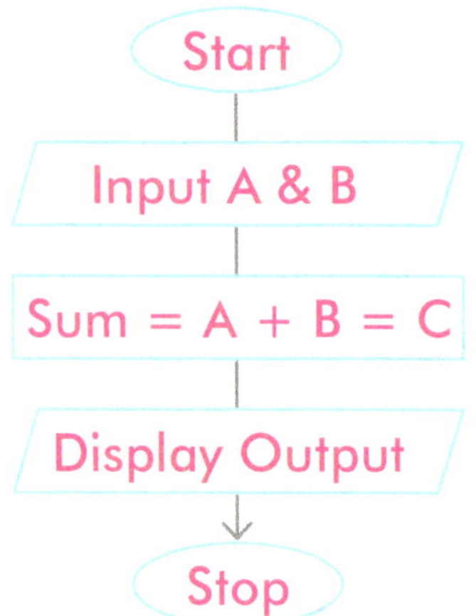

Indicates the beginning of the flowchart

Input statement giving two numbers to the computer

Processing : giving the instructions to calculate

Processing : giving the instructions to average

Output or result is displayed

Marks the end

LOOPS AND COUNTERS

Suppose you want to print your name 500 times; the flowchart will be very long. Here, you can use Counter.

A counter is used to count the number of times a process is being repeated. The counter is a variable and gets an incremented number after each repetition. This repetition is called as Looping.

When the value of the counter becomes equal to 500, it will get out of the loop.

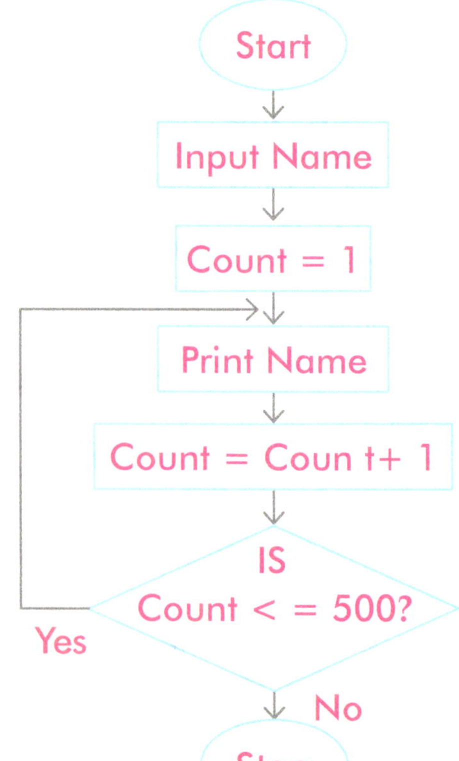

LET'S HAVE A LOOK

- A set of instructions given to the computer in a step-by-step manner to perform a specific task is called a computer program.
- An algorithm is a formal set of instructions that can be followed to perform a specific task.
- A flowchart is a visual representation of a problem-solving process.
- A flowchart acts as a guide or blueprint during the system analysis and program development phase.
- In a flowchart, each operation is represented by drawing specific geometrical shapes.

BRAIN TEASER

1. Answer each of the following in one word or line:

a. In a flowchart, name the symbol used for 'start' and 'stop'.

b. What is the shape of the circle called in a flowchart?

c. What does a rectangular box represent in a flowchart?

2. Answer the following in brief:

a. What is a computer program?

b. What is the importance of a flowchart?

c. What is an algorithm?

d.   Write two advantages and disadvantages each of a flowchart.

e.   Write any two rules of a flowchart.

f.   Name the different symbols of a flowchart.

3.   Multiple Choice Questions

Tick (✓) the correct answer:

a.   Step-by-step instructions given to the computer:
   i.   Program ☐   ii.   Algorithm ☐   iii.   Flowchart ☐

b.   A visual representation of an algorithm:
   i.   Program ☐   ii.   Algorithm ☐   iii.   Flowchart ☐

c.   The symbol used to start the flowchart is:
   i.   ⬭ ☐   ii.   ▭ ☐   iii.   ▱ ☐

d.   The symbol for processing the function of a program:
   i.   ▭ ☐   ii.   ○ ☐   iii.   ▱ ☐

e.   The connector is represented in:
   i.   Circle ☐   ii.   Rectangle ☐
   iii.   Parallelogram ☐

4.   Write an algorithm and draw the flowchart to:

a.   Make a cup of tea.

b.   Polish your shoes.

c.   Add two numbers.

5. Fill in the blanks:

a. A flowchart acts as a guide or _____________ during the system analysis.

b. A flowchart is a _____________ representation of the steps involved in a problem-solving process.

c. A process box is for _____________ .

d. A _____________ symbol is used at the beginning and in the end of a flowchart.

e. _____________ shape is used to represent input as well as output.

6. Write the names and the uses of the following symbols:

Name		USE
_____________	⬭ (pink ellipse)	_____________
_____________	◯ (green circle)	_____________
_____________	▭ (blue rectangle)	_____________
_____________	⇄ (yellow arrows)	_____________

7. Arrange the following steps of an algorithm in proper order:

a. Reach the bus stop.   Step 1. _______________________

b. Pack your bag.   Step 2. _______________________

c. Board the bus.   Step 3. _______________________

d. Start   Step 4. _______________________

e. Leave your home   Step 5. _______________________

f. Stop   Step 6. _______________________

9 Internet

You can save the pictures of your birthday party in a pen drive and give it to your friends. But how can you give these pictures to your cousins who live in another city quickly? You can do this with the help of the Internet. Let us study about it in detail.

INTERNET

The Internet is network of millions of computers and computer networks all over the world. It allows us to access and share information over the network. It contains billions of websites to provide information. These web sites contain related web pages. Websites are located by using the website address or Uniform Resource Locator (URL) which is a unique address.

REQUIREMENTS TO CONNECT TO INTERNET

The things required for having an Internet connection are:

Computer System : It is an integrated system with all the different types of input, output, processing and storage devices.

Telephone and Cable Lines : These help establish a link between the different computers and the servers.

Modem: It stands for Modulator-Demodulator. Modem Transfers digital information over telephone line and vice versa.

Web Browser : It is a software program which helps the user open and display the different web pages. The different types of web browsers are Google Chrome, Safari, Mozilla, Firefox, Microsoft Edge, etc.

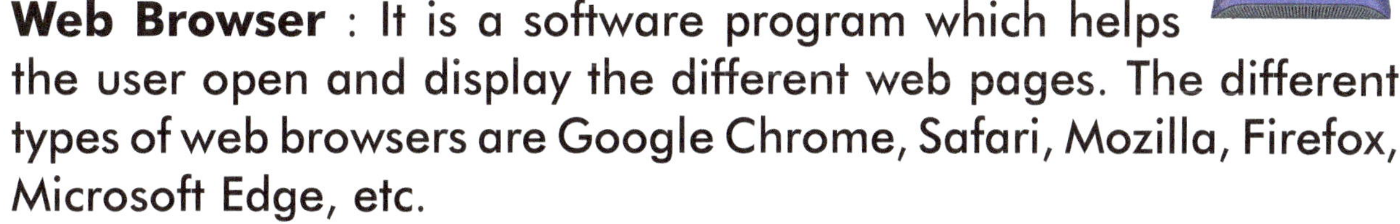

ISP : It stands for Internet Services Provider. It is a company that provides Internet access on the payment of a monthly fee. Some of the ISPs are Airtel, Vi, AT&T Internet, Xfinity, Jio, etc.

 TYPES OF INTERNET CONNECTION

To connect your computer with the Internet, you need an Internet connection. There are numerous ways to connect your computer to the Internet. Some of most widely used ways are:

Dial-up Connection

Dial-up requires users to link their phone lines to the computer in order to access the Internet. It doesn't allow users to make or receive phone calls through phone service while using the Internet.

Broadband Connection

Broadband is provided through either cable or telephone companies. It is a high-speed Internet connection. You can share a large amount of data. It is significantly faster than dial-up connection. A broadband connection provides Internet access only through cable.

Wi-Fi

Wi-Fi stands for Wireless Fidelity. It uses radio frequency to connect to the Internet. Wireless connections are possible through the modem, which picks up Internet signals and sends them to the computer. Wi-Fi doesn't require cable to provide Internet access. The main advantage of wireless is the "always on" connection that can be accessed from any location under network coverage.

Mobile Internet

It allows users to access the Internet over a smartphone provided offer voice plans with Internet access. This connection provides a good speed for the Internet. The main advantage of Mobile Internet is access the Internet anywhere within the range of a Mobile network signal.

Hotspots

Hotspots are sites that offer Internet access. They utilise Wi-Fi technology, which allows computers to connect to the Internet. They are mainly used on smartphones.

USING WEB BROWSER

As you know, Web browser is an application software which is used for finding information from different websites.

You need to connect to the Internet before opening a web browser. Once you have established a connection, open your browser following the steps given below:

1. Click on Start button on the Windows taskbar.

2. Open the list of programs. When the list of Programs opens, find the name of your browser and click it. A web browser window opens.

USING URLs

You have learnt in the previous class that every web page has a unique address called a Uniform Resource Locator, or URL. URLs are the key to navigating the web. When you provide a URL to the browser finds that URL's Web page and then transfers the Web page to your PC. The content of the web page appears in the Web Browser window.

To open a web page, follow these steps:

1. Type the URL in the browser Address bar.

2. Press the Enter key from the keyboard.

Suppose you want to visit the website of Wikipedia. To do this, you can type www.wikipedia.org in the Address bar and then press the Enter key. The home page of Wikipedia appears in the browser window.

A hyperlink is simply a part of the web page that is linked to a URL. A hyperlink can appear as text, an image, or a navigational tool such as a button or an arrow. You can click a hyperlink and jump from your present location to the URL specified by the hyperlink.

LET'S HAVE A LOOK

- The Internet is a network of millions of computers and computer networks all over the world.

- Dial-up connection is where you access the Internet using phone lines.

- Broadband is faster than the dial-up connection as it provides high-speed Internet through various transmission mediums.

- Wireless provides great speed as it uses radio frequency to connect to the Internet.

- Mobile Internet allows the the user to access the Internet using a smartphone and network provided by the service provider.

- Hotspots are the Internet access point that lies in a limited distance which is around 20 metres.

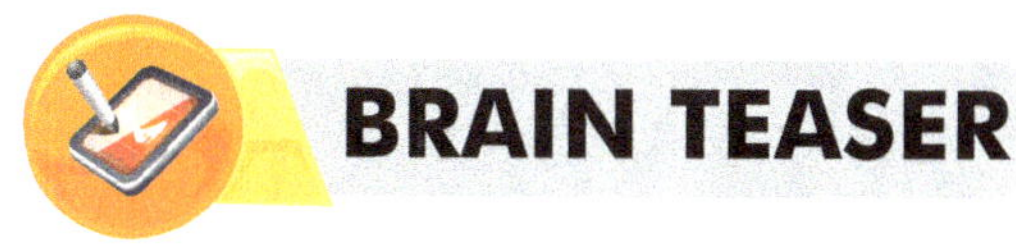

BRAIN TEASER

1.   Answer the following.

a.   What is Dial-up Connection?

b.   How wireless is different from mobile Internet?

c.   Write steps to open a web page using URL.

2.   Multiple Choice Questions

Tick (✓) the correct answer:

a.   Websites are located by using the _____________ .

i.   Web page ☐   ii.   Modem ☐   iii.   URL ☐

b.   Which of the following is an examples of ISP?

i.   Chrome ☐   ii.   Xfinity ☐   iii.   Modem ☐

3.   Write 'T' for True or 'F' for False in the boxes:

a.   Internet allows us to access and share information over the network.   ☐

b.   Websites are located by using the website address.   ☐

c.   Web browser is a software program which helps the user in opening software applications.   ☐

d.   Wi-Fi uses radio frequency to connect to the Internet.   ☐

e.   Hotspot are sites that offer Internet access on computers only.   ☐

4. Fill in the blanks:

a. The full form of Modem is ________________ .

b. Every web page has a unique address called ________________ .

c. The full form of URL is ________________________________ .

d. Web browser is an ________________ which is used for finding information from different websites.

e. The main advantage of Wi-Fi is ________________ connection that can be accessed from any location under network coverage.

f. The internet is network of ________________ and ________________ all over the world.

g. ________________________ is where you access the Internet using phone lines.

h. Hotspots are mainly used on ________________________ .

i. You need to connect to the ________________ before opening a web browser.

j. ________________________ is provided through either cable or telephone companies.

 **LAB ACTIVITY**

What kind of Internet connection you use in your school? Find out. And also write the name of the Internet Service Provider (ISP).

Formative Assessment-4
(Chapters 7-9)

1. Make a PowerPoint presentation on 'Child Labour'.

Now insert Images, Transitions and Animation to give an attractive look to your slides. Save the presentation by your name.

2. Name the purpose of the following shapes of the flowchart:

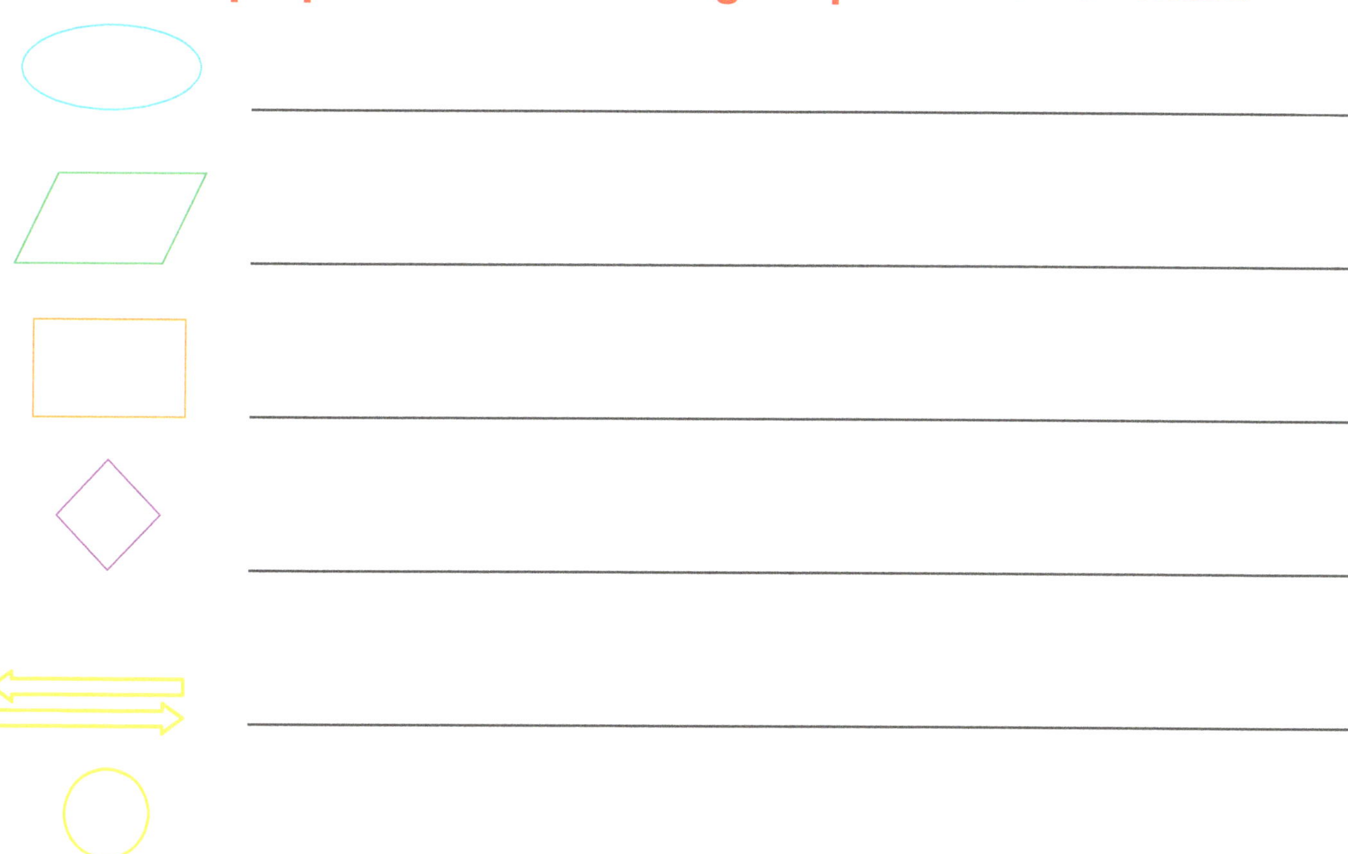

3. Write the names of the following Web Browsers:

Summative Assessment-2
(Chapters 5-9)

1. Fill in the blanks:

a. The _____________ feature is used to repeat the last action that is made while typing the text document.

b. _____________ can help you to increase your vocabulary skills.

c. MS-Word provides you with a _____________ feature to find out a particular text in your document.

d. In _____________ case, the first character of the word will be in lowercase and the rest in uppercase.

e. The _____________ are the symbols such as dots, diamonds, etc.

f. A single page of a PowerPoint presentation is called a _____________.

g. You can display the text notes for any hints or references for your presentation in the _____________ Pane.

h. MS-PowerPoint 2016 includes _____________ inbuilt slide layouts, also called _____________ layouts.

i. _____________ shows you one slide at a time in full screen.

j. A _____________ symbol is used at the beginning and in the end of a flowchart.

k. The full form of URL is _____________.

2. Tick (✓) the correct answer:

a. Shortcut key to open Thesaurus:

   i. Alt+F7 ☐   ii. Shift+F7 ☐   iii. Ctrl+F7 ☐

b. The feature in which the first letter is made larger:

   i. Indentation ☐   ii. Right Tab ☐   iii. Drop Cap ☐

c. A presentation software from Microsoft:

   i. MS-Excel ☐   ii. MS-PowerPoint ☐   iii. MS-Word ☐

d. The container in layout that holds contents:

   i. Placeholder ☐   ii. Animation ☐   iii. Slide Layout ☐

e. The bar located at the top of the window:
   i. Status bar ☐   ii. Task bar ☐   iii. Title bar ☐

f. The connector is represented in
   i. Circle ☐   ii. Parallelogram ☐   iii. Rectangle ☐

g. A Web browser designed for Google:
   i. Safari ☐   ii. Opera ☐   iii. Chrome ☐

3. Write 'T' for true or 'F' for false in the boxes:

a. MS-Word is used to create a document. ☐

b. The PowerPoint is developed by Adobe. ☐

c. The spelling error is indicated in green colour. ☐

d. The short cut key of Undo is Ctrl+z. ☐

e. Slide Show view displays the thumbnails of your slides. ☐

f. A flowchart is a visual representation of a problem-solving process. ☐

g. Links are also known as Hyperlinks. ☐

h. Google Chrome is a Web browser. ☐

4. Answer the following questions:

a. What is Thesaurus?

b. What are the different change cases provided by MS-Word?

c. Explain the different views provided in PowerPoint.

d. What is slide transition?

e. Differentiate between an algorithm and a flowchart.

f. Write five rules of making a flowchart.

g. What is URL?

h. What is instant search box?

i. Write a short note on the Internet Explorer.

j. Define a Web browser.

10 Code to Gaming in Scratch

Gaming is one of the most popular computer activities. New technologies are making it possible to develop better and powerful games that can be run on any computer.

We have already learnt the basics of Scratch. Do you remember coding you did to create an animation? Do you want to create a game in Scratch? Let us learn to create a game in Scratch.

 INTRODUCTION

Scratch is a visual programming language that helps us to make our own interactive stories, animations, games, music and more. This can be done using drag and drop block and an active object called "sprites".

> **Note**
>
> *In this chapter, we will use Scratch 3.12. You can download Scratch 3.12 from the following link:* https://scratch.mit.edu/download

Getting Started with Scratch 3.12

To open Scratch 3.12, do the following:

1. Click Start button.

2. Scroll menu and select Scratch 3.

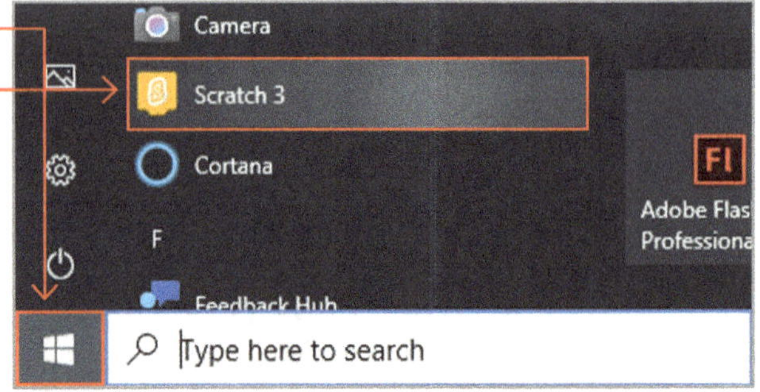

We have already learnt the basics of Scratch and now we would learn the development of games in Scratch. Scratch 3.12 makes game development easy to learn and fun to create.

Project: Let's make an underwater game in Scratch 3.12

In this game, we will have two different characters, One will be moved by the player and the second one will move randomly. When we touch the character by the other one, we score a point.

Let's start!

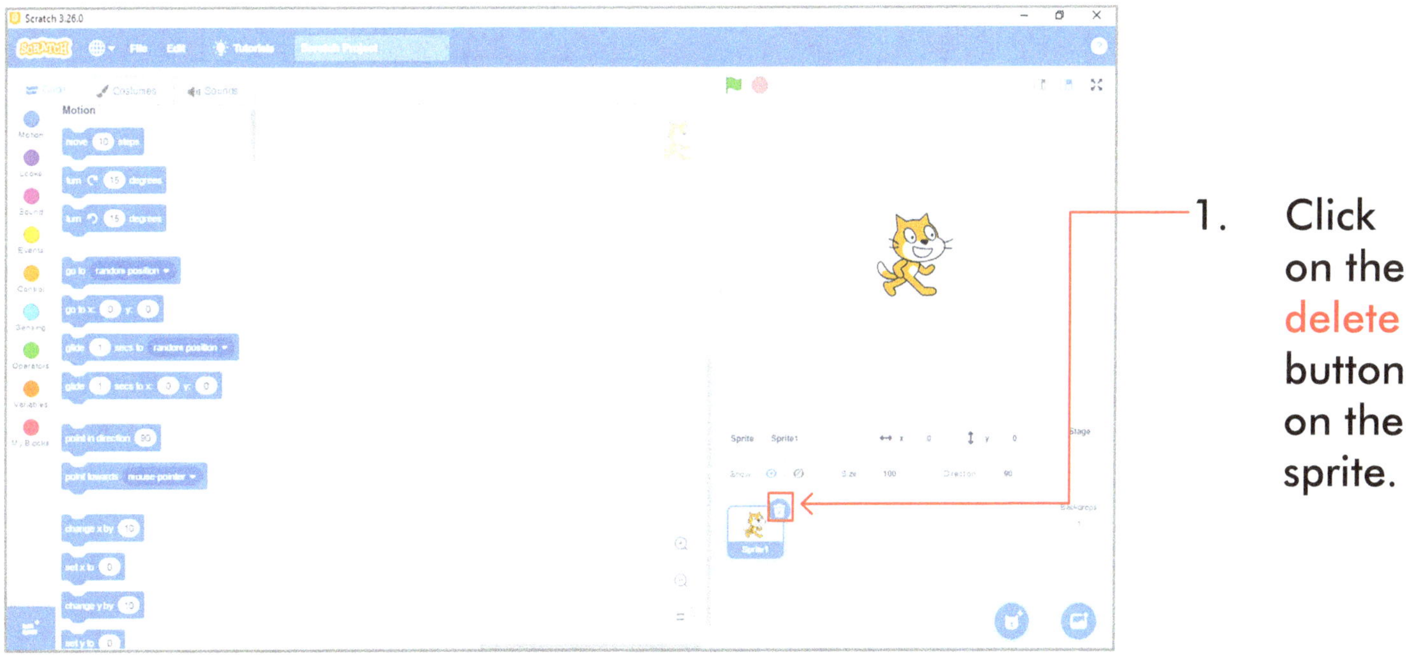

1. Click on the **delete** button on the sprite.

We need a background on the stage.

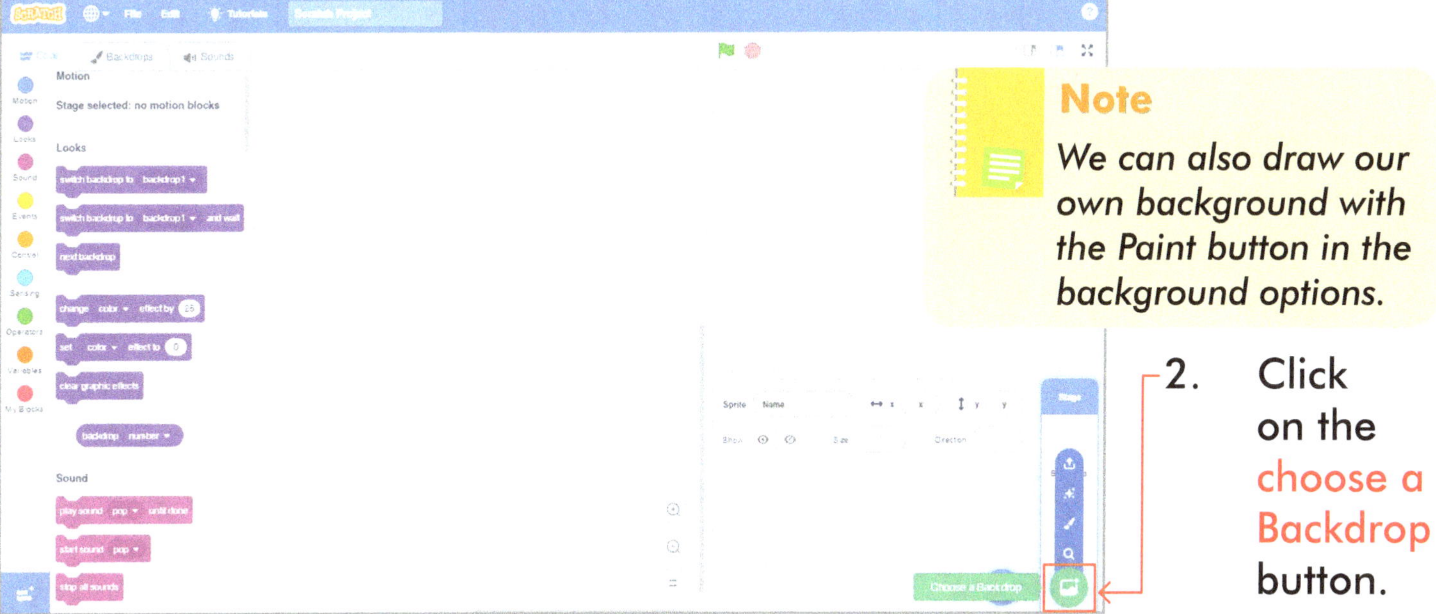

Note

We can also draw our own background with the Paint button in the background options.

2. Click on the **choose a Backdrop** button.

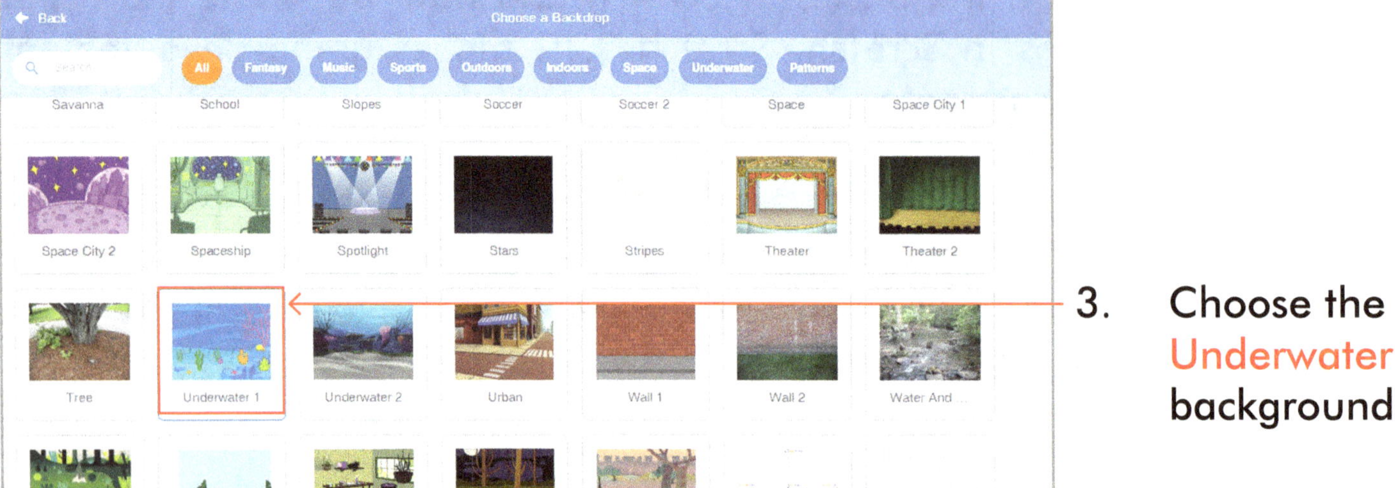

3. Choose the **Underwater 1** background.

Now, the selected background will appear on the stage. As our stage is ready, we will start adding the characters on the stage.

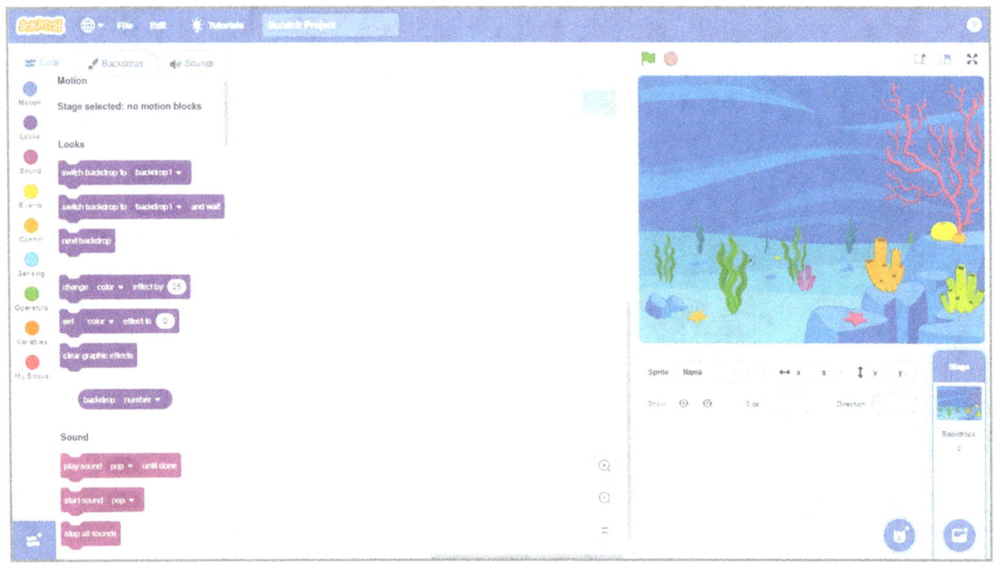

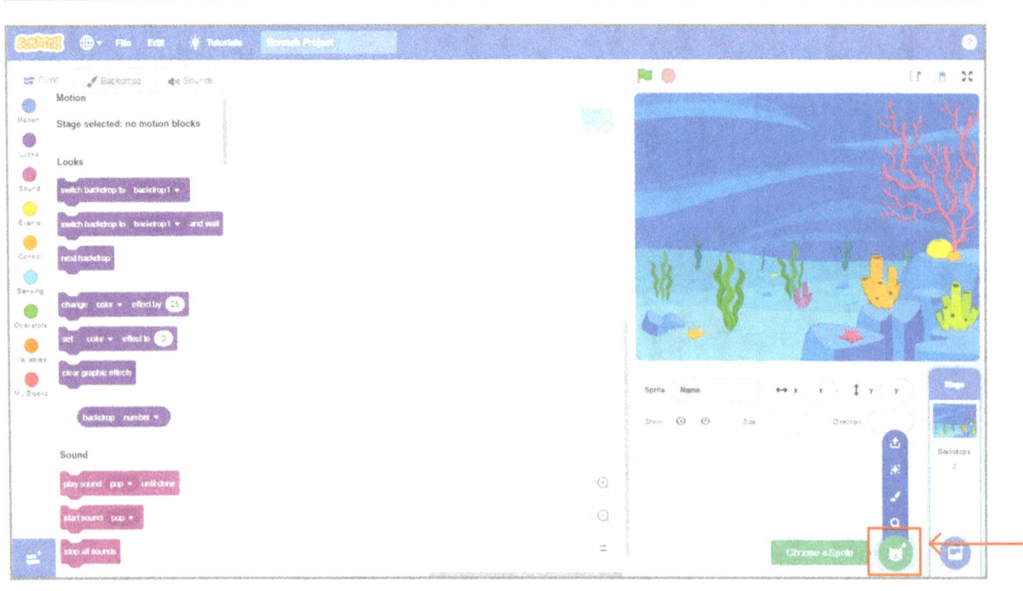

4. Click on the **choose a sprite** to choose sprite from the library.

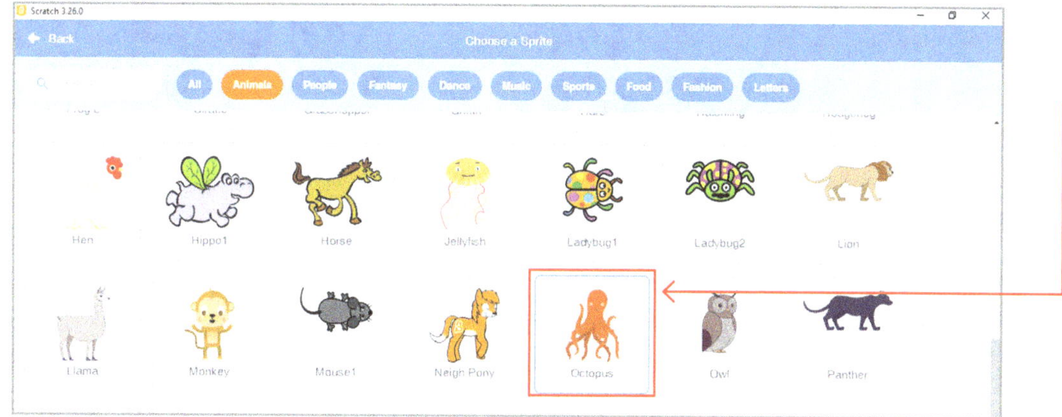

5. Click on the **Animals** section; select and click on **Octopus** as player.

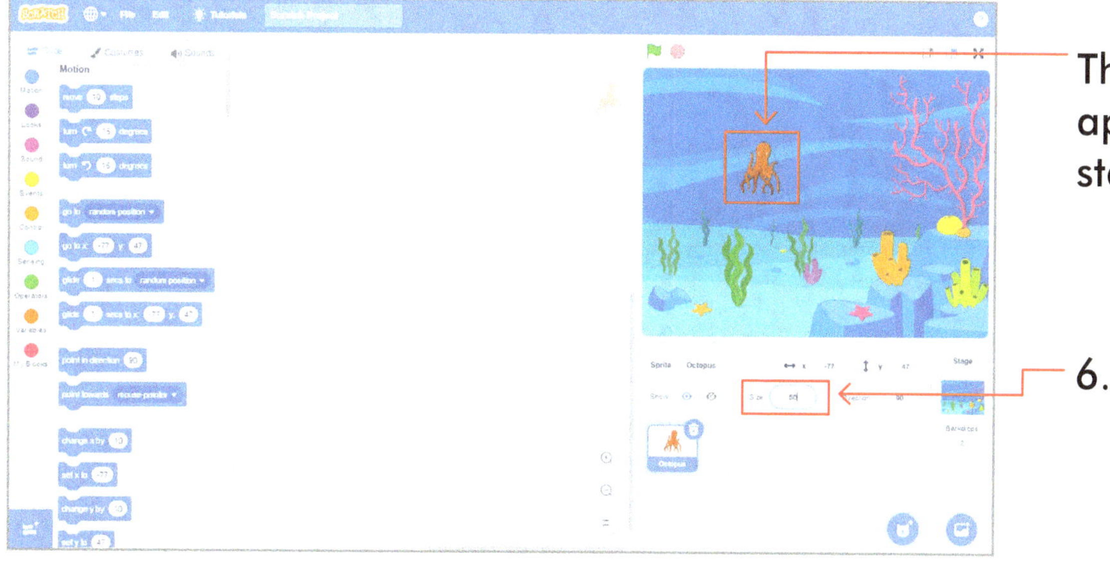

The selected sprite appears on the stage.

6. Click on the size box and change the number to **50**.

We can reduce or increase the size of the sprite. We can also change the direction or the location of the sprite on the stage.

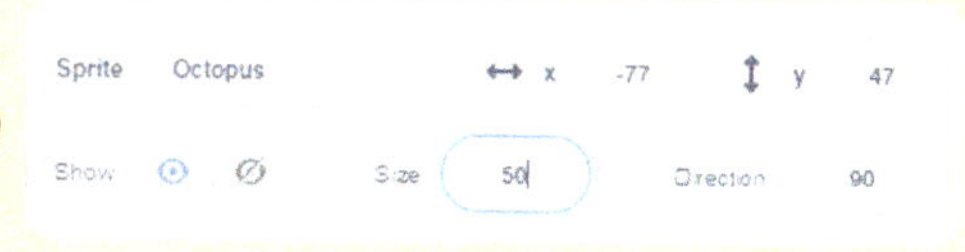

Now, we will program the sprite to move with the keys on the keyboard.

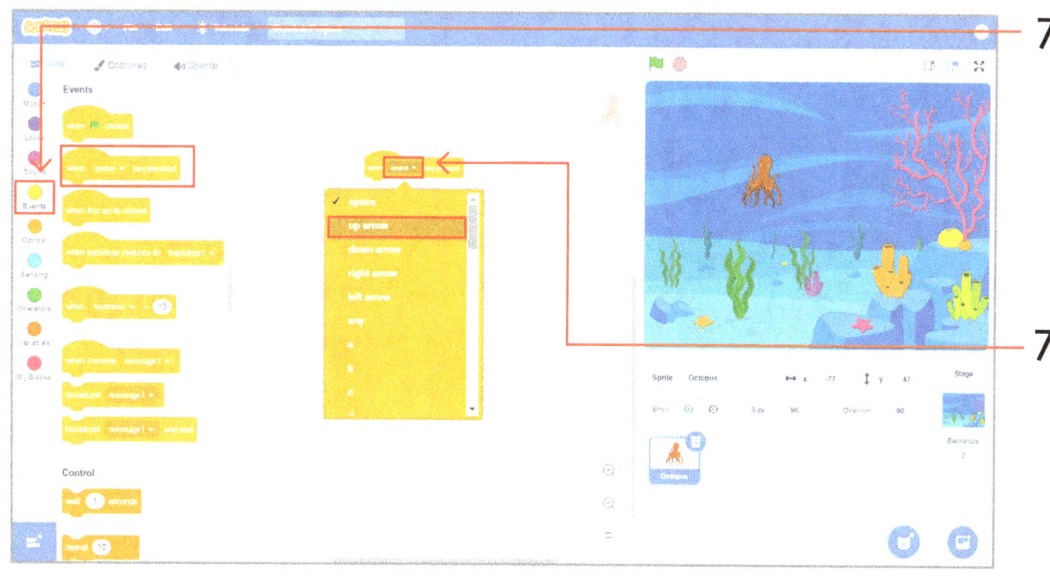

7. Click on the **Events** block category and drag **when Key pressed** block on the stage.

7a. Click on the **when Key pressed** block. Change the key to **up arrow**.

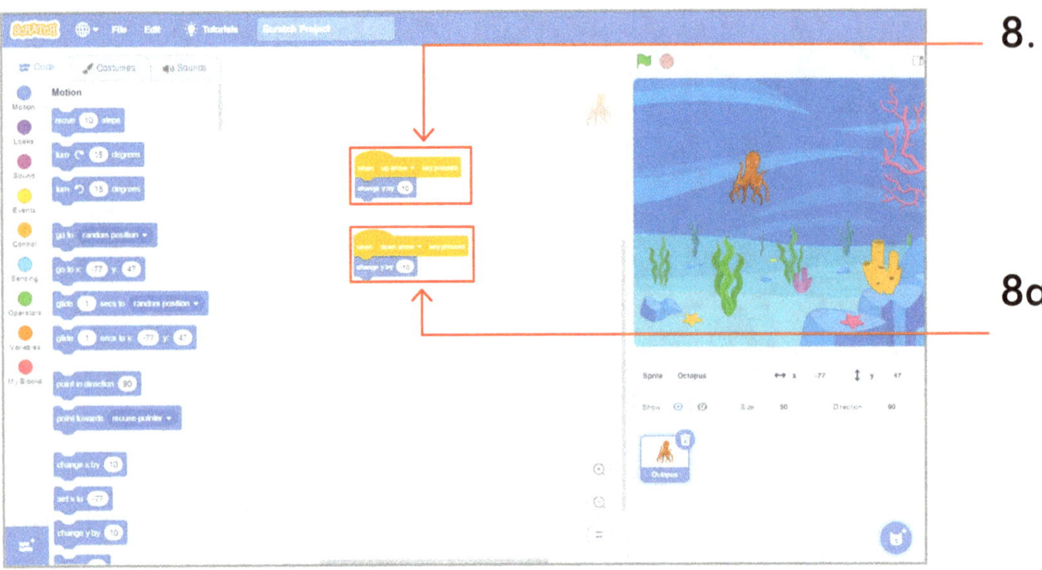

8. From the **Motion** block category, click and drag the **change y by** block.

8a. Add these two blocks, **When Key pressed** block and **change y by** block on the stage.

Change their values to **down arrow** and **-10**, as shown in the figure.

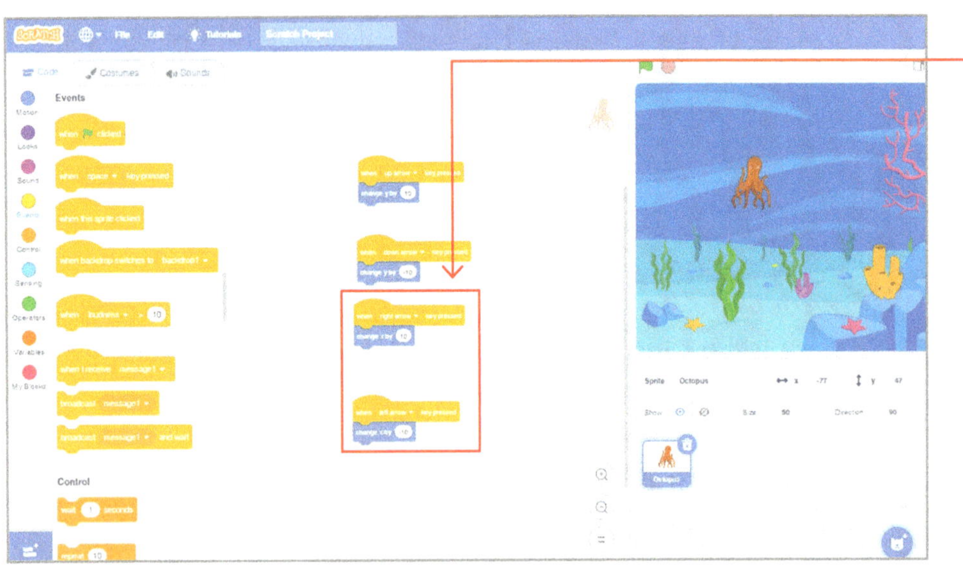

9. Add these two blocks, **When Key pressed** block and **change x by block** on the stage. Set their values as shown in the figure.

Now, check the movement of the sprite with the help of arrow keys. If you find some error, then recheck the codes.

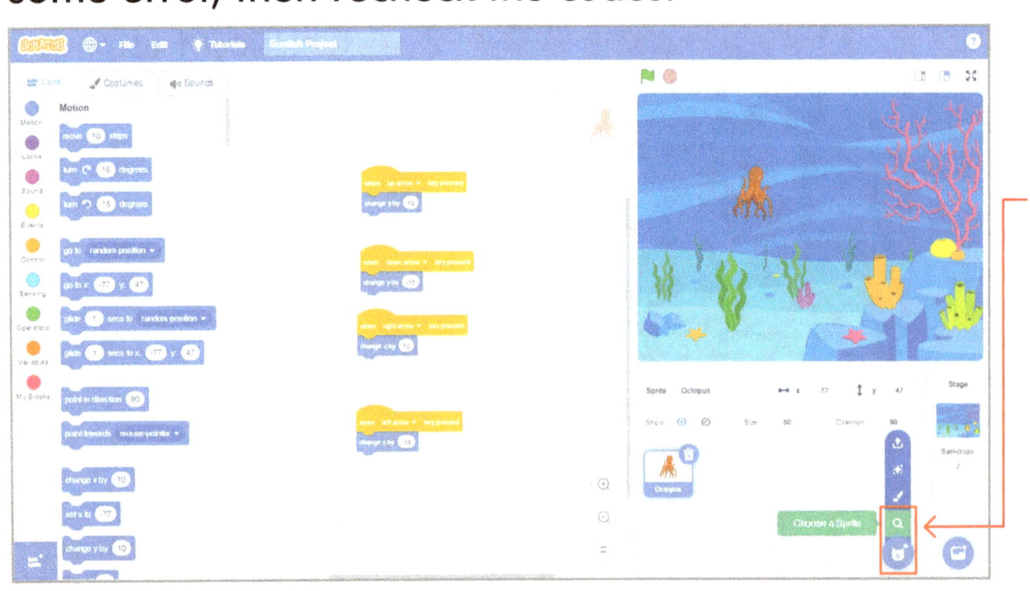

10. Add the new sprite to the stage by clicking on **Choose a new sprite**.

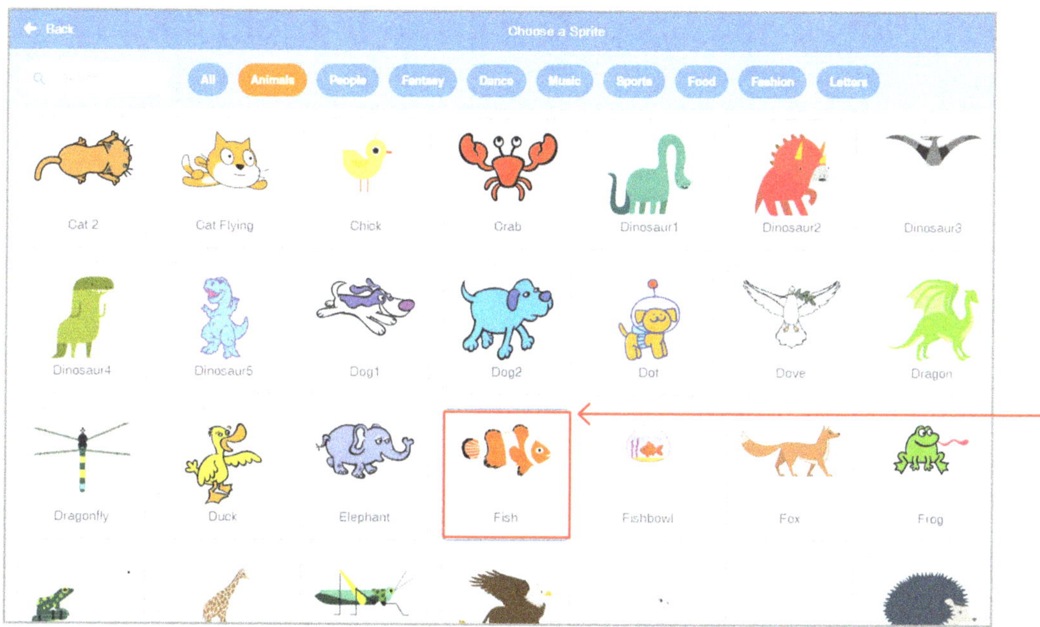

11. Click on **Fish** to add the new sprite.

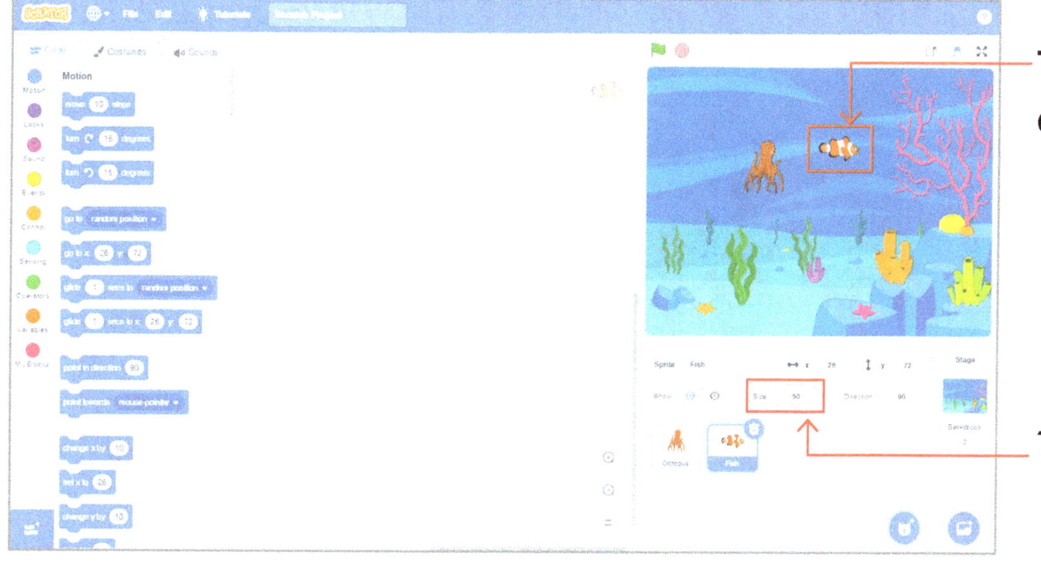

The selected sprite appears on the stage.

12. Reduce the size of sprite to **50**.

Now, we have to move the fish to the random position on the stage, for which we have to program the fish.

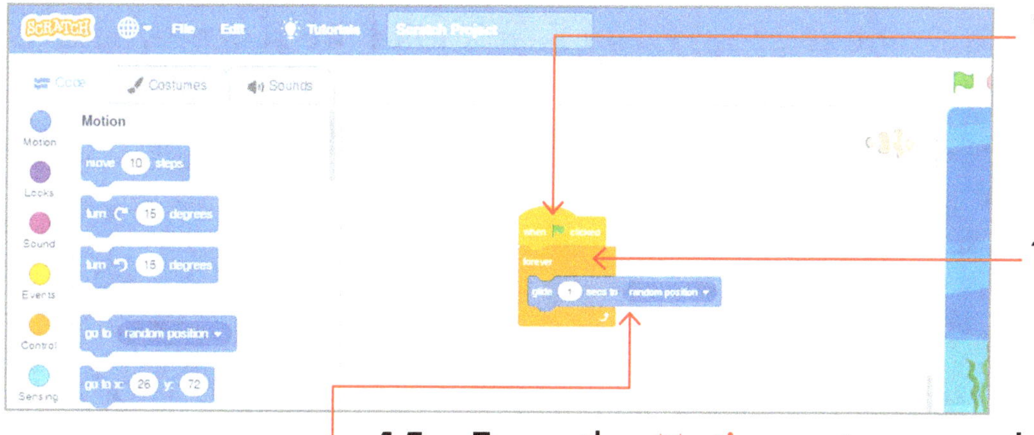

13. From the **Event category**, add the **When ⚑ Flag clicked** block.

14. From the **control** category, add **forever** block.

15. From the **Motion** category, add the **glide 1 secs to random position** block.

Now, we will write a code so that when our sprite touches the fish, it makes a sound and adds to the score.

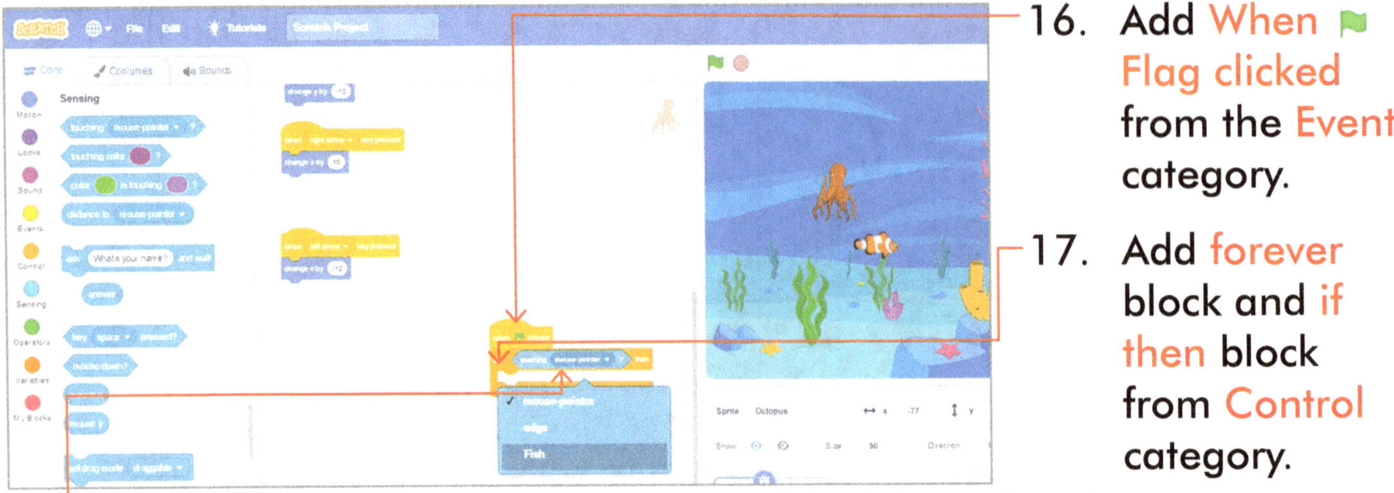

16. Add When ⚑ Flag clicked from the Events category.

17. Add forever block and if then block from Control category.

18. Add touching mouse pointer? block from Sensing category. Change mouse pointer to Fish by drop down button.

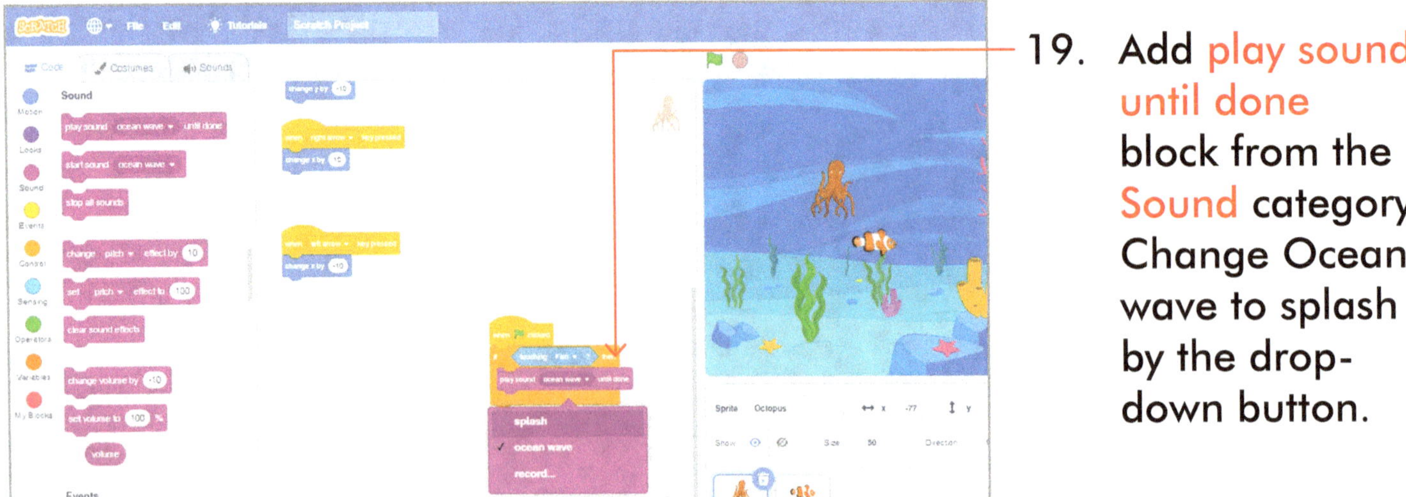

19. Add play sound until done block from the Sound category. Change Ocean wave to splash by the drop-down button.

Now, check the code by moving the Octopus with the arrow button and touch the fish; the sound of Splash should play.

Whenever, we play a game we need score as well. To make the score, we have to make a new variable.

20. Click on the Variables category.

21. Click on the Make a Variable block.

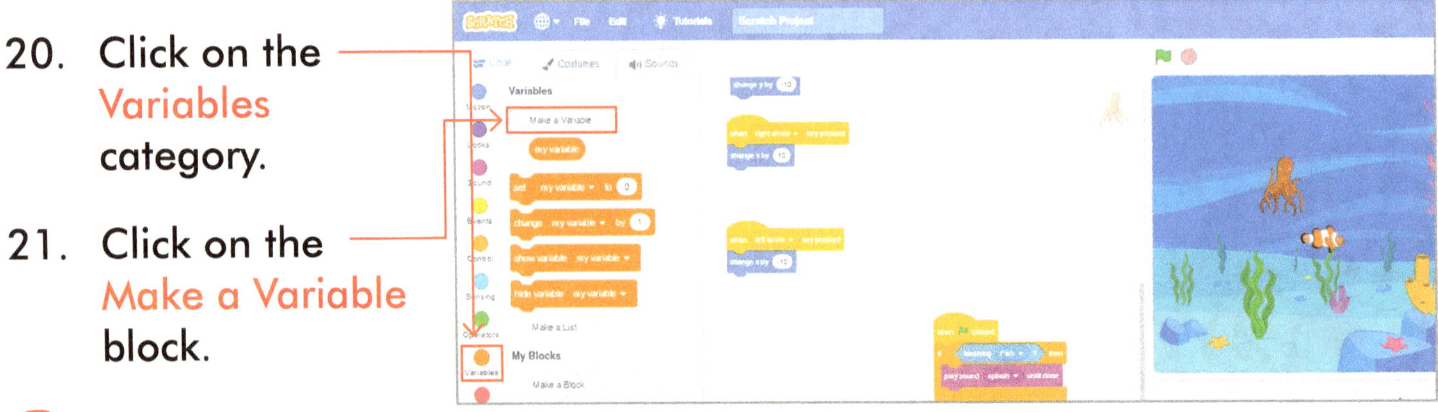

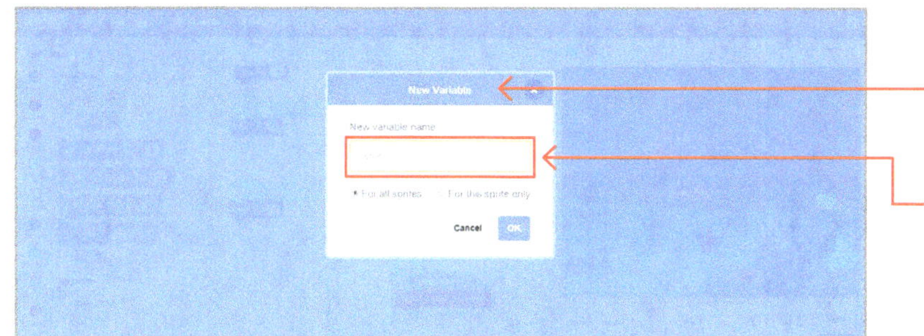

A new window will appear.

22. Click on the New Variable name block; type Score in it and click OK.

We can see that a new variable is created and appears on the left corner of the stage. Now, we want that score should move as we touch the fish, for which we need to do another coding for the scoring.

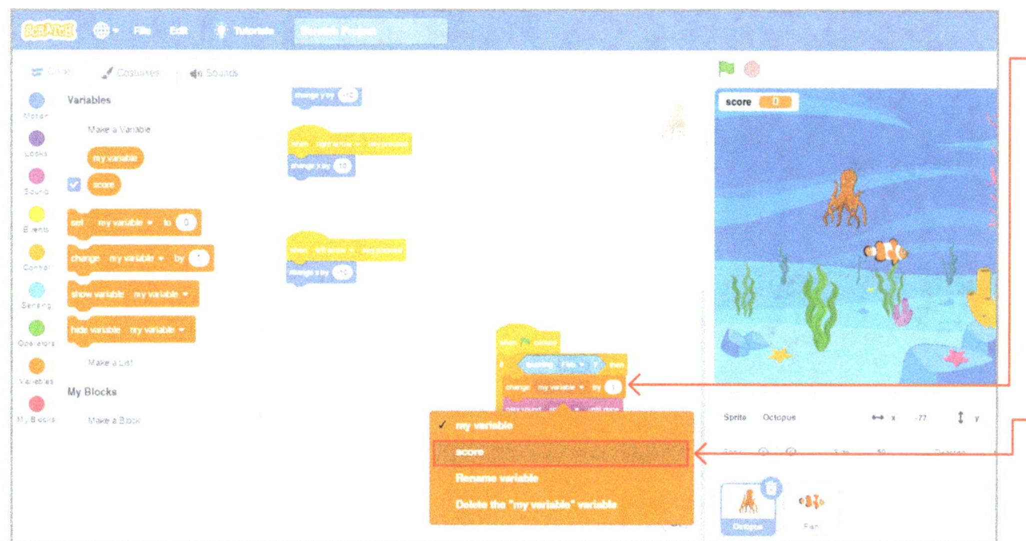

23. Add change my variable by 1 block from the Variables category.

24. By the down arrow change it to Score.

Our coding for the Under water game has been completed!

Now, we should test the game by clicking on the green flag above the stage. If you find any errors in the program, then recheck the entire coding again.

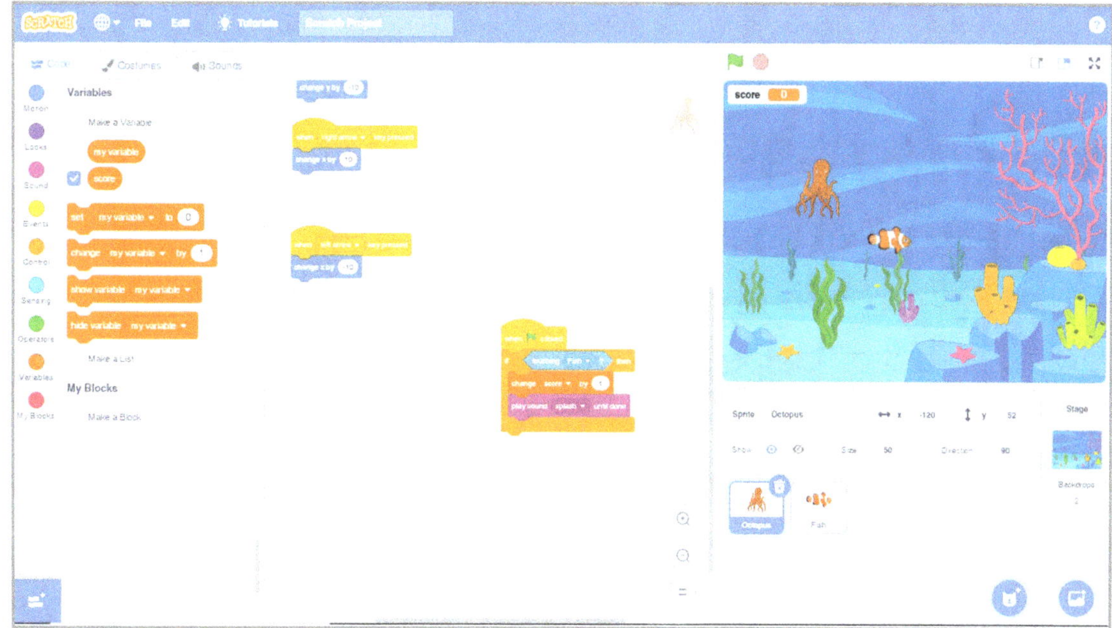

Now, click on the full screen control 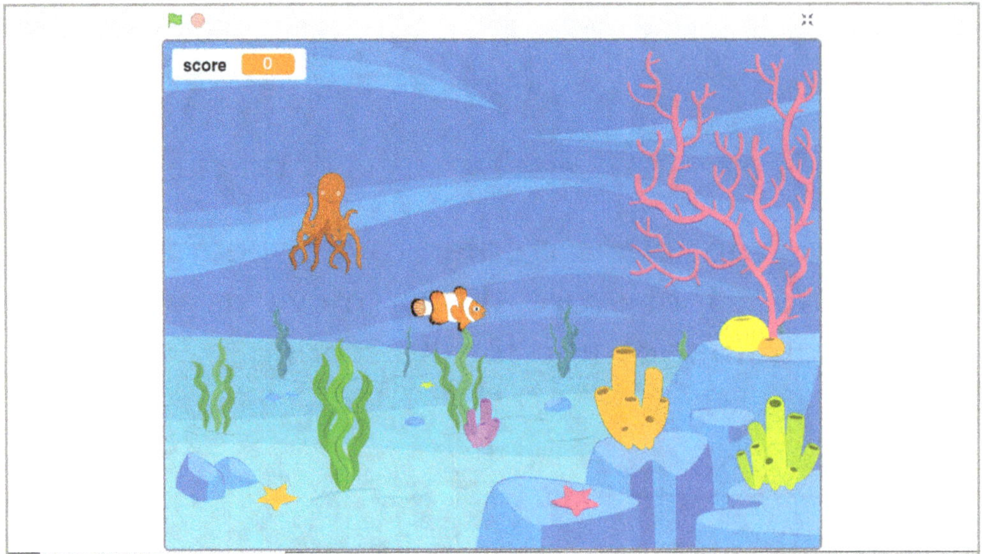 button in the right corner of the stage and play the game.

Saving your game

As we have successfully made our first game in scratch 3.12, we must save the game. Click on **File - Save to your computer** to save the game.

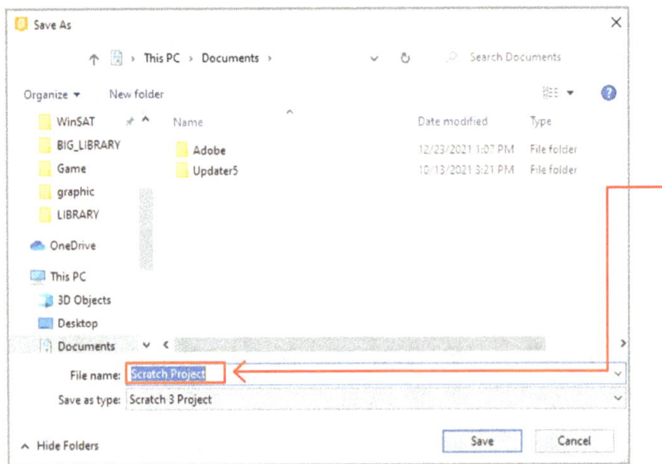

Type a name and click on the **Save** to save your game.

LET'S HAVE A LOOK

- Scratch helps us to make our own interactive stories, game, and animations.
- Paint new backdrop helps to design or draw backdrops for the Scratch project.
- Paint new sprite button helps to create a new sprite or modify an existing one.
- Control category helps to add the Forever and the If Block.
- Position of a sprite can be changed by going to x…y… block which is available in the Motion category.
- We can reduce or increase the size of the sprite.

- Flag block in the Events category helps to execute the program by clicking on the green flag and stop the program by clicking on the stop button.

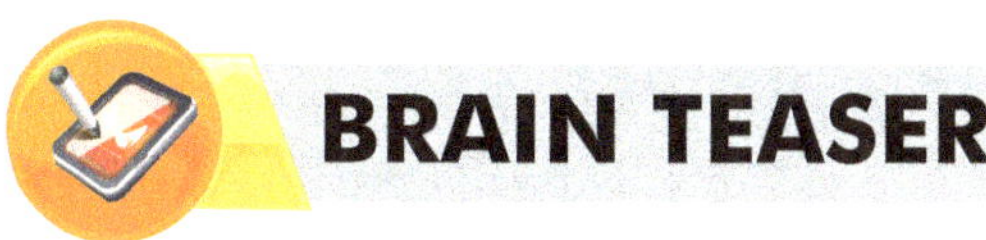

BRAIN TEASER

1. Fill in the blanks:

a. _______________ is a visual programming language that helps you to make your own interactive _______________, animations, _______________, music and more.

b. To move the sprite forward, _______________ the X-coordinate.

c. To move the sprite backward, _______________ the X-coordinate.

d. We can add sound to the Sprite by adding the _______________ block.

e. _______________ flag helps to start the program.

2. Write 'T' for true or 'F' for false in the boxes:

a. We can add scoring by making a new variable.

b. The game stops if stop button is clicked.

c. The sprite can play sound with move 10 block in the motion category.

d. The Green flag can be added from the Looks Script.

e. Change the X coordinate if you want to move the sprite upward.

f. Key pressed block can be added from the Events Scripts.

3. Answer the following in brief:

a. What is Scratch?

b.   Explain the steps to add new Backdrop to the project.

c.   Olivia is not able to understand why her sprite is moving in an awkward manner when she is pressing the arrow keys. Explain how the arrow keys should be programmed so that she may not face any problems.

d.   Sam wants to play the drum when the sprite touches the other character. Help him to do so.

e.   Write the steps to add a new sprite on the Stage in Scratch.

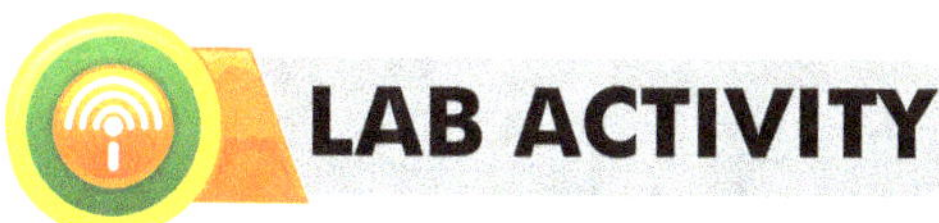 **LAB ACTIVITY**

- Revise the steps to open Scratch 3.12 window.

- Explain the logic behind game design.

- Explain how in a game a player needs to complete the task to win.

- Explain the usage of if and make a variable block.

- Explain how to control the movement of the sprites by programming the arrow keys.

For Students

- Create a hide and seek game by adding the following blocks to the sprite. Also, add a beautiful backdrop to the game.

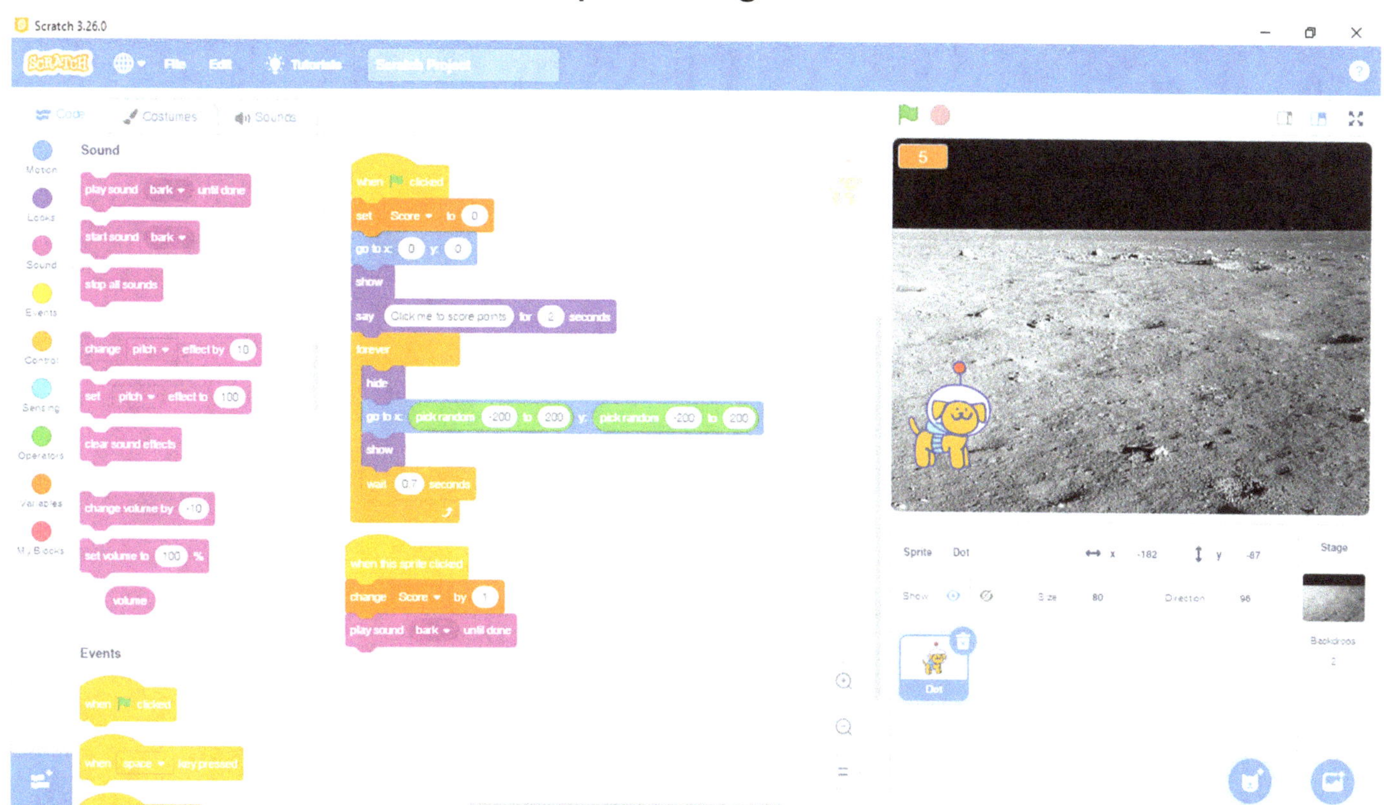

Formative Assessment-5
(Chapter 10)

1. **Lable the parts of the Scratch 3.12 window.**

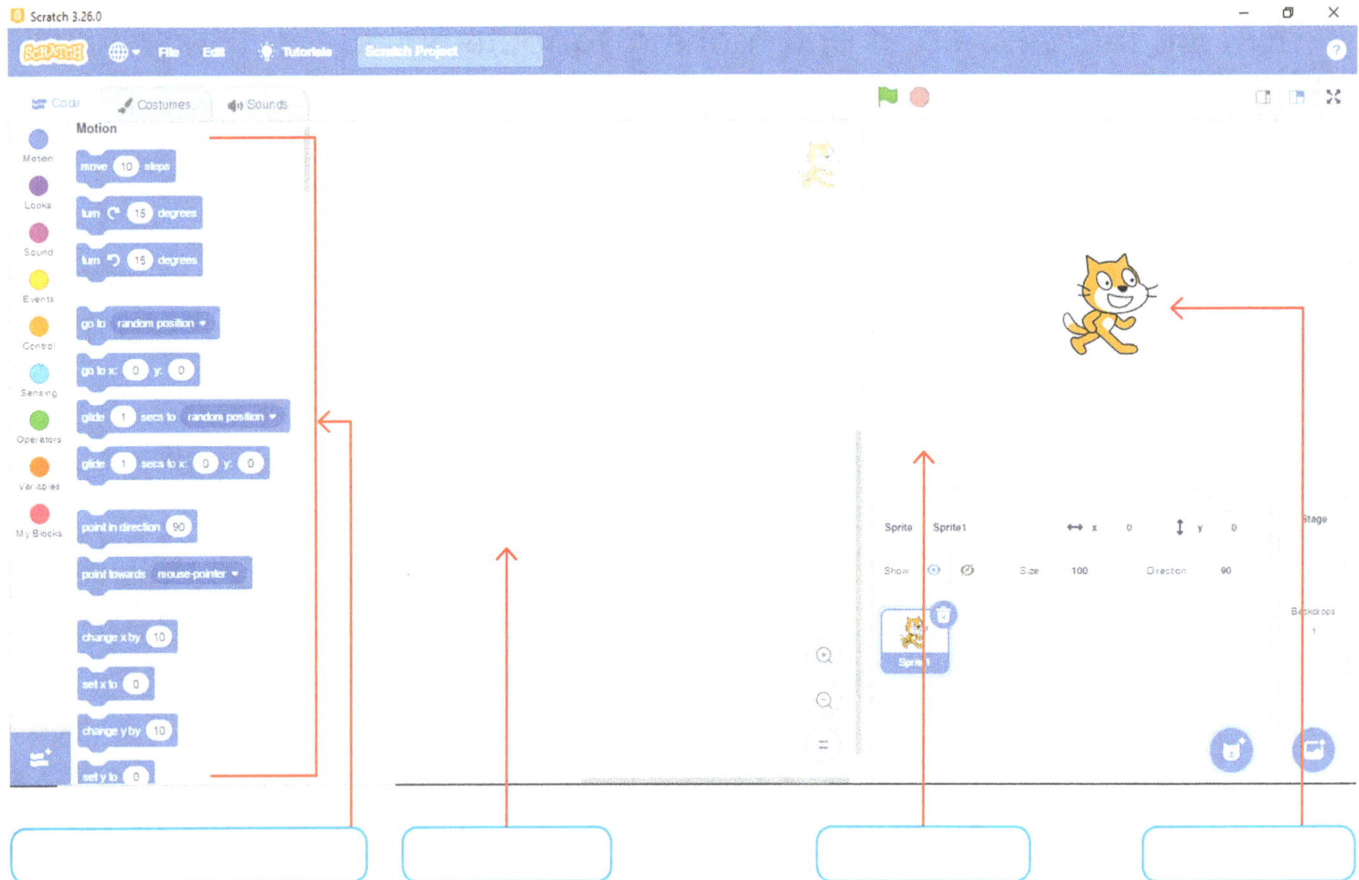

2. **Tick (✓) the correct option.**

Motion Scripts   ☐   Control Scripts   ☐

Events Scripts   ☐   Sound Scripts   ☐

3. **Do you want to create any other game on Scratch that you play on a mobile device? Which one is it? How can you create it on Scratch.**

PROJECT WORK

WINDOWS 10

Create your own folder and sub-folders to manage your files stored in the computer.

- Create a folder on a Desktop and Rename the folder as 'My First Folder'.
- Open it by double-clicking on it.
- Create a sub-folder within the My First Folder and name it 'My First Document'.
- Double-click the 'My First Document' folder and the newly created folder will open in the window. This folder does not contain any other file or sub-folder in it.
- Now in this blank window, create two new sub-folders and name them as PowerPoint and Excel respectively.
- To go back to the parent folder window, we can click on the Back button on the window's toolbar. So click on this button to go to the parent folder 'My First Folder.
- Now close the folder 'My First Folder'.

WORD 2016

Create the following document in MS-Word and perform the actions given below:

THE FLOWER

The flower is a pure and beautiful creation of Nature. It is offered to gods and presented to the dear and near ones because of its beauty and purity. It may be of different sizes, species, colours and shapes. It grows on dalicate plants.

Flowers like roses, lotuses, tropical water lilies, etc. are famous for their beauty and charm. Besides, there are many other popular and common flowers like lily, marigold, jasmine, China rose, chrysanthemum, etc. There are also small flowers like daisy and seasonal flowers of small and pretty sizes and colours planted in parks, lowns, etc.

Flawers are sold in the market. They are used for decorating houses and temples, and also used in weddings and festivals. They are loved and adored by all.

Many flowers have important symbolic meanings just like red roses are given as a symbol of love, beauty and passion.

- Save the document with the filename 'Flower'.
- Now run the spell check feature to correct the mis-spelt words in the document.
- Apply the various character formatting features, like changing the font, size, style, alignment, etc., to make it more beautiful.
- Format the title 'The Flower' in Title case, Red colour, Bold and Underline style, Size 18 points and Center aligned.

- At last add a heading 'Flowers I like the most' and make it bold.
- Now add the bulleted style to the five flowers you like the most. Also, give Bold, Italic style to these flowers.
- Now save the document once again and close Microsoft Word.

MS-POWERPOINT 2016

Create the PowerPoint presentation containing the following slides in it:

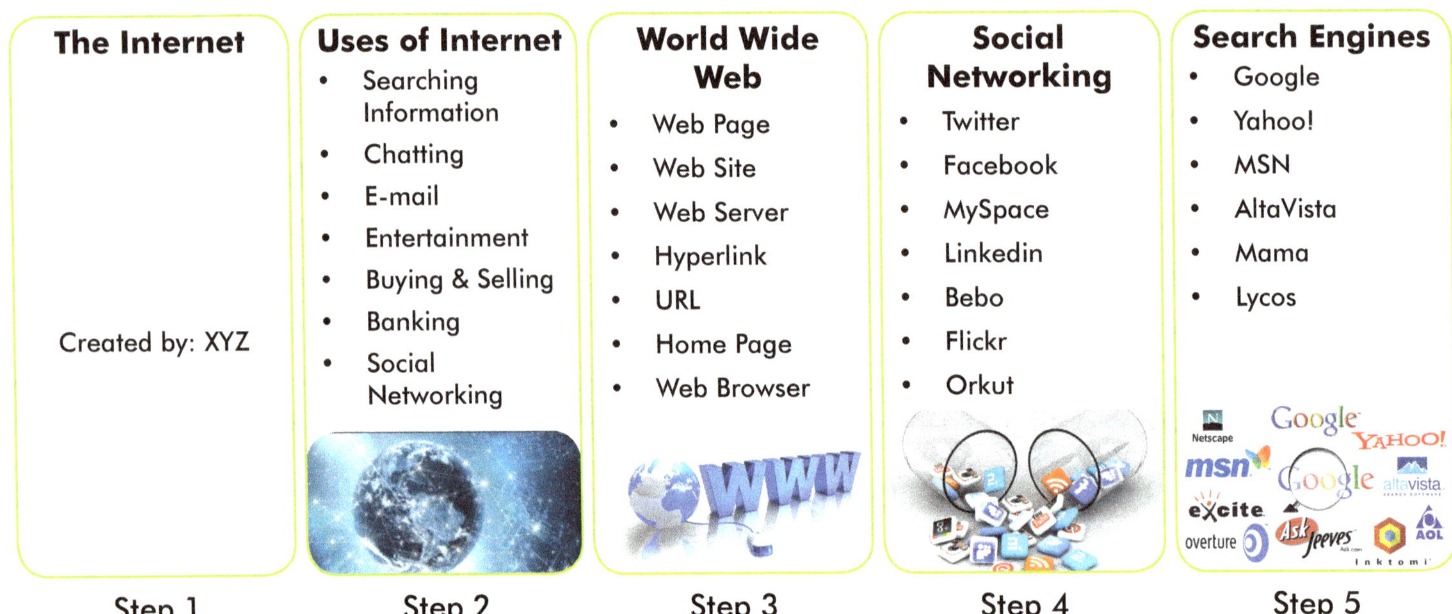

Now perform the following actions:

- Type your own name in the place of 'XYZ' in the first slide.
- Change the font for the title of each slide in the presentation to 'Comic Sans MS' and show them in Bold and Shadow style.
- Increase the font size for the title of each slide in the presentation and also change their colours into red.
- Align them to the centre of the place holder.
- Change the font on all the slides to 'Calibri'.
- Give a light yellow colour background to the first slide of the presentation.
- Apply gradient effect to the second slide with a diagonal down shading style.
- Chose a suitable texture to use it as background for the third slide of the presentation.
- Choose an Image Fill background in the fourth slide.
- Give a light blue colour background to the fifth slide of the presentation.
- Add suitable clipart or image to enhance the appearance of slides.
- Apply the Animation effect 'Fly In' to the titles of all the slides in the presentation.
- Run the slide show to view the presentation and then close the file.
- Save the presentation and close PowerPoint.